THE BOOK OF POLITICAL QUOTES

For my parents

By the same author
The Book of Rock Quotes
The Book of Sports Quotes (with Don Atyeo)
Famous Last Words
The Directory of Infamy

Reprinted by arrangement with Angus & Robertson
Publishers

123456789SEMSEM876543

ISBN 0-07-024354-9
First U.S. edition

LIBRARY OF CONGRESS CATALOGING IN PUBLICATION DATA

Main entry under title:
The Book of political quotes.
Includes index.
1. Political science—Quotations, maxims, etc.
2. Politicians—Quotations.   I. Green, Jonathon.
PN6084.P6B66 1982   081   82-25908
ISBN 0-07-024354-9

THE BOOK OF POLITICAL QUOTES

Compiled by Jonathon Green

McGraw-Hill Book Company
New York   St. Louis   San Francisco
Bogotá   Guatemala   Hamburg   Lisbon
Madrid   Mexico   Montreal   Panama   Paris
San Juan   São Paulo   Tokyo   Toronto

'Every government is run by liars, and nothing they say should be believed.' Thus spoke American commentator I. F. Stone, and who — other than a politician — would really argue with his damning appraisal. Bitter experience has taught us all, even if we seem foolishly set against absorbing the lesson, that all those fine words poured forth by our politicians add up to depressingly little: a skein of vainglorious, empty promises. The bland hypocrite, the ranting ideologue, the bloodthirsty rhetorician ... paving their paths of glory with our sacrifices. In government, in opposition too, what a seedy, self-opinionated, arrogant crew!

Yet how seductive they must be, since we fall time and time again for their dulcet blandishments, their canting calls to glory. Are they simply appealing to our baser selves, to our greed, our fears, our fantasies, our pride? The well-turned phrase, in this televised, cosmetic age, is perhaps less valuable than the good profile, but in the valley of the politically blind, the man or woman with just one sop to offer is, if not king, then certainly prime minister, president or the like. Perhaps, as American journalist David Broder has remarked: 'Anyone willing to do what is necessary to become president shouldn't be allowed the job.' But they get it all the same.

Here are more than three thousand quotations culled from around two and a half thousand years and taken from most countries of the 'civilised world'. Every one comes from the world of politics. Here you will find the speechifying, the seduction, the sweet and not so sweet delusions; the dictators, rabble-rousers, gossips, pundits, heroes, villains and even the occasional honest man or woman. Some of these lines are well known, the stuff of legend. Others stem from history's back alleys and bit players.

There is style here, of course, and there is wit and wisdom too. But how often that comes not from the politicians but from their critics — the writers and philosophers. Reading what the performers themselves have to say makes one thing endlessly clear: for all the fine words and fancy phrases politics is about power — be it national or individual — and about the human greed for domination. It is what Norman Mailer has called 'the hard dealing of hard men' — and to hell with the losers.

JONATHON GREEN

CONTENTS

POLITICS IS...

Democracy is the form of government in which the free are rulers.

Aristotle,
  Greek philosopher: *Politics*, fourth century BC

Democracy...is a charming form of government, full of variety and disorder, and dispensing a sort of equality to equals and unequals alike.

Plato,
  Greek philosopher: *The Republic*, fourth century BC

An ambassador is an honest man sent abroad to lie for the commonwealth.

Sir Henry Wotton,
  English diplomat, 1604

That which is more than lives, more than the lives and liberties of thousands, than all our goods, all our interests and faculties is the life, the liberty of the parliament, the privileges and immunities of this House which are the bases and supports of all the rest.

Sir John Eliot,
  Puritan leader, 1628

No man can be a politician, except that he be first a historian or a traveller; for except that he can see what must be, or what may be, he is no politician.

James Harrington,
  English political commentator, 1656

Freedom is the recognition of necessity.

Benedict Spinoza,
  Dutch-Jewish philosopher: *Ethics*, 1677

Government has no other end but the preservation of property.

John Locke,
  English philosopher, 1690

Law is a bottomless pit.

Dr John Arbuthnot,
  Scottish writer and physician: *The History of John Bull*, 1712

Party is the madness of the many for the gain of the few.

Alwxander Pope,
  English satirist: *Thoughts on Vrious Subjects*

Liberty is the right to do what the laws permit.

Charles, Baron de la Montesquieu,
  French philosopher: *L'Esprit des Lois*, 1748

Faction is to party what the superlative is to the positive. Party is a political evil and faction is the worst of all parties.

Viscount Bolingbroke,
  British statesman *The Patriot King*, 1749

Were there a people of gods, their government would be democratic. So perfect a government is not for men.

Jean-Jacques Rousseau,
  Genevan political philosopher, educationist and essayist *The Social Contract* 1762

That the king can do no wrong is a necessary and fundamental principle of the English Constitution.

Sir William Blackstone,
  English jurist: *Commentaries*, 1765-69

The true charter of liberty is independence, maintained by force.

Voltaire,
  French philosopher and humanitarian: *Philosophical Dictionary*, 1764

Politics are...nothing more than a means of rising in the world.

Samuel Johnson,
  English lexicographer and critic, 1775

POLITICS IS...

Liberty then, about which so many volumes have been written, is, when accurately defined, only the power of acting.

Voltaire,
French philosopher and humanitarian:
Philosophical Dictionary, 1764

Abstract liberty, like other abstractions, is not to be found.

Edmund Burke,
British statesman, 1775

Society in every state is a blessing, but government, even in its best state, is but a necessary evil, in its worst state an intolerable one.

Tom Paine,
English radical pamphleteer: ***Common Sense, 1776***

Political liberty is good only insofar as it produces private liberty.

Samuel Johnson,
English lexicographer and critic

The best party is but a kind of conspiracy against the rest of the nation...Ignorance maketh men go into a party and shame keepeth them from going out of it.

Lord Halifax,
English pamphleteer: ***The Character of a Trimmer, 1688***

Fear is the foundation of most governments.

John Adams,
future US president: ***Thoughts on Government, 1776***

Society is produced by our wants, and government by our wickedness.

Tom Paine,
English radical pamphleteer: ***Common Sense, 1776***

All political power is a trust.

Charles James Fox,
British politician, 1788

Corruption — the most infallible symptom of constitutional liberty.

Edward Gibbon,
English historian: ***The Decline and Fall of the Roman Empire, 1776-88***

It is with government as with medicine. Its only business is the choice of evils. Every law is an evil, for every law is an infraction of liberty.

Jeremy Bentham,
English philosopher: ***Principles of Legislation, 1789***

Government is a contrivance of human wisdom to provide for human wants.

Edmund Burke,
British statesman: ***Reflections on the Revolution in France, 1790***

The condition upon which God hath given liberty is eternal vigilance.

John Philpot Curran,
Irish judge, 1790

The king is not the nation's representative, but its clerk.

Maximilien de Robespierre,
French revolutionary leader, 1790

The Republican is the only form of government which is not eternally at open or secret war with the rights of mankind.

Thomas Jefferson,
US Secretary of State, 1790

Governments arise either out of the people or over the people.

Tom Paine,
   English radical pamphleteer: *The Rights of Man*, 1791

The end of all political associations is the preservation of the rights of man, which rights are liberty, property and security; that the nation is the source of all sovereignty derived from it; the right of property being secured and inviolable, no one ought to be deprived of it, except in cases of evident public necessity and on condition of a previous just indemnity.

Tom Paine,
   English radical pamphleteer: *The Rights of Man*, 1792

A monarchy is a merchantman which sails well, but will sometimes strike on a rock and go to the bottom. A republic is a raft which will never sink, but then your feet are always in the water.

Fisher Ames,
   US statesman, 1795

Anarchy is the stepping stone to absolute power.

Napoleon Bonaparte:
   ***Maxims*, 1804-15**

Politics, like religion, hold up torches of martyrdom to the reformers of error.

Thomas Jefferson

I hate liberality — nine times out of ten it is cowardice and the tenth time lack of principle.

Henry Addington,
   British statesman

Revolution is an idea which has found bayonets.

Napoleon Bonaparte:
   ***Maxims*, 1804-15**

Politics indeed make strange bedfellows.

John Spencer Bassett,
   biographer: *The Life of Andrew Jackson*

There is no act of treachery or meanness of which a political party is not capable; for in politics there is no honour.

Benjamin Disraeli:
   ***Vivian Grey*, 1824**

That is the best government which desires to make the people happy and knows how to make them happy.

Lord Macaulay,
   English historian, 1824

In politics, what begins in fear usually ends in folly.

Samuel Taylor Coleridge,
   English poet, 1830

A sect or party is an elegant incognito devised to save a man from the vexation of thinking.

Ralph Waldo Emerson,
   US poet and essayist: *Journals*, 1831

The history of the world is none other than the progress of the consciousness of freedom.

Georg Friedrich Hegel,
   German philosopher: *The Philosophy of History*, 1832

Diplomacy today is a collective education in fear.

Alexander van Humboldt,
   Prussian writer, 1832

Wine is good for adults who know what to do with it, but fatal to children. And politics is a wine which in Russia may even turn into opium.

Vissarion Belinsky,
   Russian critic, 1837

The final end of government is to create restraint but to do good.

Rufus Choate,
   US jurist, 1841

An institution is the lengthened shadow of one man.

Ralph Waldo Emerson,
   US poet and essayist: 'Self-Reliance', 1841

Communism . . . is the genuine solution of the antagonism between man and nature and between man and man. It is the true solution of the struggle between existence and essence, between objectification and self-affirmation, between freedom and necessity, between individual and species. It is the solution to the riddle of history and knows itself to be this solution.

Karl Marx:
Economical and Philosophical Manuscripts, 1844

A Conservative government is an organized hypocrisy.

Benjamin Disraeli,
British statesman, attacking Sir Robert Peel, 1845

Politics are but the cigar smoke of a man.

Henry David Thoreau,
US philosopher

Reform is affirmative, conservatism negative. Conservatism goes for comfort, reform for truth. . . . Conservatism makes no poetry, breathes no prayer, has no invention, it is all memory. Reform has no gratitude, no prudence, no husbandry.

Ralph Waldo Emerson,
US poet and essayist

The love of liberty is the love of others. The love of power is the love of ourselves.

William Hazlitt,
English essayist and critic

The closest thing to a Tory in disguise is a Whig in power.

Benjamin Disraeli,
on being accused of being 'a Tory in disguise'

Credit is . . . the economic judgement on the morality of a man. In credit, man himself, instead of metal or paper, has become the mediator of exchange, but not as man, but as the existence of capital and interest.

Karl Marx:
Economic and Philosophical Manuscripts, 1844

The democrat is a young conservative; the conservative is an old democrat. The aristocrat is the democrat ripe and gone to seed.

Ralph Waldo Emerson,
US poet and philosopher

The smallest and most inoffensive State is still criminal in its dreams.

Mikhail Bakunin,
Russian anarchist

The end of the institution, maintenance and administration of government is to secure the existence of the body politic, to protect it, and to furnish the individuals who compose it with the power of enjoying in safety and tranquillity their natural rights and the blessings of life.

Jacob Prout,
secretary to Liberia's Constitutional Convention which proclaimed the first independent African republic, 1847

A strong government, which was not to be much liked, to be preferred to a weak one. . . . Any ministry was better than a ministry without power.

Lord Brougham of Vaux,
Scottish law reformer, 1847

Political power, properly so called, is merely the organized power of one class for oppressing another.

Karl Marx:
The Communist Manifesto, 1848

Why is liberty valuable? Because it is an end in itself, because it is what it is. To bring it as a sacrifice to something else is simply to perform an act of human sacrifice.

Alexander Herzen,
Russian political thinker and writer: From The Other Shore, 1847-60

The liberty of the individual must be thus far limited, he must not make himself a nuisance to other people.

John Stuart Mill,
English philosopher: On Liberty, 1859

BOOK OF POLITICAL QUOTES

The legitimate object of government is to do for a community of people whatever they need to have done, but cannot do for themselves in their separate and individual capacities.

Abraham Lincoln

Liberty consists in doing what one desires.

John Stuart Mill,
   English philosopher: *On Liberty*, 1859

Governments exist to protect the rights of minorities. The loved and rich need no protection, they have many friends and few enemies.

Wendell Phillips,
   US abolitionist, 1860

What is conservatism? Is it not adherence to the old and tried, against the new and untried.

Abraham Lincoln,
   US presidential candidate, 1860

Liberty is the delicate fruit of a ripe civilization.

Lord Acton,
   English historian

A nihilist is a man who does not bow to any authorities, who does not take any principle on trust, no matter with what respect that principle is surrounded.

Ivan S. Turgenev,
   Russian playwright: *Fathers and Sons*, 1862

Politics is not an exact science.

Otto von Bismarck,
   future Prussian chancellor, 1863

Politics is organized opinion.

Benjamin Disraeli,
   British statesman, 1864

A parliament is nothing less than a big meeting of more or less idle people.

Walter Bagehot,
   British economist and journalist: *The English Constitution*, 1867

It has long been a grave question whether any government not too strong for the liberties of its people, can be strong enough to maintain its existence in great emergencies.

Abraham Lincoln,
   US president, 1864

The best reason why monarchy is a strong government is that it is an intelligible government. The mass of mankind understand it, and they hardly anywhere in the world understand any other.

Walter Bagehot,
   British economist and journalist: *The English Constitution*, 1867

The test of political intentions is the condition of the country whose future they regulate.

Benjamin Disraeli

A statesman is a successful politician who is dead.

Thomas B. Reed,
   US lawyer and legislator

A constitutional statesman is in general a man of common opinions and uncommon abilities.

Walter Bagehot,
   British economist and journalist: *The English Constitution*, 1867

There is no gambling like politics.

Benjamin Disraeli,
   former British prime minister: *Endymion*, 1880

Politics is perhaps the only profession for which no preparation is thought necessary.

Robert Louis Stevenson,
   Scottish author: *Familiar Studies of Men and Books*, 1882

All kings is mostly rapscallions.

Mark Twain,
   US author: *The Adventures of Huckleberry Finn*, 1884

POLITICS IS . . .

Politics ruins the character.

Otto von Bismarck,
German chancellor, 1881

The worst thing in this world, next to anarchy, is government.

Henry Ward Beecher,
US editor and clergyman, 1887

Liberal institutions straightway cease from being liberal the moment they are soundly established. Once this is attained no more grievous and more thorough enemies of freedom exist than liberal institutions.

Friedrich W. Nietzsche,
German philosopher, 1888

The Democratic Party is like a mule — without pride of ancestry or hope of posterity.

Emory Storrs,
US politician, 1888

The economic side of the democratic ideal is . . . socialism itself.

Sidney Webb,
Fabian socialist: *Fabian Essays*, 1889

Anyone has a right to do anything the law does not say is wrong.

J. Pierpoint Morgan,
US capitalist

The radical of one century is the conservative of the next.

Mark Twain,
US author: *Notebooks*, 1935

Law represents the efforts of men to organize society; government, the efforts of selfishness to overthrow liberty.

Henry Ward Beecher,
US editor and clergyman: *Proverbs from Plymouth Pulpit*, 1887

Destiny, n. A tyrant's excuse for crime and a fool's excuse for failure.

Ambrose Bierce,
US journalist and author: *The Devil's Dictionary*, 1881-1911

Politics are like a labyrinth, from the inner intricacies of which it is even more difficult to find the way of escape, than it was to find the way in to them.

William Gladstone

The purification of politics is an iridescent dream. Government is force.

John J. Ingalls,
US politician and lawyer, 1890

Government is nothing but the balance of the natural elements of a country.

Jose Marti,
Cuban patriot, 1891

Bourgeois is the epithet which the riff-raff apply to what is respectable and the aristocracy to what is decent.

Anthony Hope,
English novelist: *The Dolly Dialogues*, 1894

Democracy means simply the bludgeoning of the people, by the people, for the people.

Oscar Wilde

A mugwump is a fellow with his mug on one side of the fence and his wump on the other.

Harold Willis Dodds,
president of Princeton University

Democracy is based upon the conviction that there are extraordinary possibilities in ordinary people.

Harry Emerson Fosdick,
US Baptist minister

The Fabian is the man who does what he can and thanks heaven that things are not worse.

Elbert Hubbard,
US businessman and writer: *The Notebook*, 1927

Politics, n. A strife of interests masquerading as a contest of principles.

Ambrose Bierce,
US journalist and author: *The Devil's Dictionary*, 1881-1911

Parliaments are the great lie of our time.

Konstantin Pobedonostsev,
Russian jurist, 1896

The reactionary is always willing to take a progressive attitude on any issue that is dead.

Theodore Roosevelt

The heresy of one age becomes the orthodoxy of the next.

Helen Keller,
US essayist: *Optimism*, 1903

Liberty means responsibility. That is why so many men dread it.

George Bernard Shaw,
Irish playwright, 1903

Fanaticism consists in redoubling your effort when you have forgotten your aim.

George Santayana,
Spanish-born US philosopher, poet and
novelist: *The Life of Reason*, 1905-06

Kings are not born, they are made by universal hallucination.

George Bernard Shaw,
Irish playwright

Socialism is nothing but the capitalism of the lower classes.

Oswald Spengler,
German historicist

Liberty, n. One of Imagination's most precious possessions.

Ambrose Bierce,
US journalist and author: *The Devil's*
***Dictionary*, 1881-1911**

Modern politics is, at bottom, a struggle not of men but of forces.

Henry Adams,
US historian: *The Education of Henry*
***Adams*, 1907**

Liberty is not a means to a higher political end. It is itself the highest political end.

Lord Acton,
English historian: *The History of Freedom*,
1907

Politics, as a practice, whatever its professions, has always been the systematic organization of hatreds.

Henry Adams,
US historian: *The Education of Henry*
***Adams*, 1907**

I call democracy a superstition and a fetish: and I repeat that it is plainly both.

William R. Inge,
Dean of St Pauls: *The Church and the Age*

Democracy is the name we give to the people each time we need them.

Robert de Flers,
French playwright: *L'Habit Vert*, 1912

Freedom only for the supporters of the government — only for the members of one party, however numerous they may be — is no freedom at all. Freedom is always and exclusively for one who thinks differently. Not because of any fanatical concept of 'justice' but because all that is instructive, wholesome and purifying in political freedom depends on this characteristic.

Rosa Luxemburg,
German revolutionary, 1916

A democracy is a state which recognizes the subjection of the minority to the majority. That is, an organization for the systematic use of violence by one class against another, by one part of the population against another.

V.I. Lenin:
***The State and the Revolution*, 1917**

Communism is soviet government. Plus the electrification of the whole country.

V.I. Lenin,
1920

Freedom is a bourgeois notion devised as a cloak for the spectre of economic slavery.

V.I. Lenin,
1920

Statesmanship is housekeeping on a great scale.

Sir John Simon,
British statesman and lawyer, 1922

I tell you, all politics is apple sauce.

Will Rogers,
US humorist: *The Illiterate Digest*

Democracy substitutes election by the incompetent many for appointment by the corrupt few.

George Bernard Shaw,
Irish playwright, 1913

BOOK OF POLITICAL QUOTES

Babies in silk hats playing with dynamite.

Alexander Woollcott,
US critic and wit, on diplomats

The dictatorship of the proletariat is nothing else than power based upon force and limited by nothing — by no law and absolutely no rule!

V.I. Lenin

Communism might be likened to a race in which all competitors come in first with no prizes.

Lord Inchcape,
British shipping magnate

Newton saw an apple fall and deduced gravitation. You and I might have seen millions of apples fall and only deduced pig-feeding. It's the same story about Bolshevism. We want some Newtonian Cromwell to enunciate that Bolshevism is the reaction from repressed Freedom.

Lord Fisher,
Admiral of the Fleet: letter in *The Times*,
1920

Democracy is the theory that the common people know what they want, and deserve to get it good and hard.

H.L. Mencken,
US philologist, editor and satirist: *A Book of Burlesques*, 1920

The state is a special cudgel, nothing more.

V.I. Lenin: *The State and Revolution*, 1917

Politics, as hopeful men practise it in the world, consists mainly of the delusion that a change in form is a change in substance.

H.L. Mencken,
US philologist, editor and satirist,
***Prejudices*, fourth series, 1924**

Politics are almost as exciting as war, and quite as dangerous. In war you can only be killed once, but in politics many times.

Winston Churchill,
Secretary of State for War and Air, 1920

Liberty is nothing if it is not the organised and conscious power to resist in the last resort.

Harold J. Laski,
English political scientist and socialist: *A Grammar of Politics*, 1925

A dictatorship is a confession of political incapacity and sloth in the government.

Francesco Nitti, Italian socialist statesman,
1926

Politics is a place of humble hopes and strangely modest requirements, where all are good who are not criminal, and all are wise who are not ridiculously otherwise.

Frank Moore Colby,
US essayist and teacher: *The Colby Essays*, 1926

Orthodoxy: That peculiar condition where the patient can neither eliminate an old idea nor absorb a new one.

Elbert Hubbard,
US businessman and writer: *The Notebook*,
1927

A progressive is always a conservative, he conserves the direction of progress. A reactionary is always a rebel.

G.K. Chesterton,
English critic, novelist and poet

A liberal is a man who leaves a room before the fight begins.

Heywood Broun,
US critic and wit

The politician is an acrobat. He keeps his balance by saying the opposite of what he does.

Maurice Barrès,
French politician and journalist

Politicians . . . are the semi-failures in business and the professions, men of mediocre mentality, dubious morality and magnificent commonplaceness.

W.B. Pitkin,
US writer: *The Twilight of the American Mind*, 1928

POLITICS IS...

It is true that liberty is precious — so precious that it must be rationed.

V.I. Lenin,
attributed by Sidney and Beatrice Webb

A creed is an ossified metaphor.

Elbert Hubbard,
US businessman and writer: *The Notebook*,
1927

A reformer is a guy who rides through a sewer in a glass-bottomed boat.

James J. Walker,
mayor of New York City, 1928

Liberty is so much latitude as the powerful choose to accord to the weak.

Judge Learned Hand,
1930

Public office is the last refuge of a scoundrel.

Boies Penrose,
US politician and lawyer, 1931

I hate elections, but you have to have them — they are medicine.

Stanley Baldwin,
Lord President of the Council in the
MacDonald coalition, 1931

Democracy means government by the uneducated, while aristocracy means government by the badly educated.

G.K. Chesterton,
English critic, novelist and poet, 1931

Insurrection is an art and like all arts it has its laws.

Leon Trotsky:
***History of the Russian Revolution*, 1932**

The state is an instrument in the hands of the ruling class for suppressing the resistance of its class enemies.

Joseph Stalin

Fascism is capitalism plus murder.

Upton Sinclair,
US novelist

This is the sport of kings!

Huey Long,
governor of Louisiana, on politics

Envy is the basis of democracy.

Bertrand Russell:
***The Conquest of Happiness*, 1930**

A politician is a person with whose politics you don't agree. If you agree with him he is a statesman.

David Lloyd George,
former British prime minister, 1935

I am convinced that politics alone are incapable of solving the great problems now weighing upon us, and that it is a serious error to pin all our hopes on their development or upon arbitrary changes in their normal procedure.

Antonio de Salazar,
Portuguese dictator

Freedom of expression is the matrix, the indispensable condition of nearly every other form of freedom.

Benjamin N. Cardozo,
US jurist, 1937

The typical socialist...a prim little man with a white-collar job, usually a secret teetotaller and often with vegetarian leanings.

George Orwell,
English essayist and critic: *The Road to*
***Wigan Pier*, 1937**

A Liberal is a man who uses his legs and his hands at the behest, at the command of his head.

Franklin D. Roosevelt,
US president, 1939

Socialism is simply the degenerate capitalism of bankrupt capitalists. Its one genuine object is to get more money for its professors.

H.L. Mencken,
US philologist, editor and satirist

BOOK OF POLITICAL QUOTES

A reactionary is a somnambulist walking backwards.

Franklin D. Roosevelt,
 US president, 1939

Fascism is not in itself a new order of society. It is the future refusing to be born.

Aneurin Bevan,
 British Labour politician

Democracy is the superior form of government because it is based on a respect for man as a reasonable being.

John F. Kennedy,
 future US president: *Why England Slept*, 1940

The tragedy of modern democracies is that they have not yet succeeded in effecting democracy.

Jacques Maritain,
 French philosopher: *Christianisme et Democratie*, 1940

The object of government, in peace or war, is not the glory of rulers or races, but the happiness of the common man.

Sir William Beveridge,
 British economist, 1942

The history of liberty has largely been the history of the observance of procedural safeguards.

Justice Felix Frankfurter,
 US jurist, 1943

Diplomacy is the lowest form of politeness because it misquotes the greatest number of people. A nation, like an individual, if it has anything to say, should simply say it.

E.B. White,
 US humorist: *One Man's Meat*, 1944

In our time there is no such thing as 'keeping out of politics'. All issues are political issues and politics itself is a mass of lies, evasions, folly, hatred and schizophrenia.

George Orwell,
 English essayist and critic: 'Politics and the English Language', 1946

Politics is the art of preventing people from taking part in affairs which properly concern them.

Paul Valéry,
 French poet, 1943

Politics is the science of who gets what, when and why.

Sidney Hillman,
 ***Political Primer for All Americans*, 1944**

Government of the duds, by the duds and for the duds.

Winston Churchill,
 on socialist governments

Power politics is the diplomatic name for the law of the jungle

Ely Culbertson,
 US bridge expert, 1946

Democracy is a form of religion. It is the worship of jackals by jackasses.

H.L. Mencken,
 US philologist, editor and satirist

We shall get nowhere until we start by recognizing that political behaviour is largely non-rational, that the world is suffering from some kind of mental disease which must be diagnosed before it can be cured.

George Orwell,
 English essayist and critic, 1946

It has been said that democracy is the worst form of government, except for all those other forms that have been tried from time to time.

Winston Churchill

Liberty and democracy become unholy when their hands are dyed red with innocent blood.

Mahatma Gandhi:
 ***Non-Violence in Peace and War*, 1948**

Communism arises from poverty. End poverty and you end communism.

Bernard Baruch,
 US financier and statesman

A conservative is a man with two perfectly good legs who, however, has not learnt to walk.

Franklin D. Roosevelt

Socialism is the philosophy of failure, the creed of ignorance and the gospel of envy.

Winston Churchill,
British opposition leader, 1948

The essence of the liberal outlook lies not in *what* opinions are held, but in *how* they are held; instead of being held dogmatically they are held tentatively and with a conscience that new evidence may at any moment lead to their abandonment.

Bertrand Russell,
English philosopher: *Philosophy and Politics*, 1950

One of the evils of democracy is that you have to put up with the man you elect whether you want him or not.

Will Rogers,
US humorist: *The Autobiography of Will Rogers*, 1949

I have never regarded politics as the arena of morals; it is the arena of interests.

Aneurin Bevan,
British Labour politician

Freedom is when one hears the bell at seven o'clock in the morning and knows it is the milkman and not the gestapo.

Georges Bidault,
French prime minister, 1950

An independent is the guy who wants to take politics out of politics.

Adlai Stevenson,
governor of Illinois, 1950

Fascism...represents the exaltation of the executioner by the executioner....Russian Communism...represents the exaltation of the executioner by the victim. The former never dreamt of liberating all men, but only of liberating the few by subjugating the rest. The later, in its most profound principle, aims at liberating all men by provisionally subjugating them all.

Albert Camus,
French author and philosopher: *The Rebel*, 1951

There lies at the back of every creed something terrible and hard for which the worshipper may one day be required to suffer.

E.M. Forster,
English novelist: *Two Cheers for Democracy*, 1951

Political toleration is a by-product of the complacency of the ruling class. When that complacency is disturbed, there never was a more bloody-minded set of thugs than the British ruling class.

Aneurin Bevan,
British Labour politician

BOOK OF POLITICAL QUOTES

Democracy works as the dictatorship of organized money power, and that is a dictatorship of the Jew.

Arnold Leese,
president of the Imperial Fascist League

Conservatism is the worship of dead revolutions.

Clinton Rossiter,
US political scientist

All diplomacy is a continuation of war by other means.

Chou En-lai,
Chinese prime minister, 1954

An appeaser is one who feeds a crocodile, hoping it will eat him last.

Winston Churchill,
British prime minister, 1954

A liberal is a man too broadminded to take his own side in a quarrel.

Robert Frost,
US poet

Politics is the diversion of trivial men who, when they succeed at it, become important in the eyes of more trivial men.

George Jean Nathan,
US editor and critic, 1954

A good politician is quite as unthinkable as an honest burglar.

H.L. Mencken,
US philologist, editor and satirist, 1955

The professional politician is one of the mysteries of American life, a bundle of paradoxes, shrewd as a fox, naïve as a schoolboy. He has great respect for the people yet treats them like boobs, and is constitutionally unable to keep his mouth shut.

James Reston,
US political commentator, 1955

Liberty is always unfinished business.

American Council for Civil Liberties,
1955

Nowhere are prejudices more mistaken for truth, passion for reason, and invective for documentation, than in politics. That is a realm, peopled only by villains or heroes, in which everything is black or white and grey is a forbidden colour.

John Mason Brown,
US essayist, 1956

Liberty is the way, and the only way of perfectibility. Without liberty heavy industry can be perfected, but not justice or truth.

Albert Camus,
French author and philosopher

When I hear a man applauded by the mob I always feel a pang of pity for him. All he has to do to be hissed is to live long enough.

H.L. Mencken,
US philologist, editor and satirist: *Minority Report*, 1956

The British monarchy is one of our few contemporary pieces of good luck.

C.P. Snow,
English novelist

Democracy and socialism are means to an end, not the end in itself.

Shri Jawaharlal Nehru,
Indian prime minister, 1958

The socialists believe in two things which are absolutely different and perhaps contradictory: freedom and organization.

Elie Halévy,
French historian

Democracy is good. I say this because other systems are worse.

Shri Jawaharlal Nehru,
Indian prime minister, 1961

The sad duty of politics is to establish justice in a sinful world

Reinhold Niebuhr,
US theologian

POLITICS IS . . .

A politician is a man who understands government and it takes a politician to run a government. A statesman is a politician who's been dead for fifteen years.

Harry S. Truman,
former US president, 1958

There is one thing solid and fundamental in politics — the law of change. What's up today is down tomorrow.

Richard Nixon

Liberty is liberty, not equality or fairness or justice or human happiness or a quiet conscience.

Isaiah Berlin,
English philosopher: *Two Concepts of Liberty*, 1959

A diplomat is a person who can tell you to go to hell in such a way that you actually look forward to the trip.

Caskie Stinnett,
US writer: *Out of the Red*, 1960

The liberals can understand everything but people who don't understand them.

Lenny Bruce,
US satirist

Authority is not power, that's coercion. Authority is not knowledge, that's persuasion or seduction. Authority is simply that the author has the right to make a statement and to be heard.

Herman Kahn,
US political commentator

Democracy means government by discussion, but it is only effective if you can stop people talking.

Clement Attlee,
former British prime minister, 1962

Politics and the fate of mankind are shaped by men without ideals and without greatness. Men who have greatness within them don't go in for politics.

Albert Camus,
French author and philosopher

The British House of Lords is the British Outer Mongolia for retired politicians.

Anthony Wedgwood Benn,
British Labour politician

Terrorism is essentially the rage of literati in its last stage.

Jacob Burckhardt,
Swiss historian

Politics is property.

Murray Kempton,
US journalist

Totalitarianism is the interruption of mood.

Norman Mailer,
US novelist and journalist

Democracy without education is hypocrisy without limitation.

Iskander Mirza,
former Pakistani president

People are the common denominator of progress.

John Kenneth Galbraith,
Canadian-born US economist: *Economic Development*, 1964

Democracy . . . is the only form of government that is founded on the dignity of man. Not the dignity of some men, of rich men, of educated men or of white men, but of all men. Its sanction is not the sanction of force, but the sanction of human nature.

Robert M. Hutchins,
US educator and writer

Politics no longer means stirring speeches. Nor does it mean more talk, stirring the sentiment of the people or jockeying for power. . . . For any country that respects itself, politics means work, production . . . the transformation of society into a better one.

Gamal Abdel Nasser,
Egyptian president, 1965

The monarchy is a labour intensive industry.

Harold Wilson

BOOK OF POLITICAL QUOTES

Politics has its virtues, all too many of them — it would not rank with baseball as a topic of conversation if it did not satisfy a good many things — but one can suspect that its secret appeal is close to nicotine.

Norman Mailer,
US novelist and journalist: *Presidential Papers*, 1964

Politics is war without bloodshed, while war is politics with bloodshed.

Mao Tse-tung:
***Quotations from Chairman Mao*, 1966**

A politician is a man who can be verbose in fewer words than anybody else.

Peter de Vries,
US novelist

The function of socialism is to raise suffering to a higher level.

Norman Mailer,
US novelist and journalist

Political power grows out of the barrel of a gun.

Mao Tse-tung:
***Quotations from Chairman Mao*, 1966**

Politics is war without violence. War is politics with violence.

Stokeley Carmichael,
US black power leader, paraphrasing Mao, 1967

Being in politics is like being a football coach. You have to be smart enough to understand the game and dumb enough to think it's important.

Eugene McCarthy,
US senator

Command is getting people to go the way you want them to go — enthusiastically.

General William Westmoreland,
commander in chief US troops in Vietnam, 1966

Socialism without liberty is the barracks.

Graffito
in Paris during the student riots of 1968

Politics should be fun, politicians have no right to be dull or po-faced. The moment politics becomes dull, democracy is in danger.

Lord Hailsham,
British politician and jurist, 1966

A rich man told me recently that a liberal is a man who tells other people what to do with their money.

LeRoi Jones,
US writer, 1966

Freedom! Was it a place somewhere between Atlanta and Birmingham and you kept missing it everytime you drove that way?

Julius Lester,
US black activist: *Look Out Whitey!* 1968

The function of liberal Republicans is to shoot the wounded after the battle

Eugene McCarthy,
US senator, 1968

Politics is the hard dealing of hard men over properties, and their strength is in dealing and their virility.

Norman Mailer,
US novelist and journalist: *Miami and the Siege of Chicago*, 1968

All politics are based on the indifference of the majority.

James Reston,
US political commentator, 1968

Probably the most distinctive characteristic of the successful politician is selective cowardice.

Richard Harris,
US journalist, 1968

Everything starts as mystique and ends up as politics.

Graffito
in Paris during the student riots of 1968

Equality is a futile pursuit, equality of opportunity is a noble one.

Iain MacLeod,
British politician, 1969

POLITICS IS...

Full democracy means the dissolution of differences between the classes, which is the same as equality.

Gamal Abdel Nasser,
   Egyptian president, 1968

Power...is the simple and indestructible will of the people. That is really power!

Fidel Castro,
   Cuban president, 1970

National security lies not only at the ramparts alone, but also lies in the value of our free institutions.

Judge Murray Gurfein,
   dismissing the US Justice Department's attempt to suppress publication of the 'Pentagon Papers' in the New York Times, 1971

Politics is not an art of principles but of timing. The principles are few and soft enough to curve to political winds. The fundamental action of politics is to gain the most one can from a favourable situation and pay off as little as possible whenever necessity forces an unpopular line.

Norman Mailer,
   US novelist and journalist: St George and the Godfather, 1972

Democracy is first of all a state of feeling.

Arthur Miller,
   US playwright, 1972

I reject the cynical view that politics is inevitably, or even usually, dirty business.

Richard Nixon,
   US president, 1973

A statesman is a politician who places himself at the service of the nation. A politician is a statesman who places the nation at his service.

Georges Pompidou,
   French president, 1973

Politics is the art of acquiring, holding and wielding power.

Indira Gandhi,
   Indian prime minister, 1975

A government big enough to give you everything you want is a government big enough to take from you everything you have.

Gerald Ford,
   US president, 1974. Attributed also to Barry Goldwater, US presidential candidate, 1964

My idea of a Labour government is one which fulfills its election pledges to build a new Jerusalem, which is not a corny ideal.

Eric Heffer,
   British politician, 1975

Politics is like boxing — you try to knock out your opponent.

Idi Amin,
   Ugandan president, 1976

If dictatorship is the concentration of power, freedom consists in its diffusion.

Lord Hailsham,
   British politician and jurist, 1976

As far as socialism means anything, it must be about the wider distribution of smoked salmon and caviar.

Sir Richard Marsh,
   British politician, 1976

If you can make money and have fun and power — that's what it's all about.

Phil Walden,
   rock band manager and backer of fellow Georgian, Jimmy Carter, 1976

There's something about politicians, about becoming a politician and being a politician that is so unpalatable that most of the best people in the community won't take it on.

Senator James McLelland,
   Australian politician, 1977

Liberty is conforming to the majority.

Hugh Scanlon,
   president of the AUEW, 1977

The word 'Islam' does not need any such adjectives as 'democratic'. Precisely because Islam is everything, it means everything.

Ayatollah Khomeini,
   religious dictator of Iran, 1979

Ronald Reagan, in 1940, poses for a sculpture class, having been elected a 'Twentieth-Century Adonis'/Popperfoto

I used to say that politics was the second oldest profession, and I have come to know that it bears a gross similarity to the first.

Ronald Reagan,
US presidential candidate, 1979

HAIL TO THE CHIEF

For truly have I often thought that I could not tell what my business was, nor what I was in the place I stood in, save comparing myself to a good constable set to keep the peace of the parish.

Oliver Cromwell,
    protector of the commonwealth of England, Scotland and Ireland, 1657

Nothing has been so obnoxious to me through life as a dead calm.

John Wilkes,
    British radical politician

By God, Mr Chairman, at this moment I stand astonished at my own moderation!

Robert, Lord Clive,
    replying to allegations of governmental excesses in India, 1773

I have sworn on the altar of God eternal hostility against every form of tyranny over the mind of man.

Thomas Jefferson,
    US vice-president, 1800

If there were two Henry Clays, one of them would make the other president of the United States.

Henry Clay,
    US politician

When I want to read a novel, I write one.

Benjamin Disraeli

What is the Throne? A bit of wood gilded and covered in velvet. I am the State — I alone am here the representative of the people. Even if I had done wrong, you should not have reproached me in public; people wash their dirty linen at home. France has more need of me than I of France.

Napoleon Bonaparte,
    addressing the Senate, 1814

If I were not Napoleon I would be Alexander.

Napoleon Bonaparte,
    referring to Alexander the Great, 1814

I am proud to say that with a perseverance undismayed by difficulties, a disinterestedness that compelled respect, I have not only contributed to raise a new empire in the world, founded on a new system of government, but I arrived at eminence in political literature, the most difficult of all lines to succeed and excel in, which aristocracy, with all its aids, has not been able to reach or to rival.

Tom Paine,
    English radical pamphleteer

I was born an American, I will live an American, I shall die an American.

Daniel Webster,
    US statesman, 1850

Benjamin Disraeli delivering his maiden speech/Mary Evans Picture Library

Though I sit down now, the time will come when you will hear me.

Benjamin Disraeli,
   after the stormy reception of his maiden speech as an MP, 1837

I would rather the people should wonder why I wasn't president than why I am.

Salmon P. Chase,
   US politician

The only thing I am afraid of is fear.

Duke of Wellington

HAIL TO THE CHIEF

The mission of my life appears to be, to prepare the population of the world to understand the vast importance of the second creation of Humanity, from the birth of each individual, through the agency of man, by creating entirely new surroundings in which to place all through life, and by which a new human nature would appear to arise from the new surroundings.

Robert Owen,
 Welsh social reformer

I shall leave a name execrated by every monopolist...who clamours for protection because it accrues to his personal benefit; but it may be that I shall leave a name sometime remembered with good will in the abodes of those whose lot it is to labour, and to earn their daily bread by the sweat of their brow, when they shall recruit their exhausted strength with abundant and untaxed food, the sweeter because it is no longer leavened with a sense of injustice.

Sir Robert Peel,
 in his last speech as prime minister, 1850

I have been acting the part of a very distinguished tightrope dancer and much astounding the public by my individual performances and feats...so far so well, but even Madame Sacqui, when she had mounted her rope and flourished among her rockets, never thought of making the rope her perch but providently came down to avoid a dangerous fall.

Lord Palmerston,
 British Home Secretary in Aberdeen's coalition, 1852

I am far from insensible to the pleasure of having fame, rank and this opulence which has come so late.

Lord Macaulay,
 English historian, in his journal for 1858, a year before his death

As I would not be a slave, so I would not be a master. This expresses my idea of democracy. Whatever differs from this, to the extent of the difference, is no democracy.

Abraham Lincoln,
 US vice-president, 1858

There is always room for a man of force — and he makes room for many.

Ralph Waldo Emerson,
 US poet and essayist: *The Conduct of Life*, 1860

A man...who has faith in everybody and enjoys the confidence of nobody

William H. Seward,
 US politician, on himself, 1862

I'm not a politician and my other habits are good.

Artemus Ward,
 US wit and essayist: 'Fourth of July Oration', 1862

Let them impeach and be damned!

Andrew Johnson,
 US president, facing a motion that failed to impeach him by one vote, 1868

I was a rock of order.

Prince Clemens Metternich,
 Austrian statesman, last words, 1859

'The Artisan of German Unity'/The Mansell Collection

BOOK OF POLITICAL QUOTES

If my worst enemy was given the job of writing my epitaph when I'm gone, he couldn't do more than write: 'George W. Plunkitt. He seen his opportunities and he took 'em.'

George W. Plunkitt,
Tammany Hall politician

I will not go down to posterity talking bad grammar.

Benjamin Disraeli,
former British prime minister, correcting
Hansard proofs on his death-bed, 1881

On April 23, Shakespeare, St George and myself were all born, and I am the only survivor.

Chauncey M. Depew,
US politician

A house lamb and a street lion.

Thomas Hart Benton,
US politician, on himself

I know if I was chief I would never employ myself, for I am incorrigible.

General Charles Gordon,
British soldier, on himself, 1883

I am not concerning myself about what history will think, but contenting myself with the approval of a fellow named Cleveland whom I have generally found to be a pretty good sort of fellow.

Grover Cleveland,
US president, on himself

I will do my duty as I see it, without regard to scraps of paper called constitutions.

Wilhelm I,
German emperor, 1887

I have a tendency against which I should, perhaps, be on my guard, to swim against the stream.

Winston Churchill

I am as strong as a bull moose, and you may use me to the limit.

Theodore Roosevelt,
US president

It's no use sitting on me — for I am india-rubber, and I bounce!

Winston Churchill,
to fellow subalterns at Meerut, 1898

For the present, at any rate, I must proceed alone. I must plough my furrow alone, but before I get to the end of that furrow it is possible that I may not find myself alone.

Lord Rosebery,
British statesman, 1901

Politics, when I am in it, makes me sick.

William Howard Taft,
US president

No president has ever enjoyed himself as much as I.

Theodore Roosevelt

Thank God I am an optimist, and I believe in the common sense of the people of this country.

George V,
English king

While there is a lower class I am in it. While there is a criminal element, I am of it and while there is a soul in prison, I am not free.

Eugene V. Debs,
US socialist, on trial, 1913

I used to be a lawyer, but now I am a reformed character.

Woodrow Wilson,
US president

The fact that my father was president and Chief Justice of the United States was a tremendous help and inspiration in my public career.

Robert A. Taft,
US politician

Old people are always absorbed in something, usually themselves. We prefer to be absorbed in the Soviet Union.

Sidney and Beatrice Webb,
English Fabian social reformers and
historians

I hate fences. I always feel like knocking down every fence I come across.

David Lloyd George,
British Chancellor of the Exchequer, 1915

Non-violence is the first article of my faith. It is also the last article of my creed.

Mahatma Gandhi,
1922

I have noticed that nothing I ever said ever did me any harm.

Calvin Coolidge,
US president

I can only say that, while my own opinions as to ethics do not satisfy me, other people's satisfy me even less.

Bertrand Russell,
English philosopher: *Reply to My Critics*

In my will it will be one day written that nothing is to be engraved on my tombstone but 'Adolf Hitler'. I shall create my own title for myself in my name itself.

Adolf Hitler

My principle is take a trick while you can and go on with the game.

Lord Beaverbrook,
Canadian-born British newspaper magnate,
1930

I should like to be known as a former president who tries to mind his own business.

Calvin Coolidge,
former US president, 1930

Think of me as a coal miner and you won't make any mistakes.

John L. Lewis,
US trade union leader

I believe that Providence has chosen me for a great work.

Adolf Hitler,
German presidential candidate, 1932

I want to be a hero!

Joseph Goebbels,
Nazi Minister of Propaganda

I ask you to judge me by the enemies I have made.

Franklin D. Roosevelt,
US presidential candidate, 1932

I learnt one thing from father — and that was to hate, to hate!

Lord Beaverbrook,
Canadian-born British newspaper magnate,
1935

I pledge you, I pledge myself, to a new deal for the American people.

Franklin D. Roosevelt,
US president, announcing the New Deal in
a speech actually written by Judge Samuel I.
Rosenmann, 1932

Oh hell, say I'm *sui generis* and leave it at that.

Huey P. Long,
governor of Louisiana, asked to define
himself

A maxi-millionaire.

Lord Beaverbrook,
Canadian-born British newspaper magnate,
on himself

I go the way that Providence dictates with the assurance of a sleepwalker.

Adolf Hitler,
Nazi führer on entering the Rhineland, 1936

I suppose they asked me to show him that, if they couldn't bark themselves, they kept a dog who could bark and might bite.

Winston Churchill,
on being asked by the Chamberlain
government to meet the German ambassador
Ribbentrop

I am what I have always been — the last Renaissance man, if I may be allowed to say so.

Hermann Goering,
Nazi leader

I invented the low blow.

Fiorello LaGuardia,
mayor of New York City

If I am not France, what am I doing in your office?

Charles de Gaulle,
    making his claim to Winston Churchill to lead the Free French after the fall of France, 1940

I was not the lion, but it fell to me to give the lion's roar.

Winston Churchill

I never feel comfortable in the presence of policemen, unless they're sitting beside me at a function.

Sir Robert Menzies,
    Australian prime minister

I would rather be right than president, but I am perfectly willing to be both.

Norman Thomas,
    US socialist, 1949

There are some of us, Mr Chairman, who will fight and fight and fight again to save the party we love.

Hugh Gaitskell,
    British opposition leader, 1960

Hugh Gaitskell at the Lyceum Ballroom/Popperfoto

I can give it and I can take it.

Lord Beaverbrook,
    Canadian-born British newspaper magnate, in a letter to Tom Driberg MP, 1952

Once you get into the great stream of history you can't get out.

Richard Nixon

Boys, I may not know much, but I know chicken shit from chicken salad.

Lyndon B. Johnson,
    then Senate Majority Leader, commenting on a speech by Vice-President Richard Nixon

I went to work when eleven years old for two and six a week, though I may not have been worth more.

Aneurin Bevan,
    British Labour politician, 1952

The singing of one nightingale does not make the spring.

Josip Broz Tito,
    Yugoslav president, on himself

I never gave them hell. I just tell the truth and they think it's hell.

Harry S. Truman,
    former US president, 1956

I have never bothered with politics.

Francisco Franco

I do unto others what they do unto me, only worse.

Jimmy Hoffa,
    boss of US Teamsters Union, 1957

I always thought I was Joan of Arc and Bonaparte. How little one knows oneself.

Charles de Gaulle,
    to a speaker who compared him to Robespierre, 1958

One newspaper, I am told, has perpetually in type the headline 'Mac At Bay'. I suggest they also keep in type 'Mac Bounces Back'.

Harold Macmillan

HAIL TO THE CHIEF

I am the Congo. The Congo has made me and I am making the Congo.

Patrice Lumumba,
  leader of Congolese independence, 1960

If someone hits me on the left cheek, I would not turn my own. I would hit him on the right cheek, and so hard that it would knock his head off.

Nikita Kruschev

Lady Bird, how do you like *my* building?

Sam Rayburn,
  Speaker of the US House of Representatives, to Lady Bird Johnson as they passed the Capitol building

I had a contract with France. Things might have gone well or ill, but she was behind me.

Charles de Gaulle,
  1958

If I had not been born Perón, I should have liked to be Perón.

Juan Perón,
  exiled Argentinian president, 1960

We are all worms, but I think I am a glow-worm.

Winston Churchill

If I had the choice between smoked salmon and tinned salmon, I'd have it tinned. With vinegar.

Harold Wilson,
  British opposition leader, 1962

That's us. The President, that's my brother. The Government, that's me. And the people, that's you.

Robert Kennedy,
  US Attorney-General, replying to Willy Brandt's toast 'To the President, Government and People of the USA' and actually speaking to his brother, Edward, 1962

An idealist without illusions.

John F. Kennedy,
US presidential candidate, on himself, 1960

They may call me a twister, but I don't do the twist.

Harold Macmillan,
British prime minister, refusing to dance at a Conservative Party rally at the height of the Profumo Affair, 1963

Sure, it's a big job — but I don't know anyone who can do it better than I can.

John F. Kennedy

I myself have become a Gaullist only little by little.

Charles de Gaulle,
French president, 1963

When I get out of that car you can just see them light up and feel the warmth coming up at you...the Negroes go off the ground. They cling to my hands like I was Jesus Christ walking among them.

Lyndon B. Johnson,
US president, 1964

There is an epitaph in Boot Hill Cemetery which reads 'Here lies Jack Williams. He done his damnedest. What more could a person do?' Well, that's all I could do. I did my damnedest and that's all there is to it.

Harry S. Truman,
former US president, 1964

I am not a Kennedy. You see, I am a Johnson. I fly by the seat of my pants.

Harold Wilson,
British prime minister, 1964

What have you come to learn?

Charles de Gaulle,
French president, to a visiting Lyndon B. Johnson, 1963

I'm not smart, but I like to observe. Millions saw the apple fall, but Newton was the one who asked why.

Bernard Baruch,
US financier and presidential confidant, 1965

Organizing the middle classes.

Clive Jenkins,
general secretary of the Association of Scientific, Technical and Managerial Staffs, entry in Who's Who under 'Hobbies'

However uneasy I am about being spoken of too well by too many men, I don't feel I'm obliged to go out and smash somebody's window to prove that I'm not respectable.

Norman Thomas,
US socialist, 1966

There are two kinds of prime minister I will never be. A Ramsay MacDonald or a Dubček.

Harold Wilson

I want *loyalty.* I want him to kiss my ass in Macy's window at high noon and tell me it smells like roses. I want his pecker in my pocket.

Lyndon B. Johnson,
offering a guideline for assessing White House staffers

Abdel Nasser is no more than a transient phenomenon that will run its course and leave.

Gamal Abdel Nasser,
Egyptian president, 1967

Hell, it *is* part rattlesnake!

Lyndon B. Johnson,
replying to a CBS reporter who was watching him urinate into dense undergrowth and who asked: 'Aren't you afraid a rattle-snake might bite it?'

Yes, if you want to say that I was a drum major, say that I was a drum major for justice; say that I was a drum major for peace; I was a drum major for righteousness. And all of the other shallow things will not matter.

Martin Luther King,
US civil rights leader, suggesting his own eulogy, 1968

I was born a Tory. I am a Tory and I shall die a Tory!

Enoch Powell,
British politician

HAIL TO THE CHIEF

Why should I listen to all those student peaceniks marching up and down the streets? They wouldn't know a Communist if they tripped over one. They simply don't understand the world the way I do.

Lyndon B. Johnson

They're *all* my helicopters, son.

Lyndon B. Johnson,
  to an Air Force corporal who pointed out the presidential helicopter, saying 'This is your helicopter, sir.'

I am not one of those who think that coming second or third is winning.

Robert Kennedy,
  US politician, 1968

I am not, and have never been, a man of the right. My position was on the left and is now in the centre of politics.

Sir Oswald Mosley,
  British Fascist leader, 1968

The numeral accords with my estimate of myself. My only worry is how I will look in short pants.

Henry Kissinger,
  US National Security Adviser, after being presented with a Harlem Globetrotters' uniform inscribed 'Number One'

For years politicians have promised the moon — I'm the first one to be able to deliver it.

Richard Nixon,
  US president, after the successful landing of Apollo XI, 1969

I am very proud to be called a pig. It stands for pride, integrity and guts.

Ronald Reagan,
  governor of California, 1970

I've always acted alone. Americans admire that enormously. Americans admire the cowboy leading the caravan alone on his horse, the cowboy entering a village or city alone on his horse.

Henry Kissinger,
  US National Security Adviser

Lord George-Brown/Popperfoto

I could never be shouted down in the other place and I'm not going to be shouted down here.

Lord George-Brown,
  former deputy leader of the Labour government, after his elevation to the House of Lords, 1970

I usually make up my mind about a man in ten seconds, and I very rarely change it.

Margaret Thatcher,
  Secretary of State for Education and Science, 1970

However tired people may be of me, I think most people in the country will regard me as the lesser of two evils. I always put these things in a modest way.

Harold Wilson,
  British Labour prime minister, during his unsuccessful election campaign, 1970

I rate myself a deeply committed pacifist.

Richard Nixon,
  US president, 1971

I would have made a good pope.

Richard Nixon

I am a lone monk walking the world with a leaky umbrella.

Mao Tse-tung,
1971

When presidents begin to worry about images...they become like athletes, the football teams and the rest, who become so concerned about what is written about them and what is said about them that they don't play the game well....The President, with the enormous responsibilities he has, must not be constantly preening in front of a mirror....I don't worry about polls, I don't worry about images. I never have.

Richard Nixon,
US president, 1971

I'm not asking for popularity, I'm not seeking it. In fact, if you really want to know, I care nothing for popularity. I can afford to say what I think. I am referring to what is genuine in me. Take actors, for instance, the really good ones don't rely on mere technique. They also follow their feelings when they play a part. Like me, they are genuine.

Henry Kissinger,
US National Security Adviser

Today I am one trillionth part of history.

Arthur Bremer,
after failing to assassinate George Wallace, 1972

I did not know that I was a radical or a nationalist. I thought I was a person.

Bishop Abel Muzorewa,
Zimbabwe leader, 1972

I would have been deeply offended if they had left me off the list.

John Kenneth Galbraith,
Canadian-born US economist, on the Nixon White House's 'Enemies List', 1973

However rough the seas are, I don't get seasick.

Richard Nixon,
US president weathering the Watergate storm, 1973

You can call me bourgeois, but not decadent.

Gough Whitlam,
Australian prime minister, 1973

I don't give a damn about protocol, I'm a swinger. Bring on the beautiful spies!

Henry Kissinger,
US National Security Adviser, at an East European state banquet, 1973

It is a compliment to be criticised for giving too much importance to style.

Valery Giscard d'Estaing,
French president, 1974

I am not a product of privilege, I am a product of opportunity.

Edward Heath,
British prime minister, 1974

I think it fair to say that my own estimate of myself may be at variance with that of some of my critics.

Henry Kissinger,
US National Security Adviser, 1974

If we had a presidential system, on polls I would no doubt be a candidate.

Enoch Powell,
British politician and darling of anti-immigrant lobby, 1974

I have never been an idealist — that implies you aren't going to achieve something.

Arthur Scargill,
president of the Yorkshire branch of the National Union of Miners, 1974

There is a great amount of talent in the Parliamentary Labour Party, but I believe that I have the greatest amount of talent at the present time.

Gough Whitlam,
Australian prime minister, 1974

I see myself as a deep-lying half-back feeding the ball forward to the chaps who score the goals.

Harold Wilson,
British prime minister, 1974

Cyril Smith and friends/Popperfoto

If the fence is strong enough, I'll sit on it.

Cyril Smith,
obese British politician, 1974

BOOK OF POLITICAL QUOTES

I am a bit of a showman, and I don't mind admitting it.

Jeremy Thorpe,
   British Liberal Party leader, 1974

I am in the fortunate position of being an irresponsible academic who can say what I want.

Milton Friedman,
   monetarist guru of Chile, Israel and the UK, visiting Australia, 1975

I don't believe in the destruction of ego. I just think it got a bad press.

Abbie Hoffman,
   Yippie! leader, 1975

I've got a woman's ability to stick to a job and get on with it when everyone else walks off and leaves it.

Margaret Thatcher,
   British opposition leader, 1975

The greatest show in the world and I got the best seats there are.

Abbie Hoffman,
   former Yippie! leader, on his life on the run, 1975

He is lofty, and I am eminent.

Gough Whitlam,
   Australian prime minister, commenting on the difference between opposition leader Malcolm Fraser and himself, 1975

Few people realize that I am a conservationist at heart.

Joh Bjelke-Petersen,
   Queensland premier and die-hard supporter of mining and exporting nuclear fuels, 1976

Ladies and gentlemen, I stand before you tonight in my green chiffon evening gown, my face softly made up, my fair hair softly waved.... The Iron Lady of the Western World? Me? A cold warrior? Well, yes — if that is how they wish to interpret my defence of the values and freedom fundamental to our way of life.

Margaret Thatcher,
   British opposition leader, referring to the Soviet magazine *Red Star* which had called her the 'Iron Lady', 1976

I find a fence a very uncomfortable place to squat my bottom.

Bob Hawke,
   Australian trade union leader, 1976

I'm not trying to compare myself with Roosevelt, but he couldn't walk either.

George Wallace,
   governor of Alabama, crippled after an assassination attempt, 1976

I enjoy myself in the public bars of pubs more than anywhere else, almost.

Malcolm Fraser,
   Australian prime minister, 1977

There is no substitute for experience.

Joh Bjelke-Petersen,
   eccentric Queensland premier, killing off hopes of his retirement on his sixty-sixth birthday, 1977

I'm pretty much an out-front, straightforward chick.

Margaret Trudeau,
   playgirl wife of Canadian premier, Pierre, 1977

I do not have to tell you that preaching caution and restraint are not the most congenial roles to me.

Gough Whitlam,
   Australian Labor Party leader, 1977

Life is pleasantly tough. I don't expect it to be anything else.

Sir John Kerr,
   Australian Governor-General, 1978

A poet and a revolutionary — that is what I have been all these years and that is how I shall remain until the last breath is gone from my body.

Zulfikar Ali Bhutto,
   former Pakistani president, last words before his execution, 1979

I managed to rank in the top twenty-five per cent of our class. How that happened I can't explain.

Gerald Ford,
   former US president: *A Time to Heal*, 1979

HAIL TO THE CHIEF

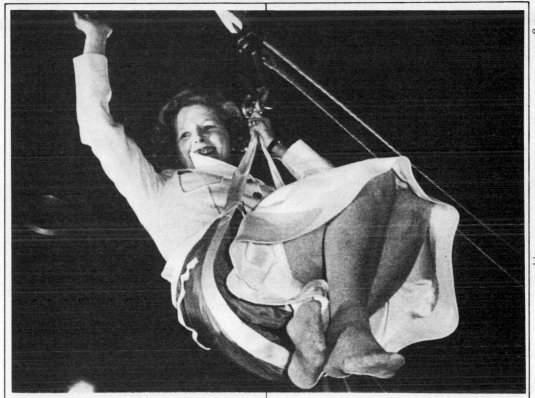

I haven't the figure for jeans.

Margaret Thatcher,
    British prime minister, 1980

I am no intellectual but just an ordinary, simple, working-class lad from the shop floor with simple tastes. I am president today because I can feel the pulse of the shop-floor.

Terry Duffy,
    newly elected president of the AUEW, 1978

I envisaged my job at the White House as that of manager and was determined to be the best manager a president ever had. That meant I had to be tough. I was tough. Add to that a reputation for puritanism and you're nearing the Nazi image.

H. R. Haldeman,
    former Nixon aide: *The Ends of Power*, 1978

I will be the one who will choose the government with the support of the people.

Ayatollah Khomeini,
    religious dictator of Iran, 1979

If someone is confronting our essential liberties, if someone is inflicting injuries and harm   by God, I'll confront them!

Margaret Thatcher,
    British prime minister, 1979

I know that during my long life I have always been right about what I said.

Ayatollah Khomeini,
    religious dictator of Iran, 1979

If a competent man, combining in himself ...supreme virtues, appears and founds a true Islamic government, it means that he has been invested by the Almighty with the same mandate as the Holy Prophet to lead the people. Therefore it is the people's absolute duty to follow him.

Ayatollah Khomeini,
    religious dictator of Iran: *Sayings*, 1980

USAGE AND ABUSAGE

I will prove you the notoriousest traitor that ever came to the bar...thou art a monster; thou hast an English face, but a Spanish heart...thou art the most vile and execrable traitor that ever lived. I want words sufficient to express thy viperous treasons. ...Thou art an odious fellow, thy name is hateful to all the realm of England....There never lived a viler viper upon the face of the earth than thou.

Sir Edward Coke,
    English jurist, to Sir Walter Raleigh at the latter's trial, 1601

The best that, perhaps, can be said of him is that on the whole, all things considered, he might have been worse.

Justin McCarthy,
    Irish politician, on George II of England: *A History of the Four Georges*

England has been a long time in labour, but she has at last brought forth a man.

Frederick the Great,
    Prussian king, on William Pitt the Elder

He was not merely a chip off the old block, but the old block itself.

Edmund Burke,
    British statesman, on William Pitt the Younger after the latter's maiden speech as an MP, 1781

Pitt is to Addington/ As London is to Paddington

George Canning,
    British statesman on the respective prime ministers: *The Oracle*, 1823

This man, I thought, had been a lord among wits; but, I find, he is only a wit among Lords!

Samuel Johnson,
    English lexicographer, critic and poet, on Lord Chesterfield after reading Chesterfield's 'Letters'

Rousseau was the first militant low-brow.

Isaiah Berlin,
    English philosopher, 1952

The great snorting bawler.

William Cobbett,
    British controversialist, on William Pitt the Younger: *Rural Rides*, 1830

The Right Honourable Gentleman is indebted to his memory for his jests and to his imagination for his facts.

Richard Sheridan,
    Irish playwright and politician, on Henry Dundas, a member of Pitt's Cabinet

For great evils, drastic remedies are necessary and whoever has to treat them should not be afraid to use the instrument that cuts the best.

Prince Clemens Metternich,
    Austrian statesman, on Talleyrand, 1808

I met Murder on the way/ He had a mask like Castlereagh

Percy Bysshe Shelley,
    English poet attacking the prime minister who had authorised the 'Peterloo Massacre': *The Mask of Anarchy*, 1819

USAGE AND ABUSAGE

Throughout the greater part of his life George III was a kind of consecrated obstruction.

Walter Bagehot,
   British economist and journalist: *The English Constitution*, 1867

He is the purest figure in history.

William Gladstone,
   on George Washington

He is too illiterate, unread, unlearned for his station and reputation.

John Adams,
   US president, on his predecessor George Washington

The indefatigable air of a village apothecary inspecting the tongue of the State.

Lord Rosebery,
   British prime minister, on Henry Addington, Viscount Sidmouth

The principles of Jefferson are the axioms of a free society.

Abraham Lincoln,
   on his predecessor, Thomas Jefferson

His flame blazed like a straw bonfire and has left behind it a shovelful of ashes. Never any public man had it in his power to do so much good for his country, nor was there ever one who accomplished so little.

J.A. Froude,
   English historian, on Irish politician Daniel O'Connell: *Short Studies*, 1867-83

He has all the characteristics of a dog except loyalty.

Sam Houston,
   US senator, on fellow legislator Thomas Jefferson Green

The Right Honourable Gentleman caught the Whigs bathing and walked away with their clothes. He has left them in full enjoyment of their liberal position and he is himself a strict conservative of their garments.

Benjamin Disraeli,
   British statesman, on Sir Robert Peel, 1837

The Right Honourable Gentleman's smile is like the fittings on a coffin.

Benjamin Disraeli,
   on Sir Robert Peel

The Right Honourable Gentleman is reminiscent of a poker. The only difference is that a poker gives off occasional signs of warmth.

Benjamin Disraeli,
   on Sir Robert Peel

If he were a horse, nobody would buy him; with that eye no one could answer for his temper.

Walter Bagehot,
   British economist and journalist, on Lord Brougham

An arch mediocrity presiding over a Cabinet of mediocrities.

Benjamin Disraeli
   on Lord Liverpool

I can't spare this man — he fights.

Abraham Lincoln
   on Ulysses S. Grant

His mind was a kind of extinct sulphur pit.

Thomas Carlyle,
   Scottish author and historian, on Napoleon III

If a traveller were informed that such a man was leader of the House of Commons he may begin to comprehend how the Egyptians worshipped an insect.

Benjamin Disraeli
   on Sir John Russell

Napoleon — mighty somnambulist of a vanished dream.

Victor Hugo
   on Napoleon Bonaparte: *Les Misérables*, 1862

As he rose like a rocket, he fell like a stick.

Tom Paine,
   English radical pamphleteer, on Edmund Burke

John Wilkes Booth assassinates Abraham Lincoln/Mary Evans Picture Library

Our country owes all our troubles to him, and God simply made me an instrument of his punishment.

John Wilkes Booth,
   Abraham Lincoln's assassin, on his victim, 1865

Lincoln was a sad man because he couldn't get it all at once. And nobody can.

Franklin D. Roosevelt
   on Abraham Lincoln

I cannot believe that the killing of two thousand Englishmen at New Orleans qualifies a person for the various difficult and complicated duties of the presidency.

Henry Clay,
   US politician, on his rival, President Andrew Jackson

When I was in high school, Abraham Lincoln was my idol. I truly admired him because, although he *never* went to college, he never gave up and *made* himself the President of the United States!

Edy Williams,
   Hollywood sex symbol, in a letter to *Esquire* **magazine, 1973**

The constitution provides for every accidental contingency in the Executive, except for a vacancy in the mind of the president.

Senator Sherman
   of Ohio on President James Buchanan

There is Jackson, standing like a stone wall. Let us determine to die here and we will conquer.

Brigadier-General Barnard E. Bee,
   coining a nickname at the First Battle of Bull Run, 1862

The only way to deal with such a man as O'Connell is to hang him up and erect a statue to him under the gallows.

Sydney Smith,
   English journalist, clergyman and wit, on Daniel O'Connell

Susan is lean and cadaverous and intellectual, with the proportions of a file and the voice of a hurdy-gurdy.

The New York *World*,
   on suffragette Susan B. Anthony, 1866

USAGE AND ABUSAGE

The arch-philistine Jeremy Bentham was the insipid, pedantic, leather-tongued oracle of the bourgeois intelligence of the nineteenth century.

Karl Marx:
   Das Kapital, **1867**

He struck me much like a steam engine in trousers.

Sydney Smith,
   English journalist, clergyman and wit, on US statesman Daniel Webster

I don't object to Gladstone always having the ace of trumps up his sleeve, but merely to his belief that God Almighty put it there.

Sir Henry Labouchère,
   British statesman, on William Gladstone

Well, if Gladstone fell into the Thames, that would be a misfortune, and if anybody pulled him out, that, I suppose, would be a calamity.

Benjamin Disraeli
   defining two words

An almost spectral kind of a phantasm of a man — nothing in him but forms and ceremonies and outside wrappings

Thomas Carlyle,
   Scottish author and historian, on William Gladstone, 1873

A sophisticated rhetorician intoxicated with the exuberance of his own verbosity.

Benjamin Disraeli,
   British prime minister, on William Gladstone, 1878

An old man in a hurry.

Lord Randolph Churchill
   on William Gladstone, 1886

He has not a single redeeming defect.

Benjamin Disraeli
   on William Gladstone

He speaks to me as if I were a public meeting.

Queen Victoria
   on William Gladstone

Why, she not only filled the chair, she filled the room.

Duke of Wellington,
   on his first audience with the young Victoria, 1837

Nowadays, a parlour-maid as ignorant as Queen Victoria was when she came to the throne would be classed as mentally defective.

George Bernard Shaw,
   Irish playwright

I never deny, I never contradict. I sometimes forget.

Benjamin Disraeli
   on handling Queen Victoria

I admire him, I freely confess it. And when his time comes I shall buy a piece of the rope for a keepsake.

Mark Twain,
   US author, on empire-builder Cecil Rhodes

The Great Panjandrum.

Alfred Munby,
   referring to Benjamin Disraeli, in his diary for 1874

He is a self-made man, and worships his creator.

John Bright,
   British radical statesman and orator, on Benjamin Disraeli

How long will John Bull allow this absurd monkey to dance on his chest?

Thomas Carlyle,
   Scottish author and historian, on Benjamin Disraeli

He sailed through American history like a steel ship loaded with monoliths of granite.

H.L. Mencken,
   US philologist, editor and satirist, on President Grover Cleveland, 1933

To President Roosevelt we ascribe that quality that medieval theology assigned to God — he was pure act.

Henry Adams,
   US historian, on Theodore Roosevelt

A nonentity with sidewhiskers.

Woodrow Wilson,
    on his predecessor Chester Arthur

Dropping the pilot

Punch
    captioning a cartoon on Bismarck's resignation, 1890

His mind was like a soup dish, wide and shallow, it could hold a small amount of nearly anything, but the slightest jarring spilled the soup into somebody's lap.

Irving Stone,
    US author, on US politician William Jennings Bryan

He can take a batch of words and scramble them together and leaven them properly with a hunk of oratory and knock the White House door-knob right out of a candidate's hand.

Will Rogers,
    US humorist, on US politician William Jennings Bryan

You show the bourgeoisie your behind. We, on the contrary, look them in the face.

Georgi Plekhanov,
    Social Democrat leader, to Lenin, 1895

One always thinks of him as a glorified bouncer engaged eternally in cleaning out bar-rooms — and not too proud to gouge when the inspiration came to him, or to bite in the clinches.

H.L. Mencken,
    US philologist, editor and satirist, on President Theodore Roosevelt: *Prejudices*, second series

McKinley shows all the backbone of a chocolate eclair.

Theodore Roosevelt
    on his predecessor William McKinley

The manners of a cad and the tongue of a bargee.

H.H. Asquith,
    British statesman, on Prime Minister Joseph Chamberlain, 1900

Austen always played the game and always lost it.

Lord Birkenhead,
    British Conservative statesman and lawyer, on Sir Austen Chamberlain

A man with the vision of an eagle but with a blind spot in his eye.

Andrew Bonar Law,
    British prime minister, on Lord Birkenhead

A good saying which I sometimes call to mind when I am confronting Bonar Law.

H.H. Asquith,
    British prime minister, recalling Boling-broke's dismissal of an opponent: 'I never wrestle with a chimney sweep.'

Black and wicked and with only a nodding acquaintance with the truth.

Lady Emerald Cunard,
    on H.H. Asquith, quoted in 'Chips' Channon's *Diary*, 1944

It is fitting that we should have buried the Unknown Prime Minister by the side of the Unknown Soldier.

H.H. Asquith,
    British statesman, after Bonar Law had been buried in Westminster Abbey, 1923

For twenty years he held a season ticket on the line of least resistance, and has gone wherever the train of events has carried him, lucidly justifying his position at whatever point he has happened to find himself.

Leo Amery,
    British politician, on H.H. Asquith, 1916

It was with a sense of awe that [the Germans] turned upon Russia the most grisly of all weapons. They transported Lenin in a sealed truck like a plague bacillus from Switzerland into Russia.

Winston Churchill:
    ***The World Crisis*, 1923-29**

Born into the ranks of the working class, the new King's most likely fate would have been that of a street-corner loafer.

James Keir Hardie,
    Labour Party pioneer, on George V, 1910

USAGE AND ABUSAGE

I feel I am getting a down on George V just now. He is all right as a gay young midshipman. He may be all right as a wise old king. But the intervening period when he was just shooting at Sandringham is hard to manage or to swallow. For seventeen years he did nothing at all but kill animals and stick in stamps.

Harold Nicolson,
   English diplomat, author and critic, on his biography of George V

Mr Baldwin, a well-meaning man of indifferent judgement who, whether he did right or wrong, was always sustained by a belief that he was acting for the best.

Lord Beaverbrook,
   Canadian-born British newspaper magnate, on Prime Minister Stanley Baldwin, 1937

This second-rate orator trails his tawdry wisps of mist over the parliamentary scene.

Aneurin Bevan,
   British Labour politician, on Prime Minister Stanley Baldwin, 1937

He spent his whole life in plastering together the true and the false and therefrom manufacturing the plausible.

Stanley Baldwin,
   quoting Carlyle to attack Lloyd George

He did not care in which direction the car was travelling, so long as he remained in the driver's seat.

Lord Beaverbrook,
   Canadian-born British newspaper magnate, on Lloyd George, quoted in the *New Statesman*, 1963

He could not see a belt without hitting below it.

Margot Asquith,
   wife of H.H. Asquith, on Lloyd George

Instead of making his violent speech without moving his moderate amendment, he had better have moved his moderate amendment without making his violent speech.

Winston Churchill,
   as a neophyte MP, on Lloyd George, 1900

Mr Chamberlain loves the working man — he loves to see him work.

Winston Churchill
   on Joseph Chamberlain

He is a young man who will go far if he doesn't overbalance.

Cecil Rhodes,
   English-born South African statesman on Winston Churchill, 1901

He can best be described as one of those orators who, before they get up, do not know what they are going to say; and when they are speaking do not know what they are saying; and when they have sat down, do not know what they have said.

Winston Churchill
   on Lord Charles Beresford, who had criticised his appointment as First Sea Lord, 1912

How can I talk to a fellow who thinks himself the first man in two thousand years to know anything about peace on earth.

Georges Clemenceau,
   French prime minister, on Woodrow Wilson, 1919

He had only one illusion — France — and only one disillusion — mankind.

John Maynard Keynes,
   English economist, on Georges Clemenceau: *The Worldly Philosophers*

Like Odysseus, he looked wiser when seated.

John Maynard Keynes,
   on Woodrow Wilson: *The Worldly Philosophers*

Well, it was the best I could do, seated as I was between Jesus Christ and Napoleon Bonaparte.

David Lloyd George,
   British prime minister, during his negotiations with Woodrow Wilson and Georges Clemenceau on the Versailles Treaty, 1919

Lloyd George believes himself to be Napoleon, but President Wilson believes himself to be Jesus Christ.

Georges Clemenceau,
   French prime minister, 1919

I feel certain that he would not recognize a generous impulse if he met it in the street.

William Howard Taft,
  US president, on his successor Woodrow Wilson

I have long heard of the reputation for wisdom and wit of the senator from Massachusetts, but his speech today has convinced me that his mind is like the land of his native state — barren by nature and impoverished by cultivation.

Senator Thaddeus Caraway,
  attacking Henry Cabot Lodge, whose speech in Congress had just destroyed Woodrow Wilson's Fourteen Points, 1919

Woodrow Wilson is gone, gone; but his spirit goes marching on! on!/ For freedom of word, thought and speech, ho! ho!!/ That was our grand President Woodrow/ Even yet his noble plans will prevail; and on earth Fatherhood of God and Brotherhood of Man is not doomed to fail, ho! ho!!/ That is the spirit of our grand President Woodrow....

The _Tacoma News_,
  a Maryland newspaper, in an obituary for Woodrow Wilson, 1925

Mr Coolidge's genius for inactivity is developed to a very high point. It is far from being an indolent activity. It is a grim, determined, alert inactivity which keeps Mr Coolidge occupied constantly....Inactivity is a political philosophy and a party programme with Mr Coolidge.

Walter Lippmann,
  US political commentator, on President Calvin Coolidge

He is the first president to discover that what the American people want is to be left alone.

Will Rogers,
  US humorist, on President Calvin Coolidge

Though I yield to no one in my admiration for Mr Coolidge, I do wish he did not look as if he had been weaned on a pickle.

Alice Roosevelt Longworth,
  Washington wit and social arbiter, her attributed verdict on President Calvin Coolidge

A Byzantine logothete.

Theodore Roosevelt
  on his successor Woodrow Wilson

He was the Messiah of the New Age, and his crucifixion was yet to come.

George Slocombe,
  British journalist and war correspondent, on Woodrow Wilson's visit to the Versailles peace talks: _Mirror to Geneva_

How do they know?

Wilson Mizner,
  US gambler and wheeler-dealer, on the death of Calvin Coolidge, 1933. Also attributed to Dorothy Parker

There is no snobbishness like that of professional equalitarians.

Malcolm Muggeridge,
  British journalist, on Sidney and Beatrice Webb, pioneer Fabians: _Chronicles of Wasted Time_, Volume I, 1978

Poor Sidney can't put the breeches on, because his wife wears them.

J.H. Thomas,
  British Labour politician, to George V, who noted that Sidney Webb — newly created Lord Passfield — refused to wear court dress for socialist reasons, 1929

If I were the Prince of Peace, I should choose a less provocative ambassador.

A.E. Housman,
  English scholar and poet, on Bertrand Russell

Harding was not a bad man. He was just a slob.

Alice Roosevelt Longworth,
  Washington wit and social arbiter, on President Warren G. Harding

His speeches left the impression of an army of pompous phrases moving over the landscape in search of an idea. Sometimes these meandering words would actually capture a straggling thought and bear it triumphantly, a prisoner in their midst, until it died of servitude and overwork.

Senator William G. McAdoo,
  on President Warren G. Harding

USAGE AND ABUSAGE

He writes the worst English that I have ever encountered. It reminds me of a string of wet sponges; it reminds me of tattered washing on the line; it reminds me of stale bean soup, of college yells, of dogs barking through endless nights. It is so bad that a sort of grandeur creeps into it. It drags itself out of the dark abysm of pish, and crawls insanely up the topmost pinnacle of posh. It is rumble and bumble. It is flap and doodle. It is balder and dash.

H.L. Mencken,
US philologist, editor and satirist, on
President Warren G. Harding

Not even a public figure. A man of no experience. And of the utmost inexperience.

Lord Curzon,
English statesman, on Prime Minister
Stanley Baldwin

I am afraid Mr Baldwin will never make a great leader as he seems to have a congenital incapacity for playing a dirty game.

Captain William Wedgwood Benn,
English Labour politician, on Prime
Minister Stanley Baldwin, 1929

I remember, when I was a child, being taken to the celebrated Barnum's Circus, which contained an exhibition of freaks and monstrosities. But the exhibit on the programme that I most desired to see was the one described as 'The Boneless Wonder'. My parents judged that the spectacle would be too revolting and too demoralizing for my youthful eyes, and I waited fifty years to see the Boneless Wonder sitting on the Treasury Bench.

Winston Churchill,
British statesman, on Prime Minister
Ramsay MacDonald, 1933

Sit down man, you're a bloody tragedy!

James Maxton,
Scottish politician, to Ramsay MacDonald
as he made his last speech in the Commons

A Winston Churchill who has never been at Harrow.

H.G. Wells,
English author, on Huey Long, governor of
Louisiana

The Honourable Gentleman should not generate more indignation than he can conveniently contain.

Winston Churchill
to a splenetic Captain William Wedgwood
Benn

He never believed in doing something that he could get someone else to do for him.

Lord Randolph Churchill,
British statesman, on Prime Minister
Stanley Baldwin

He has sufficient conscience to bother him, but not enough to keep him straight.

David Lloyd George,
British statesman, on ex-Prime Minister
Ramsay MacDonald, 1938

He is the greatest living master of falling without hurting himself.

Winston Churchill,
British statesman, on Prime Minister
Ramsay MacDonald, referring to a string of
parliamentary defeats which still failed to
bring down the government, 1931

I need not confirm my faith in the triumph of your cause, and I repeat that I shall always be its loyal follower.

Francisco Franco
to Adolf Hitler, 1938

A small, rather corpulent bourgeois...with the voice of a doctor with a good bedside manner.

Sir Samuel Hoare,
British Ambassador to Spain, on Franco,
1937

He must be the sort of orator who could thrill a multitude by declaiming the explanatory notes on an income tax form.

The Leeds *Mercury*
on British Fascist leader Sir Oswald
Mosley

No man can tame a tiger into a kitten by stroking it. There can be no appeasement with ruthlessness. There can be no reasoning with an incendiary bomb.

Franklin D. Roosevelt,
US president, on Adolf Hitler, 1940

Goering may be a blackguard, but he is not a dirty blackguard.

Sir Neville Henderson,
    British ambassador to Germany

Hitler has the advantages of a man who knows the theatre only from the gallery.

Bertolt Brecht,
    German playwright, 1923

Hitler is simply pure reason incarnate.

Rudolf Hess,
    Nazi leader

Well, he seemed such a nice old gentleman, I thought I would give him my autograph as a souvenir.

Adolf Hitler,
    after accepting Neville Chamberlain's
peace initiative at Munich, 1938

He saw foreign policy through the wrong end of a municipal drainpipe.

David Lloyd George
    on Neville Chamberlain

Listening to a speech by Chamberlain is like paying a visit to Woolworth's: everything in its place and nothing above sixpence.

Aneurin Bevan,
    British Labour politician, on Neville
Chamberlain, 1937

In the depths of that dusty soul is nothing but abject surrender.

Winston Churchill
    on Neville Chamberlain's policy of
appeasement

The worst thing I can say about democracy is that it has tolerated the Right Honourable Gentleman for four and a half years.

Aneurin Bevan,
    British Labour politician, on Neville
Chamberlain, 1940

A labour-baiting, poker-playing, whiskey-drinking evil old man.

John L. Lewis,
    US trade union leader, on Vice-President
John N. Garner

You are placing...the movement in an absolutely wrong position by hawking your conscience round from body to body asking to be told what you ought to do with it.

Ernest Bevin,
    British Labour politician, attacking fellow
Labour MP, George Lansbury, 1935

Our Billy's talk is just like bottled stout — You draw the cork and only froth comes out.

The Brisbane *Truth*
    on Australian prime minister, Billy Hughes

He may be a son of a bitch, but he's our son of a bitch.

Franklin D. Roosevelt,
    US president, on President 'Tacho' Somoza
of Nicaragua, 1938

A simple, barefoot Wall Street lawyer.

Harold Ickes,
    Roosevelt's Secretary of the Interior, on
presidential candidate Wendell Wilkie

There is no surer way of preserving the worst aspects of bourgeois style than by liquidating the bourgeoisie. Whatever else Stalin may or may not have done, he assuredly made Russia safe for the Forsyte Saga.

Malcolm Muggeridge,
    British journalist: *Chronicles of Wasted*
***Time*, Volume I, 1978**

I must remind the Right Honourable Gentleman that a monologue is not a decision.

Clement Attlee,
    British Labour leader, to Winston Churchill,
1945

Churchill on top of the wave has in him the stuff of which tyrants are made.

Lord Beaverbrook,
    Canadian-born British newspaper magnate

I welcome this opportunity of pricking the bloated bladder of lies with the poniard of truth.

Aneurin Bevan,
    British Labour politician, attacking
Winston Churchill

USAGE AND ABUSAGE

Churchill was fundamentally what the English call unstable: by which they mean anybody who has that touch of genius which is inconvenient in normal times.

Harold Macmillan,
    British Conservative elder statesman, 1975

Winston is always expecting rabbits to come out of empty hats.

Field Marshal Lord Wavell
    on Churchill's conduct of the war, 1943

The Prime Minister has got very many virtues, and when the time comes I hope to pay my tribute to them, but I am bound to say that political honesty and sagacity have never been among them.

Aneurin Bevan,
    British Labour politician, on Winston Churchill

His ear is so sensitively attuned to the bugle note of history that he is often deaf to the more raucous clamour of modern life.

Aneurin Bevan
    on Winston Churchill

He has all of the virtues I dislike and none of the vices I admire.

Winston Churchill
    on Labour's Sir Stafford Cripps

Sir Stafford has a brilliant mind until it is made up.

Lady Violet Bonham-Carter,
    Liberal politician and publicist, on Sir Stafford Cripps

There, but for the grace of God, goes God.

Winston Churchill
    on Sir Stafford Cripps

He is a magnet to all young men, and I warn you if you talk to him no good will come of it. Beware of flattery.

Clement Attlee,
    British prime minister, warning his junior ministers against Lord Beaverbrook, 1945

They are not fit to manage a whelk stall.

Winston Churchill
    on the Labour Party

Lloyd George would have a better rating in British mythology if he had shared the fate of Abraham Lincoln.

John Grigg,
    British journalist, 1963

He is like trying to pick up mercury with a fork.

David Lloyd George
    on Irish leader Eamon de Valera

He possessed in his nature all the qualities requisite for the art of civic destruction — the organizing command of a Carnot, the cold detached intelligence of a Machiavelli, the mob oratory of a Cleon, the ferocity of Jack the Ripper, the toughness of a Titus Oates.

Winston Churchill
    on Leon Trotsky: *Great Contemporaries*

After long experience in sizing up people, I definitely know you have the goods and can go a long way. Now aren't you foolish not to get all there is out of what God has given you?

Joseph P. Kennedy
    to his son John F. Kennedy, aged fourteen, 1931

My son was rocked to political lullabies.

Rose Kennedy,
    US political matriarch, on her son John

Each morning, he would take great pains in brushing his teeth, was careful to gargle and asked me to smell his breath to make sure he would not offend anyone on the school bus.

Hannah Nixon
    on her son Richard

He was the best potato masher one could wish for. Even these days, when I'm visiting Richard or Pat in Washington, or when they're visiting me, he will take over the potato mashing. My feeling is that he actually enjoys it.

Hannah Nixon
    on her son Richard

And where does she find them?

Dorothy Parker,
US wit, on hearing that diplomat Clare Booth Luce was always kind to her social inferiors

He is suffering from halitosis of the intellect; that is presuming that Emperor Long has an intellect.

Harold Ickes,
Roosevelt's Secretary of the Interior, on Huey Long

He seems determined to make a trumpet sound like a tin whistle....He brings to the fierce struggle of politics the tepid enthusiasm of a lazy summer afternoon at a cricket match.

Aneurin Bevan,
British Labour politician, on Prime Minister Clement Attlee

He would not blow his nose without moralizing on conditions in the handkerchief industry.

Cyril Connolly,
English author and journalist on George Orwell: *The Evening Colonnade*

Dewey has thrown his diaper in the ring.

Harold Ickes,
US Secretary of the Interior, on the Republican candidate for the presidency

I am against government by crony.

Harold Ickes
on resigning as Secretary of the Interior from the Truman Cabinet, 1946

Roosevelt would rather follow public opinion than lead it.

Harry Hopkins,
US administrator, on President Franklin D. Roosevelt

Clement Attlee kicks off/Popperfoto

USAGE AND ABUSAGE

He is a sheep in sheep's clothing.

Winston Churchill,
  British prime minister, on Clement Attlee,
1945

Attlee is a charming and intelligent man but as a public speaker he is, compared to Winston, like a village fiddler after Paganini.

Harold Nicolson,
  English politician and diarist, 1947

A speech from Ernest Bevin on a major occasion had all the horrid fascination of a public execution. If the mind were left immune, eyes and ears and emotions were riveted.

Michael Foot,
  British Labour politician: *Aneurin Bevan*

The familiar saying that Bevin always treated the Soviet Union as if it were a breakaway faction of the Transport and General Workers Union . . .

Kingsley Martin,
  English political journalist: *Harold Laski*

He objected to ideas only when others had them.

A.J.P. Taylor,
  English historian, on Ernest Bevin

I have always found Roosevelt an amusing fellow, but I would not employ him, except for reasons of personal friendship, as a geek in a common carnival.

Murray Kempton,
  US journalist

Eleanor is a Trojan mare.

Alice Roosevelt Longworth,
  Washington wit and social arbiter, of
Eleanor Roosevelt

He was an absolutely charming, sweet person. He was rather like a little, dejected sparrow. I felt he'd hop and sit on my shoulder any moment.

Earl Mountbatten,
  former Governor-General of India, on
Gandhi, 1975

No woman has so comforted the distressed or distressed the comfortable.

Clare Booth Luce,
  US diplomat, on Eleanor Roosevelt

The only American in *The Brothers Karamazov.*

Alfred Kazin,
  US essayist, on Whittaker Chambers,
protagonist of the Alger Hiss affair, 1946

The Dagwood Bumstead of American politics.

Time **magazine**
  on US Republican senator, Robert A.
Taft, 1940

Pierce didn't know what was going on and even if he had, he wouldn't have known what to do about it.

Harry S. Truman
  on President Franklin Pierce

Never was there a man who represented so completely in himself the distinction between Us and Them.

Francis Williams
  on Harold Nicolson, English diplomat,
author and critic, 1940

To write one's memoirs is to speak ill of everyone except oneself.

Marshal Pétain,
  former French leader, 1946

The General is suffering from mental saddle sores.

Harold Ickes,
  US Secretary of the Interior, on General
Hugh S. Johnson

Among his many weaknesses was his utter inability to discriminate between history and histrionics.

Anonymous commentator
  on President Harry S. Truman, quoted in
General Douglas MacArthur's *Reminiscences*

Never underestimate a man who overestimates himself.

Franklin D. Roosevelt
  on General Douglas MacArthur

He had almost every quality you could wish to have, except he had the brain of an average English gentleman. He lacked that extra little cubic centimetre which produces genius.

Earl Mountbatten,
   British sea lord, on Earl Alexander of Tunis

Much of what Mr Wallace calls his global thinking is, no matter how you slice it, still globaloney.

Clare Booth Luce,
   US diplomat, on Vice-President Henry Wallace, 1943

I doubt very much if a man whose main literary interests were in works by Mr Zane Grey, admirable as they may be, is particularly well-equipped to be chief executive of this country, particularly where Indian affairs are concerned.

Dean Acheson,
   US lawyer and politician, on President Dwight Eisenhower

Eisenhower is the only living Unknown Soldier.

Senator Kerr
   of Oklahoma on President Dwight Eisenhower

The incredible dullness wreaked upon the American landscape in Eisenhower's eight years has been the triumph of the corporation. A tasteless, sexless, odourless sanctity in architecture, manners, modes, styles has been the result. Eisenhower embodied half the needs of the nation, the needs of the timid, the petrified, the sanctimonious and the sluggish.

Norman Mailer
   US novelist and journalist: *The Presidential Papers*, 1963

Eisenhower is the most completely opportunistic and unprincipled politician America has ever raised to high office...insincere, vindictive, hypocritical, and a dedicated, conscious agent of the Communist conspiracy.

Robert H. Welch,
   founder of the ultra-conservative US John Birch Society

The General has dedicated himself so many times, he must feel like the cornerstone of a public building.

Adlai Stevenson,
   US politician, on President Dwight Eisenhower

Well, if you give me two weeks....

Dwight D. Eisenhower,
   US president, when asked to sum up the contribution of his Vice-President, Richard Nixon

Nixon is the kind of politician who would cut down a redwood tree then mount the stump for a speech on conservation.

Adlai Stevenson,
   US politician, on Vice-President Richard Nixon

I don't think the son of a bitch knows the difference between truth and lying.

Harry S. Truman
   on Richard Nixon

Mr Nixon seems to equate criticism with subversion and being hard on Republicans as being soft on Communism.

Adlai Stevenson,
   US politican

JUST PLAIN DICK ... DICK'S OTHER INCOME

Variety magazine
   headlines on Richard Nixon's theatrical 'Checkers' speech, reminiscent — as was the speech — of currently popular soap operas, 1952

He was like a fire in a room on a cold day.

Constance Cummings
   on Aneurin Bevan

He can hardly enter a railway train because there is no Fourth Class.

Daily Express
   on Aneurin Bevan, 1932

Nye was born old and died young.

Jennie Lee,
   British politician, on her husband, Aneurin Bevan

USAGE AND ABUSAGE

He enjoys prophesying the imminent fall of the capitalist system and is prepared to play a part, any part, in its burial — except that of a mute.

Harold Macmillan
on Aneurin Bevan

Why should I question the monkey when I can question the organ-grinder?

Aneurin Bevan,
British Labour politician, ceasing his attack on Foreign Secretary Selwyn Lloyd on seeing Prime Minister Anthony Eden enter the Commons; during the Suez Crisis, 1956

I know that the right kind of political leader for the Labour Party is a dessicated calculating machine.

Aneurin Bevan
in what was generally taken to be an attack on Labour leader Hugh Gaitskell although Bevan always denied this, 1954

The juvenile lead.

Aneurin Bevan
on Prime Minister Sir Anthony Eden

Beneath the sophistication of his appearance and manner, he has all the unplumbable stupidities and unawareness of his class and type.

Aneurin Bevan
on Sir Anthony Eden

He is forever poised between a cliché and an indiscretion.

Harold Macmillan
on Sir Anthony Eden

A benzedrine Napoleon and a pinchbeck Foreign Office Machiavelli all in one.

Malcolm Muggeridge,
British journalist, recalling Sir Anthony Eden at Suez, 1964

Aneurin Bevan/Popperfoto

BOOK OF POLITICAL QUOTES

An over-ripe banana, yellow outside, squishy in.

Reginald Paget,
    British MP, attacking Sir Anthony Eden over Suez, 1956

Eden did not face the dictators. He pulled faces at them.

A.J.P. Taylor,
    English historian

John Foster Dulles...a diplomatic bird of prey smelling out from afar the corpses of dead ideals.

James Cameron,
    British journalist: *Point of Departure,* **1967**

The power of positive brinking.

Adlai Stevenson,
    US politician, on John Foster Dulles, the apostle of 'brinkmanship'

Smooth is an inadequate word for Dulles. His prevarications are so highly polished as to be aesthetically pleasurable.

I.F. Stone,
    US political commentator, on John Foster Dulles, 1953

McCarthy is the only major politician in the country who can be labelled 'liar' without fear of libel.

Joseph and Stewart Alsop,
    US syndicated columnists, on witch-hunting Senator Joe McCarthy, 1953

One of the most unlovely characters in our history since Aaron Burr.

Dean Acheson,
    US lawyer and politician, on Joe McCarthy, 1954

Joe McCarthy bought Communism in much the same way as other people purchase a new automobile.

Roy Cohn,
    leading US anti-Communist attorney, 1950

This Typhoid Mary of conformity.

Richard Rovere,
    US journalist, on Joe McCarthy

The most charming guy in the world...one of the most beautiful characters of the twentieth century.

Harvey Matusow,
    former Communist turned professional informer for Joe McCarthy, on his mentor

I hope Mr Acheson will write a book explaining how he persuaded himself to believe that a government could be conducted without the support of the people.

Walter Lippmann,
    US political commentator

Not only did he not suffer fools gladly, he did not suffer them at all.

Lester Pearson,
    former Canadian prime minister, on Dean Acheson, 1971

Every great leader is the reflection of the people he leads and Stalin, in this sense, was Russia.

I.F. Stone,
    US political commentator, on Stalin's death, 1953

Nasser knew what he did not want, but not quite what he wanted.

Mohammad Heikal,
    Egyptian journalist, on President Gamal Nasser

I've met millions of self-made highbrows... but Estes is the first self-made lowbrow.

Max Ascoli,
    US editor, on crime-busting Senator Estes Kefauver

Mr Luce is like a man that owns a shoe store and buys all the shoes to fit himself. Then he expects other people to buy them.

Earl Long,
    governor of Louisiana, during a libel suit against Henry Luce and Luce Publications

The Right Honourable Gentleman has inherited the streak of charlatanry in Disraeli without his vision, and the self-righteousness of Gladstone without his dedication to principle.

Harold Wilson,
    British opposition leader, on Prime Minister Harold Macmillan

USAGE AND ABUSAGE

From Lord Hailsham we have had a virtuoso performance in the art of kicking a fallen friend in the guts....When self indulgence has reduced a man to the shape of Lord Hailsham, sexual continence requires no more than a sense of the ridiculous.

Reginald Paget,
   British MP, defending Harold Macmillan during the Profumo Affair, 1963

If Harold Wilson ever went to school without any boots, it was merely because he was too big for them.

Harold Macmillan,
   British prime minister, on Wilson's much vaunted poverty-stricken childhood. Also attributed to Ivor Bulmer-Thomas, British MP, 1949

After a half a century of democratic advance, the whole process has ground to a halt with a Fourteenth Earl.

Harold Wilson,
   on the new Conservative prime minister, Lord Home (subsequently Sir Alec Douglas-Home), 1963

The most notorious liar in the country.

J. Edgar Hoover,
   FBI chief, on Martin Luther King Jr, 1964

A mythical person first thought up by the *Reader's Digest*.

Art Buchwald,
   US humorist, on J. Edgar Hoover

Harold Wilson holds court/Poppe-foto

51

As far as the Fourteenth Earl is concerned, I suppose that Mr Wilson, when you come to think of it, is the fourteenth Mr Wilson.

Lord Home,
    replying to Wilson's jibe, 1963

It's always been my theory that you keep the door open to your enemies. You know all about your friends.

Jimmy Hoffa,
    US union boss, referring to his relationship with anti-corruption campaigner Robert Kennedy, 1957

Jimmy Hoffa's most valuable contribution to the American labour movement came at the moment he stopped breathing on July 30 1975.

Dan E. Moldea,
    US investigative journalist: *The Hoffa Wars*, 1978

I'd rather have him inside the tent pissing out, than outside, pissing in.

Lyndon B. Johnson,
    US president, refusing to fire long-time FBI chief J. Edgar Hoover, 1963

Barry tried to tell us a number of things that a number of years ago we weren't quite ready to hear. He was perhaps a little ahead of his time. He was John the Baptist. There had to be a Barry Goldwater.

Ronald Reagan,
    US presidential candidate, 1976

It was hard to listen to Goldwater and realize that a man could be half Jewish and yet sometimes appear twice as dense as the normal gentile.

I.F. Stone,
    US political commentator, on Barry Goldwater, 1968

You know when you're milking a cow and you have all that foamy white milk in the bucket and you're just about through when all of a sudden the cow switches her tail through a pile of manure and slaps it into that foamy white milk? Well, that's Bill Fulbright.

Lyndon B. Johnson,
    US president, on Senator William Fulbright, 1967

John ain't been worth a damn since he started wearing $300 suits.

Lyndon B. Johnson
    on John Connally, Governor of Texas, who opposed much of his social legislation

Johnson would knock on my door, dressed in his robe and pajamas. As I sat in a chair by the window, he climbed into the bed, pulling the sheets up to his neck, looking like a cold and frightened child.

Doris Kearns
    in her account of Lyndon B. Johnson's last days in office, 1976

His social vision did not go beyond the classic prescriptions for dealing with injustice: give everybody an equal start, above all in education, and meanwhile keep the niggers off your porch.

Christopher Lasch,
    US academic, on Lyndon B. Johnson: *The Presidential Mystique*

People said that my language was bad, but Jesus, you should have heard LBJ!

Richard Nixon,
    former US president, on his predecessor Lyndon B. Johnson, 1976

He is a master of the art of the possible in politics.

Adlai Stevenson,
    US politician, on Lyndon B. Johnson

Johnson's instinct for power is as primordial as a salmon's going upstream to spawn.

Theodore H. White,
    US political author: *The Making of the President — 1964*

To thoughtful people then, John Kennedy possessed some hope, simply because he was educable. Johnson was not. Nixon is not.

Philip Berrigan,
    US anti-war activist, 1971

That was the Kennedy way: you bit off more than you could chew, and then you chewed it.

Gerald Gardner,
    US author: *Robert Kennedy in New York*

My brother need not be idealized or enlarged in death beyond what he was in life. He should be remembered simply as a good and decent man who saw wrong and tried to right it, saw suffering and tried to heal it, saw war and tried to stop it...

Edward Kennedy
  in a eulogy for Robert Kennedy, 1968

If there were anything I could take back to France with me it would be Mrs Kennedy.

Charles de Gaulle

Now he is a legend, when he would have preferred to be a man.

Jacqueline Kennedy
  on her late husband, 1964

Bobby Kennedy is so concerned about poverty because he didn't have any as a kid.

Ronald Reagan,
  Governor of California, 1968

Macmillan, Kennedy and Kruschev are the wickedest people in the history of man.

Bertrand Russell,
  English philosopher, 1961

He'll be remembered for just one thing — he was the first Roman Catholic elected President. Period.

Richard Scammon,
  John F. Kennedy's Census Bureau Director, on his late chief, 1963

The liberals like his rhetoric and the conservatives like his inaction.

Norman Thomas,
  US socialist, on John F. Kennedy, 1960

I didn't think John Diefenbaker was a son of a bitch. I thought he was a prick.

John F. Kennedy
  on the Canadian Prime Minister, quoted by Benjamin Bradlee: *Conversations with Kennedy***, 1975**

He spoke like a poor man and walked like a king.

Dick Gregory,
  US comedian and black activist, on Malcolm X

Fuck you, you Jew sonofabitch! You lousy motherfucker! Go home!!

Richard Daley,
  mayor of Chicago, attacking Senator Abraham Ribicoff, who had just announced to the delegates at the Democratic National Convention that Chicago police were beating demonstrators outside, 1968

The most insensitive and brazen pay claim made in the last two hundred years.

Willie Hamilton,
  Scottish anti-monarchist MP, attacking provisions to increase the Civil List (the Queen's salary), 1969

All Norman Mailer the politician accomplished was to prove that in New York City almost anyone can get 41,000 votes if a million people go to the polls.

Richard Reeves,
  US journalist, on Mailer's campaign to become mayor of New York City, 1969

The Winston Churchill of Asia.

Lyndon B. Johnson,
  US president, on South Vietnamese president, Ngo Dinh Diem, 1963

You are like a nightingale. It closes its eyes when it sings and sees nothing and hears nobody but itself.

Nikita S. Khruschev
  to US labour leader, Walter Reuther, 1960

A foul caricature of himself, a man with no soul, no inner convictions, with the integrity of a hyena and the style of a poison toad.

Hunter S. Thompson,
  US gonzo journalist, on Richard Nixon, 1968

Wasn't Dean Rusk really a good Secretary of State, apart from Vietnam?

Jody Powell,
  President Jimmy Carter's press secretary, to reporters, 1977

Mr Thieu is probably one of the four or five best political leaders in the world.

Richard Nixon,
  US president, on the last president of South Vietnam, 1969

BOOK OF POLITICAL QUOTES

I doubt even the Premier's ability to handle the petty cash box at a hot-dog stand at the local Sunday School picnic.

George Moss,
    Australian politician, on Sir Henry Bolte, premier of Victoria, 1969

It is rare to see a man with foot in mouth, but that man Gorton must have an enormous jaw — for that's a kangaroo hoof sticking out of it.

Nestor Mata,
    Filipino journalist, on Australian Prime Minister Gorton, 1969

The most complete man of his age.

Jean Paul Sartre,
    French existentialist philosopher, on Che Guevara

A charming companion and a virtuoso conversationalist and not a selfish one. He was a wonderful hand at conducting a general conversation and could bring out the best in the shy and the alien. But he had his handicaps. The chief of these was his failure to tell the truth. He also had no sense of humour.

Dame Rebecca West,
    British novelist and critic, on Labour politician and diarist, Richard Crossman, 1977

Macnamara voices all the stereotypes of liberal humanitarianism, but he keeps them free from the grime of reality. . . .He reminds one of a mid-Victorian novelist writing without mention of sex or sweat.

I.F. Stone,
    US political commentator on the US Secretary of Defense, Robert Macnamara, 1968

Governor Maddox has the face of a three-month-old infant who is mean and bald and wears eye-glasses.

Norman Mailer,
    US novelist and journalist, on Governor Lester Maddox of Georgia: *Miami and the Siege of Chicago,* 1968

No shirt is too young to be stuffed.

Larry Zolf,
    opposition member in the Canadian parliament, on Prime Minister Joe Clark, 1977

The greatest resurrection for nineteen centuries.

Gough Whitlam,
    Australian Labour leader, on the reappearance in politics of the ageing Sir Robert Menzies, 1977

Billy Hughes was the ugliest man ever to enter politics. He was deaf, wizened and had a masseur, under the guise of a private secretary, who unravelled him every day. He was never born. I think he was quarried.

Fred Daly,
    Australian MP, on former Prime Minister Hughes, 1977

Billy Snedden couldn't go two rounds with a revolving door.

Vince Gair,
    Australian politician, on the leader of the Liberal Party, 1974

Ronald Reagan doesn't dye his hair — he's just prematurely orange.

Gerald Ford,
    US president, 1974

He's just a little man who has been stupid.

Lord George-Brown,
    on Labour leader Harold Wilson, after George-Brown resigned from the party, 1976

Malcolm Fraser could be described as a cutlery man — he was born with a silver spoon in his mouth and he uses it to stab his colleagues in the back.

Bob Hawke,
    Australian trade union leader, on Prime Minister Fraser, 1975

Hubert Humphrey talks so fast that listening to him is like trying to read *Playboy* magazine with your wife turning over the pages.

Barry Goldwater,
    US senator

Muskie talked like a farmer with terminal cancer trying to borrow on next year's crop.

Hunter S. Thompson,
    US gonzo journalist, on Ed Muskie: *Fear and Loathing on the Campaign Trail,* 1972

USAGE AND ABUSAGE

A treacherous, gutless old ward-heeler who should be put in a bottle and sent out with the Japanese current.

Hunter S. Thompson,
  US gonzo journalist, on Hubert Humphrey:
  Fear and Loathing on the Campaign Trail,
  1972

If he were any dumber, he'd be a tree.

Barry Goldwater,
  US senator, on Senator William Scott of Virginia, 1976

A triumph of the embalmer's art.

Gore Vidal,
  US author, of Ronald Reagan

We sit up there on our bed. He has a phone on his side of the bed and I have a phone on my side of the bed and I just sit there while he makes his calls. I just sit there and think what a man he must be.

Cornelia Sniveley Wallace,
  wife of George Wallace, governor of Alabama, 1971

One of the prominent operators chosen by the Hidden Forces that are hurling the countries of Western Europe towards the Animal Farm world willed by Lenin.... This Force of Darkness has already brought the world near to the point of no return and the enthronement of the Antichrist.

Zad Rust
  (Prince Michel Sturdza), US right-wing alarmist, on Edward Kennedy: ***Teddy Bare,***
  1972

In any civilized country Heath would have been left hanging upside down from a petrol pump years ago.

Auberon Waugh,
  English author and diarist, on Prime Minister Edward Heath, 1974

I am sure Mr Heath thinks he is honest, but I wish he didn't have to have his friends say it so often.

Roy Jenkins,
  Labour politician, 1970

A loose cannon on a rolling deck.

George Bush,
  US presidential candidate, on Andrew Young, 1980

He is not well-suited to the small-scale plot.

Barry Jones,
  Australian politician, on Gough Whitlam, 1978

Well may he say God save the Queen — because nothing will save the Governor-General.

Gough Whitlam,
  Australian prime minister ousted by the use of royal prerogative by Sir John Kerr, the Governor-General

He doesn't waffle, he lays it on the line.

Flo Bjelke-Petersen
  on her outspoken, ultra-conservative husband Joh, Queensland premier, 1977

It's the same as Jesus. A prophet is never recognized in his own time.

Robyn Sully,
  leader of the 'Christian Fair Go for Joh' — Joh Bjelke-Petersen supporters, 1976

Is he a tyrant? Oh my word! It's me who's paddywhacked the drumsticks around here!

Flo Bjelke-Petersen
  refuting allegations of her husband's excesses, 1977

A perfect gentleman on the field. He just kept knocking them over.

John Kelly
  on Idi Amin, a former rugby team-mate, 1977

Amin? He's just a goddamn cannibal. A goddamn cannibal asshole. He'd eat his own mother. Christ! He'd eat his own grandmother!

Richard Nixon,
  former US president, on a fellow world leader, 1976

I envisage President Amin pissing on the American Embassy from the Ugandan Mission.

Andrew Young,
  US ambassador to the United Nations, 1977

A lunatic.

Anwar Sadat,
  Egyptian president, on the Ayatollah Khomeini, 1980

I have seen Mr Carter's future, and it is Lyndon Johnson's past.

Barry Goldwater,
  US politician, 1976

We're realists. It doesn't make much difference between Ford and Carter. Carter is your typical smiling, brilliant, back-stabbing, bull-shitting southern nut-cutter.

Lane Kirkland,
  US trade union leader 1976

I would not want Jimmy Carter and his men put in charge of snake control in Ireland.

Eugene McCarthy,
  US senator, 1976

I can't possibly believe Jerry's a dumb-dumb. He couldn't possibly have been re-elected from the district all these years.... How many really intelligent presidents have we had? I think a president has to be able to think like the people think.

Betty Ford
  on her husband President Gerald Ford, 1974

I wish I'd married a plumber. At least he'd be home by five o'clock.

Betty Ford,
  1975

Jerry's the only man I ever knew who can't walk and chew gum at the same time.

Lyndon B. Johnson
  on Gerald Ford

If it took a football player who played centre without a helmet to pull us through, I say, thank God we've had him to lead the team.

Nelson Rockefeller,
  US vice-president, 1976

To support him, they'll have to reaffirm the divine right of kings.

Sam Ervin,
  chairman of the Watergate Hearings Committee, on the Supreme Court's decision to release the Nixon tape-recordings, 1973

Jimmy Carter has the potential and proclivity of a despot.

Eugene McCarthy,
  1976

Richard Nixon impeached himself. He gave us Gerald Ford as his revenge.

Bella Abzug,
  US politician, 1974

If he wants to do his country a favour, he'll stay over there.

Barry Goldwater,
  US politician, on Richard Nixon's trip to China, 1972

If ever there was a man ill-suited by his own nature for the full and relentless exposure of national politics, the fierce give and take, it is Richard Nixon.

David Halberstam,
  US journalist, in *Esquire* magazine, 1974

The Eichmann trial taught the world the banality of evil, now Nixon is teaching the world the evil of banality.

I.F. Stone,
  US political commentator, on the decision to bomb Cambodia, 1970

When the cold light of history looks back on Richard Nixon's five years of unrestrained power in the White House, it will show that he had the same effect on conservative/Republican politics as Charles Manson and the Hell's Angels had on hippies and flower power.

Hunter S. Thompson,
  US gonzo journalist: *The Great Shark Hunt*, 1979

President Nixon represents a cross-section of American ethics and morality.

Gerald Ford,
  US president, 1974

James Callaghan, living proof that the short-term schemer and the frustrated bully can be made manifest in one man.

Hugo Young,
  British journalist, 1980

MY COUNTRY RIGHT AND LEFT

England, the heart of a rabbit in the body of a lion/ The jaws of a serpent in an abode of popinjays.

Eustache Deschamps,
  French poet

I know that I have the body of a weak and feeble woman, but I have the heart and stomach of a king, and of a king of England, too.

Elizabeth I
  to her troops as the Spanish Armada approached, 1588

It is lamentable that to be a good patriot we must become the enemy of the rest of mankind.

Voltaire,
  French author, 1724

Neither holy, nor Roman, nor an empire.

Voltaire,
  French author, on the Holy Roman Empire:
  Essai sur le Moeurs et l'Esprit des Nations,
  1756-59

Patriotism is the last refuge of a scoundrel.

Samuel Johnson,
  English lexicographer, critic and poet, 1775

Absolutism tempered by assassination.

Ernst F. Münster,
  Hanoverian envoy to St Petersburg, commenting on the Russian Constitution

There. I guess King George will be able to read that.

John Hancock,
  first signatory of the US Declaration of Independence, 1776

To found a great empire for the sole purpose of raising up a nation of shopkeepers may at first sight appear a project fit only for a nation of shopkeepers. It is, however, a project altogether unfit for a nation of shopkeepers, but extremely fit for a nation whose government is influenced by shopkeepers.

Adam Smith,
  Scottish economist and philosopher: *The Wealth of Nations,* **1775**

If I were an American as I am an Englishman while a foreign troop was landed in my country, I would never lay down my arms. Never! Never! Never!

William Pitt, Earl of Chatham,
  British statesman, speaking against war with America, 1777

A great and lasting war can never be supported on that principle alone. It must be aided by a prospect of interest, or some reward.

George Washington
  on patriotism

Sir, I have not yet begun to fight.

John Paul Jones,
  captain of the sinking USS *Bon Homme Richard,* **hearing a demand to surrender from Captain Pearson of HMS** *Serapis,* **1779**

My country is the world and my religion is to do good.

Tom Paine,
  English radical pamphleteer: *The Rights of Man,* **1791**

I desire what is good; therefore everyone who does not agree with me is a traitor.

George III,
  English king

Let Pitt then boast of his victory to his nation of shopkeepers.

Bertrand Barere
  speaking to the French Convention, 1794. Generally attributed to Napoleon Bonaparte, but on no solid grounds.

The English have no exalted sentiments. They can all be bought.

Napoleon Bonaparte

Peace, commerce and honest friendships with all nations — entangling alliances with none.

Thomas Jefferson,
  US president, 1801

My country is the world, my countrymen are mankind.

William Lloyd Garrison,
  US abolitionist, 1803

It is cowardly to commit suicide. The English often kill themselves. It is a malady caused by the humid climate.

Napoleon Bonaparte

To write this Act of Independence we must have white man's skin for parchment, his skull for an ink-well, his blood for ink and a bayonet as a pen.

Boisrond Tonnere,
  leader of the Haitian War of Independence against the French, 1804

All empires die of indigestion.

Napoleon Bonaparte:
  Maxims, 1804-15

Europe is not to be saved by any single man. England has saved herself by her exertions and will, I trust, save Europe by her example.

William Pitt the Younger
  in his final public speech at a banquet to celebrate the victory of Trafalgar, 1805

What a place to plunder!

Field Marshal Gebhard Blücher,
  Prussian military leader, visiting London, 1814

This is the true character of the English government: that it presents the singular phenomenon of a nation, the individuals of which are as faithful to their private engagements and duties, as honourable, as worthy as those of any nation on earth, and yet whose government is the most unprincipled at this day known.

Thomas Jefferson

The less we have to do with the enmities of Europe the better. Not in our day, but at no distant one, we may shake a rod over the heads of all, which may make the stoutest tremble. But I hope our wisdom will grow with our power and teach us that the less we use our power the greater it will be.

Thomas Jefferson

Our country! In her intercourse with foreign nations may she always be in the right. But our country, right or wrong!

Stephen Decateur,
  US naval commander, in a toast to America, 1816

'My country right or wrong' is a thing that no patriot would think of saying except in a desperate case. It is like saying 'My mother, drunk or sober'.

G.K. Chesterton,
  English critic, novelist and poet: The Defendant

The single most important impediment to global institutions is the concept of 'My country right or wrong'.

U Thant,
  Secretary-General of the United Nations

The American continents...are henceforth not to be considered as subjects for future colonization by any European powers.

James Monroe,
  US president: 'The Monroe Doctrine', 1823

The United States appear to be destined by providence to plague America with misery in the name of liberty.

Simon Bolivar,
  liberator of Venezuela

Italy is only a geographical expression.

Prince Clemeñs Metternich,
   Austrian statesman, in a memo to the
Great Powers, 1814

France was long a despotism tempered by epigrams.

Thomas Carlyle
   Scottish author and historian: *The French Revolution,* **1837**

We know no spectacle so ridiculous as the British public in one of its periodical fits of morality.

Lord Macaulay,
   English historian: *Literary Essays,* **1843**

Our manifest destiny to overspread the continent allotted by providence for the free development of our yearly multiplying millions.

John L. O'Sullivan,
   US journalist and diplomat, coining a phrase in *US Magazine and Democratic Review,* **1845**

Nationality is the miracle of political independence, race is the principle of physical analogy.

Benjamin Disraeli,
   British statesman, 1848

As the Roman, in days of old, held himself free from indignity when he could say *'Civis Romanus sum'*, so also a British subject, in whatever land he may be, shall feel England will protect him against injustice and wrong.

Lord Palmerston
   defending the citizenship of Don Pacifico, a man actually Spanish but a British subject from his birth in Gibraltar and thus defended by the Foreign Office in a property suit against Greeks, 1850

Turkey is the sick man of Europe.

Lord Palmerston,
   British home secretary, 1853

Poor Mexico, so far from God and so near to the United States.

Porfirio Diaz,
   Mexican president

In England the prolonged prosperity has demoralized the workers. . . . The ultimate aim of this most bourgeois of lands would seem to be the establishment of a bourgeois aristocracy and a bourgeois proletariat, side by side with the bourgeoisie. . . . The revolutionary energy of the British workers has oozed away.

Karl Marx

Men destined to the highest places should beware of badinage. . . . An insular country, subject to fogs, and with a powerful middle class, requires grave statesmen.

Benjamin Disraeli
   warning politicians against wit in England

It is not my duty to make this country the knight-errant of the human race.

John Bright,
   British radical statesman and orator, 1855

Patriotism is a kind of religion, it is the egg from which wars are hatched.

Guy de Maupassant,
   French author: *My Uncle Sosthenes*

A nation may be said to consist of its territory, its people and its laws. The territory is the only part which is of certain durability.

Abraham Lincoln,
   US president, 1862

There are only three men who have ever understood it: one was Prince Albert, and he is dead; the second was a German professor who became mad; I am the third and I have forgotten all about it.

Lord Palmerston,
   British prime minister, on the Schleswig-Holstein Question, 1863

England is the mother of Parliaments.

John Bright,
   British radical statesman and orator, 1865

The only good Indians I ever saw were dead.

Philip Henry Sheridan,
   US soldier, 1869

English policy is to float lazily downstream, occasionally putting out a diplomatic boat-hook to avoid collisions.

Lord Salisbury,
      English Conservative statesman, 1877

I would call out the police to arrest them.

Otto von Bismarck,
      when asked how he would deal with an invading British army

National injustice is the surest road to national downfall.

William Gladstone,
      British statesman, 1878

Oh, if the Queen were a man, she would like to go and give those horrid Russians whose word one cannot trust such a beating.

Queen Victoria
      in a letter to Disraeli, 1878

No man has a right to say to his country, 'Thus far shalt thou go and no further.' And we have never attempted to fix the *ne plus ultra* to the progress of Ireland's nationhood and we never shall.

Charles Parnell,
      Irish patriot, in a speech commemorated by a plaque fixed to his statue in Dublin, 1885

Our country has liberty without license and authority without despotism.

Cardinal James Gibbons,
      US clergyman, 1887

Talking of patriotism, what humbug it is; it is a word which always commemorates a robbery. There isn't a foot of land in the world which doesn't represent the ousting and re-ousting of a long line of successive owners.

Mark Twain,
      US author: *A Connecticut Yankee at King Arthur's Court*, 1889

The universal brotherhood of man is our most precious possession — what there is of it.

Mark Twain,
      US author: *Following the Equator*, 1897

The crude commercialism of America, its materialistic spirit...are entirely due to the country having adopted for its national hero a man who was incapable of telling a lie.

Oscar Wilde,
      Irish poet, wit and dramatist: *The Decay of Lying*

In these troublesome days, when the great Mother Empire stands splendidly isolated in Europe.

George E. Foster,
      Canadian politician, coining a phrase, 1896. Also attributed to Lord Salisbury, 1898

A place in the sun.

Bernhard von Bulow,
      German chancellor, making a claim for a German colonial empire, 1897

The mission of the US is one of benevolent assimilation, substituting the mild sway of justice and right for arbitrary rule.

William McKinley,
      US president, justifying the Spanish-American War, 1898

A nation is a historical group of men of recognizable cohesion, held together by a common enemy.

Theodor Herzl,
      pioneer Zionist, 1898

Peace, n. In international affairs, a period of cheating between two periods of fighting.

Ambrose Bierce,
      US journalist and author: *The Devil's Dictionary*, 1881-1911

God has not been preparing the English-speaking and Teutonic peoples for one thousand years for nothing but vain and idle self-contemplation and self-admiration. No! He has made us the master organizers of the world to establish system where chaos reigns. He has made us adept in government that we may administer government among savage and senile peoples....He has marked the American people as His chosen nation to finally lead in the regeneration of the world. This is the divine mission of America....

Albert J. Beveridge,
      US senator, 1900

MY COUNTRY RIGHT AND LEFT

I have been called the Apostle of the Anglo-Saxon race and I am proud of the title. I think the Anglo-Saxon race is as fine as any on earth.

Joseph Chamberlain,
British statesman, 1900

Alliance, n. In international politics, the union of two thieves that have their hands so deeply inserted into each other's pockets that they cannot safely plunder a third.

Ambrose Bierce,
US journalist and author: *The Devil's Dictionary*, 1881-1911

Englishmen will never be slaves. They are free to do whatever the government and public opinion allow them to do.

George Bernard Shaw,
Irish dramatist: *Man and Superman*, 1903

Remember, my son, that any man who is bear on the future of this country will go broke.

J. Pierpoint Morgan,
US capitalist, to his son, 1908

The maxim of the British people is 'Business as usual'.

Winston Churchill,
First Lord of the Admiralty, 1914

To be the spiritual battlefield of European antagonisms — that's what it means to be a German.

Thomas Mann,
German novelist: *Reflections of an Unpolitical Man*, 1916

America is the only nation in history which miraculously has gone directly from barbarism to degeneration, without the usual interval of civilization.

Georges Clemenceau,
French prime minister

Sometimes people call me an idealist. Well, that is the way I know I am an American. America is the only idealistic nation in the world.

Woodrow Wilson

The remedy for Bolshevism is bullets.

The Times
in an editorial, 1917

A ghoul descending from a pile of skulls.

Winston Churchill,
Secretary of State for War and Air, on Communism, 1919

America is the place where you cannot kill your government by killing the men who conduct it.

Woodrow Wilson,
US president, on political assassinations, 1919

We will get everything out of her that you can squeeze out of a lemon and a bit more. I will squeeze her until you can hear the pips squeak.

Sir Eric Geddes,
British politician on international plans for Germany, 1918

We actually got down to work at half past ten and finished remaking the map of the world as we would have it at half past twelve o'clock.

Colonel Edward House,
US representative at the Versailles peace talks, 1919

I know of no method by which an aristocratic nation like England can become a democracy.

Hilaire Belloc,
Anglo-French writer, 1921

The British Empire must behave like a gentleman.

David Lloyd George,
British prime minister, 1921

As an ultimate objective, 'peace' simply means communist world control.

V.I. Lenin

The less a statesman amounts to, the more he loves the flag.

Frank McKinney 'Kin' Hubbard,
US humorist

Americans live like pigs, but in luxury sties.

Adolf Hitler

If you talk to an Englishman about class war, revolution or things of that kind, he will tell you in forcible language that he has no use for foreign theories or foreign crimes.

Viscount Cave,
British Lord Chancellor, 1925

I wish to be buried standing, facing Germany.

Georges Clemenceau,
former French prime minister and intransigent Germanophobe, in his last will, 1929

Patriotism is a lively sense of responsibility. Nationalism is a silly cock crowing on its own dunghill.

Richard Aldington,
English author and editor: *The Colonel's Daughter*, 1931

There are no unemployed, either in Russia or in Dartmoor jail, and for the same reason.

Philip Snowden,
British politician, 1932

Patriotism is often a veneration of real estate above principles.

George Jean Nathan,
US editor and critic

Much of the trouble in Russia, politics apart, is due, I believe, to the fact that Russia is not a games-playing nation.

W.W. Wakefield,
1928

Countries are like fruit — the worms are always inside.

Jean Giraudoux,
French playwright, *Siegfried*, 1928

They hired the money, didn't they.

Calvin Coolidge,
US president, refusing to cancel Europe's war debts

What they call today the will of the people is nothing but the organized corruption of the press, cinema and parliament, which is called democracy, but which is ruled by alien Jewish finance — the same finance which has hired alien mobs to yell here tonight.

Sir Oswald Mosley,
British Fascist leader, 1934

No nation will ever let its fingers be burnt twice. The trick of the Pied Piper of Hamelin catches people only once.

Adolf Hitler

Peace is indivisible.

Maxim Litvinov,
Russian ambassador to the League of Nations, 1934

Bolshevism is knocking at our gates. We can't afford to let it in. We have got to organize ourselves against it and put our shoulders together and hold fast. We must keep America whole and safe and unspoiled. We must keep the worker away from Red literature and Red ruses, we must see that his heart remains healthy.

Al Capone
in a letter from jail

MY COUNTRY RIGHT AND LEFT

The Irish people do not gladly suffer common sense.

Oliver St John Gogarty,
Irish writer, 1935

A Corridor for Camels.

The Times
heading of the first leader on the Hoare-
Laval Pact, 1935

Jewish international finance, the nameless, homeless and all-powerful force which stretches its greedy fingers from the shelter of England to throttle the trade and menace the peace of the world.

Sir Oswald Mosley,
British Fascist leader

So they go on in strange paradox: decided — only to be undecided, resolved — to be irresolute, adamant — for drift, solid — for fluidity, all-powerful — to be impotent.

Winston Churchill,
British statesman, on appeasement, 1936

Today Spain has the honour to be the bulwark of humanity on which breaks the attack of destructive communism. She will fulfil her mission in the gigantic work of liberation with the admirable German example to assist her and renew her strength.

Francisco Franco,
1937

The nation that destroys its soul destroys itself.

Franklin D. Roosevelt,
US president, 1937

It pays in England to be a revolutionary and a bible-smacker most of one's life, and then come round.

Lord Alfred Douglas,
English poet, 1938

We have seen today a gallant, civilized and democratic people betrayed and handed over to a ruthless despotism.

Clement Attlee,
British Labour leader, on the Munich
agreement, 1938

How horrible, fantastic, incredible it is that we should be digging trenches and trying on gas masks here because of a quarrel in a far-away country between people of whom we know nothing.

Neville Chamberlain,
1938

I know of no existing nation that deserves to live, and I know of very few individuals.

H.L. Mencken,
US philologist, editor and satirist

I cannot forecast to you the action of Russia — it is a riddle wrapped in a mystery inside an enigma.

Winston Churchill,
First Lord of the Admiralty, 1939

Let us therefore brace ourselves to our duties and so bear ourselves that, if the British Empire and Commonwealth last for a thousand years, men will still say: 'This was their finest hour.'

Winston Churchill,
British prime minister, 1940

Distilled, drop by crystal drop, from our manhood's triumph and its tribulations, from the patience and courage of our womanhood, and from the recklessness and the sacrifice of our youth, and above all from that sublime quality of mateship, this spirit is something more than a mundane asset, it is the very essence of Australia itself.

Reveille magazine
quoting 'An Old Soldier of the 2nd
Australian Imperial Force', 1940

I would say to this House as I have said to those who have joined this Government, I have nothing to offer but blood, toil, tears and sweat.

Winston Churchill,
British prime minister, 1940

A family with the wrong members in control.

George Orwell,
English essayist and critic, on England:
'The Ruling Class', 1941

We had the moral right, we had the duty to our people, to kill this people that wanted to kill us.... By and large we can say that we have performed this task in love of our people. And we have suffered no damage from it in our inner self, in our soul, in our character.

Heinrich Himmler,
    Nazi leader, on the 'Final Solution'

When I warned [the French] that Britain would fight on alone...their General told their Prime Minister: 'In three weeks England will have her neck wrung like a chicken.' Some chicken. Some neck!

Winston Churchill,
    British prime minister, to the Canadian Parliament, 1941

They hope to see established a peace which will afford to all nations the means of dwelling in safety within their own boundaries and which will afford assurance that all the men in all the lands may live out their lives in freedom from fear and want.

The Atlantic Charter,
    signed by Winston Churchill and Franklin D. Roosevelt, 1941

The German carries in his racial character a feature that must be taken infinitely seriously: an unusual need for justice and sensitivity concerning justice.

Hans Frank,
    Nazi Governor-General of Poland

When the race is in danger of being oppressed, the question of legality plays only a secondary role.

Adolf Hitler

It is not healthy when a nation lives within a nation, as coloured Americans are living inside America. A nation cannot live confident of its tomorrow, if its refugees are among its own citizens.

Pearl S. Buck,
    US novelist: *What America Means to Me*, 1943

We must be decent, honest, loyal and comradely to members of our own blood and to no one else.... Whether the other peoples live in comfort or perish in hunger interests me only in so far as we need slaves for our culture, apart from that it does not interest me. Whether or not ten thousand Russian women collapse from exhaustion while digging a tank ditch interests me only in so far as the tank ditch is completed for Germany. We shall never be rough or heartless where it is not necessary, that is clear. We Germans, who are the only people in the world to have a decent attitude to animals, will also adopt a decent attitude to these human animals, but it is a crime against our blood to worry about them and bring them ideals.

Heinrich Himmler,
    Nazi leader, in a speech to the SS, 1943

Most of you know what it means to see a hundred corpses lying together, or five hundred, or a thousand. To have gone through this and yet — apart from a few exceptions, examples of human weakness — to have remained decent, this has made us hard. This is a glorious page in our history that has never been written and never shall be written.

Heinrich Himmler,
    Nazi leader, in a speech to the SS, 1943

It is natural anywhere that people like their own kind, but it is not necessarily natural that their fondness for their own kind should lead them to the subjection of whole groups of other people not like them.

Pearl S. Buck,
    US novelist: *What America Means to Me*, 1943

Nationalism is power-hunger tempered by self-deception.

George Orwell,
    English essayist and critic: 'Notes on Nationalism', 1945

It is no shame to stand on this scaffold. I served my fatherland as others before me.

General Karl Brandt,
    Nazi war criminal, last words, 1946

MY COUNTRY RIGHT AND LEFT

Men, this stuff some sources sling around about America wanting to stay out of the war and not wanting to fight is a lot of baloney. Americans love to fight, traditionally. All real Americans love the sting and clash of battle. America loves a winner. America will not tolerate a loser. Americans despise a coward. Americans play to win. That's why America has never lost and never will lose a war.

General George S. Patton
  in a D-Day pep talk to US troops, 1944

From what I hear about Communism, I don't like it because it isn't on the level.

Gary Cooper, Hollywood star, 1947

We are in the midst of a cold war.

Bernard Baruch,
  US financier and statesman, coining a phrase, 1947

Nothing has ever contributed so much to the corruption of the original idea of Socialism as the belief that Russia is a Socialist country, and that every act of its rulers must be excused, if not imitated.

George Orwell,
  English essayist and critic: Introduction to the Ukrainian edition of *Animal Farm*

Either men will learn to live like brothers or they will die like beasts.

Max Lerner,
  US editor: *Actions and Passions*, 1949

What is Communism? *A system by which one small group seeks to rule the world.* Is it aimed at me? *Right between the eyes.* What is the difference between a Communist and Fascist? *None worth noticing.* Was Marx crazy? *Perhaps. But Marx was not the first evil and crazy man to start a terrible world upheaval, nor was he the last. Hitler was like that, too, and look what he did.*

House Un-American Activities Committee:
  'A Hundred Things You Should Know About Communism in the USA', a catechism for the masses, 1949

Communists have the same right to vote as anyone else, don't they?

Joseph McCarthy,
  US senator, before his witch-hunting era, when taxed with using Communist support in his campaign for the Senate

If I must have foreign friends I prefer them black or brown.

Clement Attlee,
  British prime minister, opposing his country's membership of the EEC

Foreign policy is a thing you have got to bring down to its essence as it applies to an individual. It is not something that is great and big; it is common sense and humanity as it applies to my affairs and to yours, because it is somebody and somebody's kindred that are being persecuted and punished and tortured, and they are defenceless. That is a fact.

Ernest Bevin,
  British foreign minister, 1950

In America everybody is of the opinion that he has no social superiors, since all men are equal. But he does not admit that he has no social inferiors.

Bertrand Russell,
  English philosopher: *Unpopular Essays*, 1950

I have here in my hand a list of 205, a list of names that were known to the Secretary of State as being members of the Communist party and who are nevertheless working and shaping the policy in the State Department.

Joseph McCarthy,
  US senator, launching the witch-hunts at a Women's Republican Club in Wheeling, Virginia, 1950

An anti-Communist is a dog.

Jean-Paul Sartre,
  French Marxist philosopher, on fellow intellectual Raymond Aron, 1950

Let us try to create the whole man, whom Europe has been incapable of bringing to triumphant birth.

Frantz Fanon,
  French radical

I think the British have the distinction above all other nations of being able to put new wine into old bottles without bursting them.

Clement Attlee,
  British Prime Minister, 1950

If I had to choose between betraying my country and betraying my friend I hope I should have the guts to betray my country.

E.M. Forster,
  English novelist: *Two Cheers for Democracy*, 1951

Gratitude, like love, is never a dependable international emotion.

Joseph Alsop,
  US political columnist, 1952

McCarthyism is Americanism with its sleeves rolled.

Joseph McCarthy,
  US senator, 1952

America is a political reading of the Bible.

Richard Nixon,
  US vice-president

In America any boy may become president, and I suppose that's just the risk he takes.

Adlai Stevenson,
  US politician, 1952

Paralytic sycophants, effete betrayers of humanity, carrion-eating servile imitators, arch-cowards and collaborators, gang of woman-murderers, degenerate rabble, parasitic traditionalists, playboy soldiers, conceited dandies.

East German Government's
  approved terms of vilification for use by orators talking about the UK, 1953

There is no way to peace. Peace is the way.

Abraham Muste,
  US pacifist

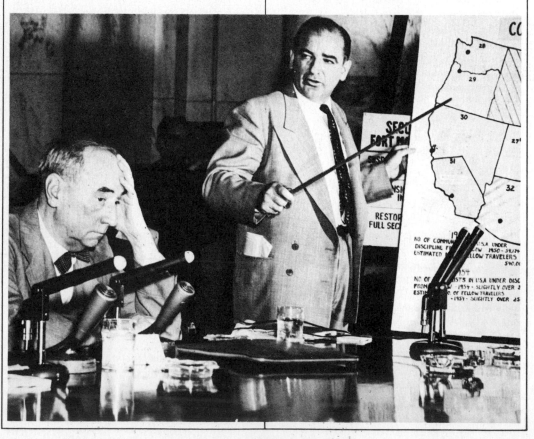

Joseph McCarthy/Popperfoto

MY COUNTRY RIGHT AND LEFT

It is a race of wolves. He who arrives does so only at the expense of the failure of others.

Che Guevara,
Argentinian-born Communist revolutionary, on Western individualism: *Man and Socialism in Cuba*

America is a large, friendly dog in a very small room. Every time it wags its tail it knocks over a chair.

Arnold Toynbee,
English historian, 1954

The only alternative to co-existence is co-destruction.

Shri Jawaharlal Nehru,
Indian prime minister, 1954

Russian Communism is the illegitimate child of Karl Marx and Catherine the Great.

Clement Attlee,
former British prime minister, 1956

The objection to a Communist always resolves itself into the fact that he is not a gentleman.

H.L. Mencken,
US philologist, editor and satirist: *Minority Report*, 1956

We know how to repel pirates.

Gamal Abdel Nasser,
Egyptian president, during the Suez fighting, 1956

You asked me why we Communist leaders travel so often to Moscow. I will tell you. We go there to learn how better to wring your capitalist necks.

Klement Gottwald,
East German president

The head of the Iranian Army said . . . that the Army was in good shape thanks to US aid. It was now capable of coping with the civilian population.

Hubert Humphrey,
US senator, during an investigation of his country's involvement in Iran, 1957

Democracy is meaningless to children.

Albert Schweitzer,
German medical missionary, on African independence

French political thought is either nostalgic or utopian.

Raymond Aron,
French historian: *The Opium of the Intellectual* 1957

Science is the search for truth — it is not a game in which one tries to beat his opponent, to do harm unto others. We need to have the spirit of science in international affairs, to make the conduct of international affairs the effort to find the right solution, the just solution of international problems, not the effort by each nation to get the better of other nations, to do harm when it is possible.

Linus Pauling,
US scientist: *No More War!*, 1958

Jaw-jaw is better than war-war.

Harold Macmillan,
British prime minister, echoing Churchill's 1954 dictum 'Talking jaw to jaw is better than going to war', 1958

Harold Macmillan/Popperfoto

Let us not be afraid of debate or dissent — let us encourage it. For if we should ever abandon these basic American traditions in the name of fighting Communism, what would it profit us to win the whole world when we have lost our soul?

John F. Kennedy,
US presidential candidate, campaigning, 1959

You can read the Declaration of Independence and the Constitution and the Gettysburg Address and you won't find even once in them the word 'efficiency'. And you can read all of Marx, all of Lenin, all of Stalin and all of Engels and you won't find even once in them the word 'love'.

Hubert Humphrey,
US senator, 1960

When I search for man in the technique and style of Europe, I see only a succession of negations of man and an avalanche of murders.

Frantz Fanon,
French radical: *The Wretched of the Earth*, 1961

Every government is in some respects a problem for every other government. And it will always be this way so long as the sovereign state, with its supremely self-centred rationale, remains the basis of international life.

George F. Kennan,
US administrator, 1961

We are not entitled to sell our friends and kinsmen down the river for a problematical and mathematical advantage in selling washing machines in Dusseldorf.

Harold Wilson,
British opposition leader, opposing his country's entry into the EEC, 1961

The nation-state system that enables one or two men to decide life or death for the planet is the common enemy — not the Russians or Americans, capitalists or Communists. The rest is delusion.

I.F. Stone,
US political commentator, 1962

Any nation is heathen that ain't strong enough to punch you in the jaw.

Will Rogers,
US humorist: *A Rogers Thesaurus*, 1962

Let us never negotiate out of fear, but let us never fear to negotiate.

John F. Kennedy,
US president, in his inaugural address, 1961

In our democratic society the Jew is like a poisonous maggot feeding off the body in an advanced state of decay.

John Tyndall,
English National Socialist leader, 1962

You cannot deny that Russian Communism succeeded in making Russia one of the world's most powerful nations. There must be some good in it.

Francisco Franco,
on signing trade agreements with Eastern Europe, 1963

Treaties are like roses and young girls — they last while they last.

Charles de Gaulle,
French president, 1963

In the first analysis it is their war. They are the ones who have to win it or lose it. We can help them. We can give them equipment, we can send our men out there as advisers, but they have to win it, the people of Vietnam.

John F. Kennedy,
US president, 1963

The great nations have always acted like gangsters and the small nations like prostitutes.

Stanley Kubrick,
US film director, 1963

In Western Europe there are now only small countries — those that know it and those that don't know it yet.

Théo Lefèvre,
Belgian foreign minister, 1963

MY COUNTRY RIGHT AND LEFT

We are the greatest power in the world. If we behave like it.

Walt W. Rostow,
US presidential adviser

To see freedom sent around the world, this is our mission. It was God's charge to us.

Senator Barry Goldwater
on the USA, 1964

Aggression by terror against the peaceful villages of South Vietnam has now been joined by open aggression on the high seas against the USA...yet our response for the present will be limited and fitting. We Americans know — though others appear to forget — the risks of spreading conflict. We still seek no wider war.

Lyndon B. Johnson,
US president, using the Tonkin Gulf
incident to escalate US involvement in
Vietnam, 1964

If you live amongst wolves, you have to act like a wolf.

Nikita Khruschev,
1964

This is the devilish thing about foreign affairs — they are foreign and will not always conform to our whim.

James Reston,
US political commentator, 1964

Of course we acted out of enlightened self-interest...but the pages of history can be searched in vain for another power whose purpose of self-interest was so infused with grandeur of spirit and morality of purpose.

Lyndon B. Johnson,
US president, on the US involvement in
Vietnam, 1964

We're a Conservative country that votes Labour from time to time.

Reginald Maudling,
British Conservative politician, on England

Progress to us is death for Israel.

Gamal Abdel Nasser,
Egyptian president, 1965

All humanity is involved in a single process and all men are brothers. To the degree that I harm my brother, no matter what he is doing to me, to that extent I harm my self.

Martin Luther King,
US civil rights leader

You're not supposed to be so blind with patriotism that you can't face reality. Wrong is wrong, no matter who does it or who says it.

Malcolm X,
US black activist, 1965

Sitting at the table doesn't make you a diner, unless you eat some of what's on the plate. Being here in America doesn't make you an American.

Malcolm X,
1965

Australia needs the patriots who spend their money on grog, girls and the gee-gees.

W.C. Coutts,
Australian politician, 1966

We must remember that in time of war what is said on the enemy's side of the front is always propaganda and what is said on our side of the front is truth and righteousness, the cause of humanity and a crusade for peace. Is it necessary for us at the height of our power to stoop to such self-deceiving nonsense?

Walter Lippmann,
US political commentator, 1966

Don't forget, there are two hundred million of us in a world of three billion. They want what we've got, and we're not going to give it to them.

Lyndon B. Johnson,
US president, 1966

That's a part of American greatness, is discrimination. Yes sir. Inequality, I think breeds freedom and gives a man opportunity.

Lester Maddox,
Governor of Georgia, 1966

We are too powerful to be infuriated.

Dean Rusk,
  US Secretary of State, 1966

I see nothing but danger in the idea that the conflict in Vietnam is a kind of holy war between two powerful ideologies.

U Thant,
  Secretary-General of the United Nations, 1966

Men may be linked in friendship, nations are only linked in interests.

Rolf Hochhuth,
  German dramatist: *The Soldiers,* 1967

They ain't like the folk you were reared with.

Lyndon B. Johnson
  complaining about dealing with foreigners

The very definition of a great power is that not only its actions, but the cases in which it declines to act have major consequences.

Irving Kristol,
  US writer, 1967

Nations, like individuals, have to limit their objectives or take the consequences.

James Reston,
  US political commentator: *Sketches in the Sand,* 1967

This nation will do whatever has to be done as long as one American remains in enemy hands.

Ronald Reagan,
  governor of California, on the US in Vietnam

In the Orient, life is cheap.

General William Westmoreland,
  Commander in Chief US troops in Vietnam

Foreign relations are like human relations. They are endless. The solution of one problem usually leads to another.

James Reston,
  US political commentator: *Sketches in the Sand,* 1967

Spiro Agnew with belly-dancer friend/Popperfoto

We're sick and tired of having this country run down by a group of phoney intellectuals who don't understand what we mean by hard work and patriotism.

Spiro T. Agnew,
  US vice-presidential candidate, 1968

A young white today cannot help but recoil from the base deeds of his people. On every side, on every continent, he sees racial arrogance, savage brutality. There seems to be no end to the ghastly deeds of which his people are guilty. *Guilty.*

Eldridge Cleaver,
  US black activist: *Soul on Ice,* 1968

Americans think of themselves collectively as a huge rescue squad on 24-hour call to any spot on the globe where dispute and conflict may erupt.

Eldridge Cleaver,
  US black activist: *Soul on Ice,* 1968

For every voice in Britain calling for a policy to Keep Britain White, there is a corresponding call to Keep Africa Black.

Dr Kenneth Kaunda,
  Zambian president, 1968

MY COUNTRY RIGHT AND LEFT

We have a three to one advantage over the Russians, which I understand means that we have the potential to kill all the Russians twice, and they have the potential to kill us one and a quarter times.

Senator Eugene McCarthy,
    1968

If we have to start over again with another Adam and Eve, I want them to be Americans, not Russians.

Senator Richard Russell,
    1968

I only wish I could take the entire US into the locker room at half time. I would simply say that we must not look at the points we have lost, but at the points we can gain. We have a winner. Americans are winners.

Gerald Ford,
    US president, at a football awards dinner,
1969

Criminal elements are truly the enemies of our country. They weaken its governmental structure by corrupting weak officials and framing others. In one way or another they affect local political processes. They weaken the economy by infiltrating legitimate businesses and labour unions, by cheating on taxes and other frauds. These then are the enemy: the organized criminal, the street criminal, the white-collar criminal, the tax cheat, the embezzler, the dishonest repairman and the dishonest businessman. Like all those who threaten the life and health of the nation, they must be fought with every weapon available and consistent with our Constitution.

Spiro T. Agnew,
    US vice-president, 1970

We shall never stop until we can go back home and Israel is destroyed. The goal of our struggle is the end of Israel and there can be no compromises or mediations.... We don't want peace, we want victory. Peace for us means Israel's destruction and nothing else.

Yasser Arafat,
    Palestinian leader, 1970

There is not a single injustice in Northern Ireland that is worth the loss of a single British soldier or a single Irish citizen either.

James Callaghan,
    British Home Secretary, 1970

I don't see why we need to stand by and watch a country go Communist due to the irresponsibility of its own people.

Henry Kissinger,
    President Nixon's adviser on national security affairs, justifying the US subversion of Chile, 1970

Countries cannot become free. Countries cannot be oppressed. Only men can be free or not free.

Anthony Lejeune,
    British journalist: *Freedom and the Politicians*

France is a widow.

Georges Pompidou,
    French president, announcing the death of Charles de Gaulle, 1970

Two Wongs don't make a white.

Arthur Calwell,
    Australian politician, explaining his anti-Asian-immigrant attitudes

There is no anti-semitism in Russia. Some of my best friends are Jews.

Alexei Kosygin,
    1971

A sporting system is a by-product of society and its political system, and it is just boyhood dreaming to suppose that you can ever take politics out of sport.

Peter Hain,
    British anti-apartheid activist, 1971

No red-blooded Australian wants to see a chocolate-coloured Australia.

Arthur Calwell,
    Australian politician, 1972

Privilege could be as harmful to the future welfare of Aborigines as discrimination.

Joh Bjelke-Petersen,
    Queensland premier, 1973

BOOK OF POLITICAL QUOTES

The most important thing in war preparation...is that we educate our people in the spirit of hating the enemy. Without educating our people in that spirit, we cannot defeat the United States, which is superior in technology.

Kim Il Sung,
North Korean president, 1972

We are really just a nation of two hundred million used-car salesmen with all the money we need to buy guns and no qualms about killing anybody else in the world who tries to make us uncomfortable.

Hunter S. Thompson,
US gonzo journalist: *Fear and Loathing on the Campaign Trail*, 1972

The pursuit of peace must...begin with the pragmatic concept of existence — especially in a period of ideological conflict.

Henry Kissinger,
US National Security Adviser, 1973

Threat and extortion can make an impression for a limited period, but one cannot make friends that way.

Willy Brandt,
West German chancellor, 1973

The old dangers to Europe were conquest by sword and fire. Now it is oil, bluster and blackmail.

Gideon Raphael,
Israeli ambassador to the United Kingdom, 1974

The Israelis must not be so ambitious as to think there is instant peace. It is an evolutionary process at the end of which you have normal relations.

Anwar Sadat,
Egyptian president, 1974

Vietnam was a country where America was trying to make people stop being Communists by dropping things on them from airplanes.

Kurt Vonnegut,
US novelist, *Breakfast of Champions*, 1973

What impressed me about China was the way everybody can do their own thing.

Margaret Whitlam,
wife of Australian prime minister Gough Whitlam, 1973

For God's sake don't try to apply logic to Rhodesia.

Roy Welensky,
former Rhodesian prime minister, 1974

Young people are the prized possession of all people. We love young Polish people as I am sure you love young American people.

Gerald Ford,
US president, visiting Poland

I'm glad the British have to put up with the Irish. They deserve them. But just get them out.

Colonel Muammar Gaddafi,
Libyan president, 1975

I do not see the EEC as a great love affair. It is more like nine middle-aged couples with failing marriages meeting at a Brussels hotel for a group grope.

Kenneth Tynan,
English critic, 1975

If the human race is to survive, we must all come to see that 'the world is my country and all mankind my countrymen'.

Roger Baldwin,
US civil rights lawyer, 1976

Just because a few immigrants want their spicy tucker, I fail to see why the Australian community as a whole should suffer the possibility of disease.

Joh Bjelke-Petersen,
Queensland premier, arguing over the quality of pig-swill, 1976

The six shooter is hanging on the wall. But it is oiled and loaded. If and when High Noon arrives, America will strap that holster on again and step out into the street.

James Hargrove,
US ambassador to Australia, 1976

MY COUNTRY RIGHT AND LEFT

I've never been one to say that Britain was joining a happy band of brothers.

James Callaghan,
British prime minister, on the EEC, 1976

The people of this country are not a community of boy scouts. They don't really want to rally round anyone.

Lord Goodman,
British lawyer, 1976

No American who works for the CIA is a spy. A spy is a foreign agent who commits treason.

Jim Keehner,
CIA psychologist, 1976

The political alternatives in America now are like putting a Band-Aid on cancer.

Shirley MacLaine,
Hollywood activist, 1976

We should tell Panama's tin-horn dictator just what he can do with his demands for sovereignty over the Canal Zone. We bought it, we paid for it, and they can't have it.

Ronald Reagan,
US presidential candidate, on Panamanian claims to the Canal Zone, 1976

How far would we go to stop someone taking the state of Alaska?

Ronald Reagan,
when asked how far he would go to keep the Panama Canal, 1976

Anyone signing a contract with a Japanese firm must ask himself: will they honour it?

Joh Bjelke-Petersen,
Queensland premier, 1977

Don't forget that unlike the French, unlike the British and unlike the Portuguese, we Afrikaners have no other place to go.

Roelof Botha,
South African author, 1977

Europe is nothing but a collection of unjust dictatorships; all of humanity must strike these trouble-makers with an iron hand if it wishes to regain its tranquillity.

Ayatollah Khomeini,
religious dictator of Iran: _Sayings_, 1980

I declare to the whole world that we agree to live with you in a permanent and just peace.

Anwar Sadat,
Egyptian president, to the Israeli Knesset, 1977

Perhaps this country needs an Iron Lady.

Margaret Thatcher,
British opposition leader, replying to Russian taunts, 1977

Marxism has placed its stake on force — which Marx called the midwife of history. And though the midwife perpetually delivers monsters...Marxists never tire of promising that the next child will be a splendid one.

Andrei Amalrik,
Soviet dissident, receiving a Human Rights Award, 1977

If you want to make peace you don't talk to your friends, you talk to your enemies.

General Moshe Dayan,
Israeli politician, 1977

It gives me great pleasure to refer to Aborigines as fellow citizens.

Sir John Kerr,
Governor-General of Australia, 1977

I am a great friend of Israel. Any country that can stand Milton Friedman as an adviser has nothing to fear from a few million Arabs.

John Kenneth Galbraith,
Canadian-born US economist, 1979

If you foreigners don't understand, too bad for you. It is none of your business. You have nothing to do with our choices. If some Iranians don't understand it, too bad for them.

Ayatollah Khomeini,
religious dictator of Iran, 1979

73

BOOK OF POLITICAL QUOTES

When it came to the survival of South Africa, morality flew out of the window.

Eschel Rhoodie,
key figure in South Africa's 'Muldergate' propaganda scandal, 1979.

For us in Russia, Communism is a dead dog, while for many people in the West it is still a living lion.

Alexander Solzhenitsyn,
Russian dissident author

When Mother gets back we will either have good relations with India or they will have been destroyed.

Jimmy Carter,
US president, after sending his mother, Miz Lillian, on a mission to India, 1977

Iran is rich enough to support revolution as an industry.

Shimon Peres,
Israeli politician, 1980

Fine goals matter less than the right strategy.

Stanley Hoffman,
Professor of Foreign Affairs, Harvard University, 1980

The British disease is old age — old institutions, old industrial assets and old attitudes. You could call it maturity, but there is only a thin line between maturity and senility.

Len Murray,
British trade union leader, 1980

Jimmy and Rosalynn Carter/Publisher's files

THE CLASSES AND THE MASSES

Money is like muck — no good unless it be spread.

Francis Bacon,
English statesman and philosopher: 'Of Seditions and Troubles', 1626

All communities divide...into the few and the many. The first are the rich and well-born; the other the mass of the people...turbulent and changing, they seldom judge or determine right. Give therefore to the first class a distinct, permanent share in the Government.

Alexander Hamilton,
US statesman, 1789

When you make men slaves you deprive them of half their virtue; you set them in your own conduct an example of fraud, rapine and cruelty...and yet you complain that they are not honest or faithful.

Gustavus Vassa,
black slave

The surest way to remain poor is to be an honest man.

Napoleon Bonaparte:
Maxims, 1804-15

A man will fight harder for his interests than his rights.

Napoleon Bonaparte:
Maxims, 1804-15

The Almighty Dollar, that great object of universal devotion throughout the land.

Washington Irving,
US essayist: The Creole Village, 1837

Property is theft.

Pierre Joseph Proudhon,
French socialist: Qu'est-ce que la Propriété? 1840

It is to be regretted that the rich and powerful too often bend the acts of government to their selfish purposes... when the laws undertake...to make the rich richer and the potent more powerful, the humble members of society have a right to complain of the injustice of their government.

Andrew Jackson,
US president, 1832

The right of man to freedom is not based on the union of man with man, but on the separation of man from man....The right of man to property is the right to enjoy his possessions and dispose of the same arbitrarily, without regard for other men, independently of society and is the right of selfishness.

Karl Marx:
On the Jewish Question, 1843

The ruling ideas of each age have ever been the ideas of its ruling class.

Karl Marx,
1848

Labour disgraces no man. Unfortunately you occasionally find men disgrace labour.

Ulysses S. Grant,
1877

Money is the alienated essence of a man's work and existence; this essence dominates him and he worships it.

Karl Marx,
1884

Whoever controls the volume of money in any country is the master of all its legislation and commerce.

James A. Garfield,
US president, 1881

Labour is prior to, and independent of capital. Capital is only the fruit of labour and could never have existed if labour had not first existed.

Abraham Lincoln

The intellectual desolation produced by converting immature human beings into machines.

Karl Marx:
Das Kapital, 1867-83

Within the capitalist system all methods for raising the social productiveness of labour are brought about at the cost of the individual labourer; all means for the development of production transform themselves into means of domination over and exploitation of the producers.

Karl Marx:
Das Kapital, 1867-83

I believe the power to make money is a gift of God...to be developed and used to the best of our ability for the good of mankind. Having been endowed with the gift I possess, I believe it is my duty to make money and still more money and to use the money I make for the good of my fellow man according to the dictates of my conscience.

John D. Rockefeller,
US capitalist

As soon as the goal of the proletarian movement, the abolition of classes, shall have been reached, the power of the state, whose function is to keep the great majority of the producers beneath the yoke of a small minority of exploiters, will disappear and governmental functions will be transformed into simple administrative functions.

Karl Marx:
Das Kapital, 1867-83

The public be damned!

William H. Vanderbilt,
US railroad millionaire, when told by a reporter that the public expected an interview with him, 1879

I was told that the privileged and the people formed two nations.

Benjamin Disraeli,
British statesman: *Sybil,* 1845

Few rich men own their property. Their property owns them.

Robert G. Ingersoll,
US lawyer, 1896

Landlords, like all other men, love to reap where they have never sowed.

Karl Marx

The danger is not that a particular class is unfit to govern. Every class is unfit to govern.

Lord Acton,
English historian, 1881

I can hire one half of the working class to kill the other half.

Jay Gould,
US railroad millionaire, 1886

We'll hang Jay Gould from a sour-apple tree!

**Campaign song
in Grover Cleveland's presidential campaign, 1884**

The formation of a class with radical chains, a class in civil society that is not a class of civil society, of a social group that is the dissolution of all social groups, of a sphere that has a universal character because of its universal sufferings and lays claim to no particular right, because it is the object of no particular injustice but of injustice in general. This class can no longer lay claim to a historical status but only to a human one. It is, finally, a sphere that cannot emancipate itself without emancipating these other spheres themselves. In a word, it is the complete loss of humanity and can only recover itself by a complete redemption of humanity. This dissolution of society, as a particular class, is the proletariat.

Karl Marx

THE CLASSES AND THE MASSES

All the world over I will back the masses against the classes.

William Gladstone,
British prime minister, 1886

The communism of combined wealth and capital, the outgrowth of overweening cupidity and selfishness which assiduously undermines the justice and integrity of free institutions is not less dangerous than the communism of oppressed poverty and toil which, exasperated by injustice and discontent, attacks with wild disorder the citadel of misrule.

Grover Cleveland,
US president, 1888

The more is given, the less the people will work for themselves and the less they work, the more their poverty will increase.

Leo Tolstoy,
Russian author, 1892

I shall not help crucify mankind upon a cross of gold; I shall not aid in pressing down upon the bleeding brow of labour this crown of thorns.

William Jennings Bryan,
US politician, 1896

The history of all hitherto existing societies is the history of class struggles.

Karl Marx:
the first line of *The Communist Manifesto*,
1848

What do I care about the law? Hain't I got the power!

Cornelius Vanderbilt,
US capitalist

The trade unions are the legitimate outgrowth of modern societary and industrial conditions.... They were born of the necessity of workers to protect themselves from encroachment, injustice and wrong.... To protect the workers in their inalienable rights to a higher and better life; to protect them, not only as equals before the law, but also in their health, their homes, their firesides, their liberties as men, as workers and as citizens; to overcome and conquer prejudices and antagonism, to secure to them the right to life, and the opportunity to maintain that life; the right to be full sharers in the abundance which is the result of their brain and brawn, and the civilization of which they are the founders and mainstay; to this the workers are entitled—the attainment of these is the glorious mission of the trade unions.

Samuel Gompers,
US unionist, 1898

I never knew the working classes had such white skins.

Lord Curzon,
British statesman

The American Beauty Rose can be produced in all its splendour only by sacrificing the early buds that grow up around it.

John D. Rockefeller,
US capitalist, his business philosophy,
1905

It is an axiom enforced by all the experience of the ages, that they who rule industrially will rule politically.

James Connolly,
Irish Republican politician: *Socialism Made
***Easy*, 1905**

The open door.

John Hay,
  US Secretary of State, abolishing all trade tariffs, 1900

Pure and simple trades unionism means the ideological subordination of the workers to the bourgeoisie.

V.I. Lenin:
  'What Is To Be Done?', 1902

There is always some basic principle that will ultimately get the Republican Party together. If my observations are worth anything, that basic principle is the cohesive power of public plunder.

A.J. McLaurin,
  US politician, 1906

I am a working man and in every nerve, in every fibre, in every aspiration, I am on the side which will advance the interests of my fellow working men. I represent my side, the side of the toiling, wage-earning masses, in every act and in every utterance.

Samuel Gompers,
  US unionist

To secure for the producers by hand and brain the full fruits of their industry and the most equitable distribution thereof that may be possible upon the basis of the common ownership of the means of production, distribution and exchange.

The British Labour Party Constitution

With all their faults, trade unions have done more for humanity than any other organization of men that ever existed. They have done more for decency, for honesty, for education, for the betterment of the race, for the developing character of man, than any other association of men.

Clarence Darrow,
  US radical lawyer, 1909

The price of an article is exactly what it will fetch.

Sir Marcus Samuel,
  founder of Shell Oil, defending a price rise, 1911

It is not good for trade unions that they should be brought into contact with the courts, and it is not good for courts. Where class issues are involved, it is impossible to pretend that the courts command the same degree of general confidence.

Winston Churchill,
  British Home Secretary, 1911

The masters of government of the United States are the combined capitalists and manufacturers.

Woodrow Wilson,
  US president, 1913

Pity the poor millionaire — for the way of the philanthropist is hard.

Andrew Carnegie,
  US millionaire and philanthropist, 1913

How these dukes harass us. They're as expensive to keep up as a dreadnought, and not half as useful.

David Lloyd George,
  British Chancellor of the Exchequer, 1909

There is a dreadful fallacy fermenting in men's minds that all they want is higher wages.

Sir Auckland Geddes,
  British politician, 1919

I do not believe that you could point to any case where men work better for the state than they work for syndicates.

David Lloyd George,
  British prime minister, 1919

They are a lot of hard-faced men who look as if they have done well out of the war.

John Maynard Keynes,
  English economist, quoting a Conservative politician, often thought to have been Stanley Baldwin: *Economic Consequences of the Peace*, 1919

If people are going to drink champagne, the larger the share of taxation on that wine, the greater will be their patriotism.

Sir Austen Chamberlain,
  British politician, 1920

THE CLASSES AND THE MASSES

I've got to keep breathing. It'll be my worst business mistake if I don't.

Sir Nathan Meyer Rothschild,
   British financier, 1915

When the State endeavours to function as a charitable institution it does more harm than good.

Arthur Hopkinson,
   British politician, 1921

Unionism seldom, if ever, uses such power as it has to ensure better work. Almost always it devotes a large part of that power to safeguarding bad work.

H.L. Mencken,
   US philologist, editor and satirist:
   ***Prejudices,* third series, 1922**

A society without an aristocracy, without an elite minority, is not a society.

José Ortega y Gasset,
   Spanish philosopher and statesman, 1922

Of what use is culture to a labourer?

Emanuel Shinwell,
   British Labour politician, 1923

Although I know that there are those who work for different ends from most of us in this house, yet there are many in all ranks and in all parties who will re-echo my prayer: 'Give us peace in our time, oh Lord.'

Stanley Baldwin,
   British prime minister, referring to the unions, 1925

Until our educated and politically minded democracy has become predominantly a property-owning democracy, neither the national equilibrium nor the balance of the life of the individual will be restored.

A Skelton,
   British author: *Constructive Conservatism,* 1925, quoted by both Anthony Eden and Winston Churchill in 1946

There is too often today a tendency for trade unions to abuse their powers.

J.H. Thomas,
   British Labour politician, 1926

We must respect those above us. It pays. Be loyal to your employer. Don't be fooled by wrong talk. Speak well of your bosses to other workmen.

US Department of Labor:
   ***Federal Citizenship Textbook,* 1925**

American business is not a monster, but an expression of a God-given impulse to create, and the saviour of our happiness.

Warren G. Harding

Show me the country that has no strikes and I'll show you the country in which there is no liberty.

Samuel Gompers,
   US unionist, 1925

The most conservative man in the world is the British trades unionist when you want to change him.

Ernest Bevin,
   British Labour politician, 1927

Eats first, morals after.

Bertolt Brecht,
   German dramatist: *The Threepenny Opera,* 1928

An angry god may have endowed capitalism with inherent contradictions. But at least as an afterthought he was kind enough to make social reform surprisingly consistent with improved operation of the system.

John Kenneth Galbraith,
   Canadian-born US economist: *The Great Crash,* 1955

What is robbing a bank compared with founding a bank?

Bertolt Brecht,
   German dramatist: *The Threepenny Opera,* 1928

Men have been swindled by other men on many occasions. The autumn of 1929 was perhaps the first occasion when men succeeded on a large scale in swindling themselves.

John Kenneth Galbraith,
   Canadian-born US economist: *The Great Crash,* 1955

WALL STREET LAYS AN EGG

Sime Silverman,
    editor and founder of *Variety* magazine,
headlining the Great Crash, 1929

The end had come, but it was not yet in sight.

John Kenneth Galbraith,
    Canadian-born US economist: *The Great Crash,* 1955

Look, we trade every day out there with hustlers, deal-makers, shysters, con-men... that's the way businesses get started. That's the way this country was built.

Hubert Allen,
    US financier

There is no problem about money, except who has it.

Montagu Norman,
    governor of the Bank of England, 1931

Had the employers of the past generation dealt fairly with men, there would have been no trade unions.

Stanley Baldwin,
    British prime minister, 1931

Concentration of economic power in all-embracing corporations...represents private enterprise become a kind of private government which is a power unto itself, a regimentation of other people's money and other people's lives.

Franklin D. Roosevelt,
    US president, 1936

No one who has wealth to distribute ever omits himself.

Leon Trotsky,
    exiled Russian revolutionary leader, 1937

To the ordinary working man, the sort you would meet in any pub on a Saturday night, Socialism does not mean much more than better wages and shorter hours and nobody bossing you about.

George Orwell,
    English novelist and essayist: *The Road to Wigan Pier,* 1937

You cannot mine coal without machine guns.

Richard Mellon,
    US mine owner, to a Congressional investigation of strike breaking and brutality, 1937

For the ordinary man is passive. Within a narrow circle...he feels himself master of his fate, but against major events he is as helpless as against the elements. So far from endeavouring to influence the future, he simply lies down and lets things happen to him.

George Orwell,
    English novelist and essayist

The strike weapon is out of date.

Joseph Jones,
    leader of the Yorkshire miners, 1938

Enterprise doesn't have to be private to be enterprise.

Herbert Morrison,
    British politician, 1942

The history of the world is the history of a privileged few.

Henry Miller,
    US author: *Sunday After the War*, 1944

True individual freedom cannot exist without economic security and independence. People who are hungry and out of a job are the stuff of which dictatorships are made.

Franklin D. Roosevelt,
    US president, 1944

The trouble with the profit system has always been that it was highly unprofitable to most people.

E.B. White,
    US humorist: *One Man's Meat*, 1944

We are the masters at the moment, and not only for the moment, but for a very long time to come.

Lord Shawcross,
    English lawyer, on the Labour government's repeal of Conservative legislation to control trade unions, 1946

Bertrand Russell/Popperfoto

It is preoccupation with possession, more than anything else, that prevents men from living freely and nobly.

Bertrand Russell,
  English philosopher

It is an unfortunate human failing that a full pocketbook often groans more loudly than an empty stomach.

Franklin D. Roosevelt,
  US president, 1940

No country has ever been ruined on account of its debts.

Adolf Hitler,
  German führer, 1940

There is a good deal of solemn cant about the common interests of capital and labour. As matters stand, their only common interest is that of cutting each other's throat.

Brooks Atkinson,
  US essayist: 'Once Around the Sun', 1951

The Tories always hold the view that the State is an apparatus for the protection of the swag of the property owners.....Christ drove the moneychangers out of the temple, but you inscribe their initials on the altar cloth.

Aneurin Bevan,
  British Labour politician, to the Tory party

Deportations, massacres, forced labour, slavery have been the principal means used by capitalism to augment its reserves of gold and diamonds, its wealth, and to establish its power.

Frantz Fanon,
  French radical

I thought what was good for the country was good for General Motors, and vice versa.

Charles E. Wilson,
  president of General Motors, reluctantly selling his GM stock after being appointed US Secretary of Defense, 1953

The state is, or can be, master of money, but in a free society it is master of very little else.

**Lord Beveridge,
  British economist**

We know that you, the organized workers of the country, are our friends — as for the rest, they do not matter a tinker's curse.

**Emanuel Shinwell,
  British Labour politician, to the Electrical Trade Union's conference, 1947**

All forms of exploitation are identical because all of them are applied against the same 'object': man.

**Frantz Fanon,
  French radical: _Black Skin White Masks_, 1952**

Oilmen are like cats. You can never tell from the sound of them whether they are fighting or making love.

**Calouste Gulbenkian,
  Turkish-born British oil millionaire**

Right now, the basic insecurity the workers feel is this — they are haunted by the spectre of the van driving up to the door to take away the TV set.

**Bessie Braddock,
  British MP, 1955**

The meek shall inherit the earth, but _not_ its mineral rights.

**J. Paul Getty,
  US multi-millionaire**

The shop steward is a little like an egg. If you keep him in hot water long enough, he gets hard-boiled.

**Jack Tanner,
  president of the British TUC, 1954**

The genius of our ruling class is that it has kept a majority of the people from ever questioning the inequity of a system where most people drudge along paying heavy taxes for which they get nothing in return.

**Gore Vidal,
  US author**

I look forward to the day when there is a strike not because a firm has introduced automation, but because it has not.

**Jo Grimond,
  British Liberal Party leader, 1956**

What men value in this world is not rights, but privileges.

**H.L. Mencken,
  US philologist, editor and satirist: _Minority Report_, 1956**

...and all those financiers, all the little gnomes of Zurich and other financial centres about whom we keep on hearing, started to make their dispositions about sterling.

**Harold Wilson,
  British Labour politician, coining a phrase, 1956**

There is a great deal of truth in Andrew Carnegie's remark 'The man who dies rich, dies disgraced'. I should add, the man who lives rich, lives disgraced.

Aga Khan III: _Memoirs_

If capitalism had been conducted all along as if the theory of private enterprise were a matter of principle, we should have had civil war long ago.

**Harold Macmillan,
  British prime minister**

Oil friendships are greasy.

**Calouste Gulbenkian,
  Turkish-born British oil millionaire**

Nothing so weakens a government as persistent inflation.

**John Kenneth Galbraith,
  Canadian-born US economist: _The Affluent Society_, 1958**

It's a recession when your neighbour loses his job; it's a depression when you lose yours.

**Harry S. Truman,
  former US president, 1958**

THE CLASSES AND THE MASSES

If you can count your money, you don't have a billion dollars.

J. Paul Getty,
   multi-millionaire

You can tell me all you want about 'fair play' on the picket line, but violence and union organizing go hand in hand. Hell, it can't be avoided. Either the union, the employer, or the employees themselves will start it if the economic pressure is there.

Teamster official
   quoted in Dan E. Moldea: *The Hoffa Wars*, 1978

To be a trade unionist is to align oneself with those at the bottom of the social ladder at a time when the predominant urge is to climb it. In an age of social mobility — and social snobbery — the activities and still more the language and propaganda of trade unions seem increasingly anachronistic, dowdy and 'unsmart'.

Michael Shanks,
   English author: *The Stagnant Society*, 1961

If a free society cannot help the many who are poor, it cannot save the few who are rich.

John F. Kennedy

It is no part of the State's duty to facilitate the spiritual redemption of rich men by impoverishing them in this life.

John Grigg,
   British journalist, 1964

The TUC has arrived. It is an estate of the realm, as real, as potent, as essentially part of the fabric of our national life, as any of the historic estates.

Harold Wilson,
   British prime minister, 1968

The hatred Americans have for their own government is pathological...at one level it is simply thwarted greed: since our religion is making a buck, giving a part of that buck to any government is an act against nature.

Gore Vidal,
   US author

Taxation should be an energizer, not a penalizer.

James Callaghan,
   British Labour politician, 1963

It is difficult for us to appreciate the pressures which are put on men...in the highly organized strike committees in the individual ports by this tightly knit group of politically motivated men...who are now determined to exercise back-stage pressures ...endangering the security of the industry and economic welfare of the nation.

Harold Wilson,
   British prime minister, blaming the seamen's strike on communist infiltrators, 1966

The dynamic of capitalism is postponement of enjoyment to the constantly postponed future.

Norman O. Brown,
   US philosopher

An almost unlimited faith in the ability of people to get what they want through price, capital, profit and a competitive market.

Enoch Powell,
   British politician, on his economic credo, 1968

If we reach the stage where a minister cannot have interests outside Parliament then you would have a lot of people without any experience of the business world.

Sir Henry Bolté,
   premier of Victoria, 1968

You talk about capitalism and communism and all that sort of thing, but the important thing is the struggle everybody is engaged in to get better living conditions and they are not interested too much in the form of government.

Bernard Baruch,
   US financier and statesman, 1964

My lads come first, to hell with the critics.

Clive Jenkins,
   General Secretary of the Association of Scientific, Technical and Managerial Staffs, 1970

Selsdon Man is designing a system of society for the ruthless and the pushing, the uncaring.....His message to the rest is: you're out on your own.

Harold Wilson,
   British opposition leader, referring to the recent Conservative policy-forming meeting at Selsdon Park, Croydon, 1970

The taxpayer, that's someone who works for the Federal government but doesn't have to take a civil service examination.

Ronald Reagan,
   governor of California, 1968

To be an official of a union representing lower-paid workers is no career for a self-respecting man.

Clive Jenkins,
   General Secretary of the Association of Scientific, Technical and Managerial Staff, 1971

I've always known that the whole society line was bullshit from wall to wall, but what society does is to cover the bullshit with chocolate so you think it's bridge mix.

Flo Kennedy,
   US feminist, 1973

The TUC is not just a platform of people who meet once a year by the seaside, nor is it merely the name on top of official headed notepaper.

Len Murray,
   General Secretary of the TUC, 1973

Our job as trade unionists is not merely to haggle about slices of the economic 'cake'. We are in politics. We are concerned about where the power lies, and concerned that that power is not abused.

David Basnett,
   president of the General and Municipal Workers Union, 1973

It is the unpleasant and unacceptable face of capitalism, but one should not suggest that the whole of British industry consists of practices of this kind.

Edward Heath,
   on the Lonrho scandal, 1973

One man's wage rise is another man's price increase.

Harold Wilson,
   British opposition leader, 1970

Like the common cold there is no guaranteed cure for inflation, but there are a lot of things you can do to keep it within reasonable bounds.

William McMahon,
   Australian prime minister, 1971

Money made by money should be taxed at the same rate as money made by men.

Senator George McGovern,
   1972

Labour is nothing without the trade unions. But the trade unions can survive without the Labour Party.

Eric Heffer,
   British politician, 1973

This is a free country and anybody is entitled to ask for anything.

Len Murray,
   General Secretary of the TUC, 1974

A fair price for oil is whatever you can get plus ten per cent.

Dr Ali Ahmed Attiga,
   delegate to OPEC, 1974

We see trade unions not simply as fruit machines in which workers put tanners to get the jackpot — we see trade unionists as agents of social change.

Bernard Dix,
   Secretary of the National Union of Public Employees, 1974

Unemployment insurance provides a pre-paid vacation for a section of our society which has made it a way of life.

Ronald Reagan

The company is not bust. We are merely in a cyclical decline.

Lord Stokes,
   chairman of British Leyland, 1974

THE CLASSES AND THE MASSES

I have told the country before that capitalism has its unacceptable face. If you want to see the acceptable face of capitalism, go out to an oil rig in the North Sea.

Edward Heath,
  British opposition leader, 1974

I have only got one social contract which I honour and that is with the members of my union.

Arthur Scargill,
  president of the Yorkshire branch of the National Union of Miners, referring to the 'social contract' policy of voluntary wage restraint between the TUC and the Labour government, 1974

Trade unionism is killing socialism in this country and it is time socialists did something about it.

Paul Johnson,
  British journalist, 1975

One thing that terrifies the trade union bureaucrats more than anything is the independent action of workers. Nothing is better calculated to cut down their importance, their status, their prestige.... And nothing is more likely to strengthen their attachment to the status quo. The bureaucrat is not a capitalist, but he is not a worker either. He lives off the class struggle, but can't let it go beyond the point of mediation or negotiation. His basic rule is to keep the contestants alive and able to fight — gently.

Tony Cliff,
  Socialist Workers' Party, 1975

The capitalist society belongs in the dustbin of history. The ideal of a socialist society belongs to the youth of today and to the future. I have seen the vision of the socialist tomorrow and it works.

Arthur Scargill,
  president of the Yorkshire branch of the National Union of Miners, 1975

Never in the history of human credit has so much been owed.

Margaret Thatcher,
  British opposition leader, 1975

Trade unions cannot determine a greater part of the experience to which their members react.

Allan Flanders,
  English author: *Management and Unions*, 1975

We have been slow in accepting that a more equal society means levelling down.

John Kenneth Galbraith,
  Canadian-born US economist, 1975

Solidarity, understanding and friendship are the trade union answer to international tension.

Jack Jones,
  General Secretary of the Transport and General Workers Union, 1975

The Chancellor is not like Robin Hood, taking wealth from the rich and giving it to the poor. He is taking it from the rich and giving it to the Sheriff.

John Pardoe,
  British Liberal MP, 1975

We have a love-hate relationship with inflation. We hate inflation, but we love everything that causes it.

William Simon,
  US Secretary of the Treasury, 1975

British trade unionism has become a formula for national misery.

Paul Johnson,
  British journalist, 1975

I don't know, it may be that the poor people are the only ones who commit crimes, but I do know they are the only ones who serve prison sentences.

Jimmy Carter,
  US presidential candidate, campaigning, 1976

We are in a desperate state...as to the state of national leadership, there is none. The state is zero. This is the era of the chairman of the board, not leadership.

Henry Steele Commager,
  US historian, 1976

To those who say it is time to reform this organization and that it's time that its officers stopped selling out its members, I say: 'Go to hell!'

Frank Fitzsimmons,
president of the Teamsters Union, 1976

The value of the pound is what the market says it is.

Milton Friedman,
monetarist guru of Chile, Israel and the UK, 1976

I believe that once people realise they will be better off with a low pay limit rather than a higher one, they will see the sense of it.

Denis Healey,
British Chancellor of the Exchequer, 1976

If a state is mismanaged, you can move elsewhere.

Ronald Reagan,
US presidential candidate, referring to changes in the state's welfare programmes that would deprive many needy people, 1976

Unfortunately good economics is not always perceived to be good politics.

William Simon,
US Secretary of the Treasury, 1976

Money matters are very complex, but there are straightforward simple remedies.

Joh Bjelke-Petersen,
premier of Queensland, 1977

If I could get the devil to help the trade union movement, I would.

Bob Hawke,
Australian union leader, 1977

We must destroy the work ethic. No longer must a person's social position be judged by his paid occupation.

Clive Jenkins,
General Secretary of the ASTMS, 1978

The motto of 'every man for himself' was taken down from the wall when the first trade union was formed, and it does not become an acceptable motto if we change it to every union for itself.

Len Murray,
General Secretary of the TUC, 1977

We must not allow ourselves to be shackled by legal rules and regulations. The law we have is a fall-back, not a weapon of first resort. We have not reached the highest ever membership...by relying on the law.

Harry Urwin,
Assistant General Secretary of the Transport and General Workers Union, 1977

It is a matter of markets, not morals.

Gough Whitlam,
Australian prime minister, on Australia's decision to export uranium, 1977

What's good politics is bad economics; what's bad politics is good economics; what's good economics is bad politics, what's bad economics is good politics.

Eugene W. Baer
quoted in Paul Dickson: *The Official Rules*, 1978

Sitting and listening at the TUC often resembles a play. The actors strut across the stage mouthing their lines, breathing defiance or simulating sympathy, every now and then glancing at their prompter for assistance. Off stage most of them revert to ordinary human beings, facing ordinary human problems in the empirical and reasonable way that trade unionists always have done.

Frank Chapple,
General Secretary of the EEPTU, 1978

Industrial action is merely the continuation of negotiation by other means.

Denis McShane,
President of the National Union of Journalists, 1978

THE CLASSES AND THE MASSES

Workers and their families have always distrusted the law, and rightly so. It is not an instrument geared to our needs and the people who administer it are unrepresentative, out of touch and antagonistic to our demands.

Jeremy McMullen,
British author: *Rights at Work,* 1978

The entire graduated income tax structure was created by Karl Marx.

Ronald Reagan

To suggest that the Conservative Party would seek to be in conflict with trade unions is to suggest that we are in favour of cutting off one of our own limbs.

James Prior,
British Shadow Employment Minister, 1978

Those who invented the law of supply and demand have no right to complain when this law works against their interest.

Anwar Sadat,
Egyptian president, on the West's oil crisis, 1978

If I cannot afford to buy food, why should anyone else have it?

Bill Astbury,
Chairman of the Greater Manchester Lorry Drivers' Strike Committee, 1978

Everyone has a right to work and everyone has the right to pass a picket line.

James Callaghan,
British prime minister, 1979

It has no goal, but possesses an astute and sensitive awareness of what it wants to protect: the economic standard of employed, working class men. It is really very similar to the position taken up by the party leadership before 1914.

H. M. Drucker,
British author, on the link between unions and Labour: *Doctrine and Ethos of the Labour Party,* 1979

Paying people more just because they get so little is a recipe for disaster.

Frank Chapple,
General Secretary of the EEPTU, 1979

All trade union leaders are divided into two groups — those who are descended from Irishmen and those who wish they were.

Herman Rebhan,
General Secretary of the International Metalworkers Federation, 1979

We are selling the labour of our members for the highest and best price. Using any and every related reason to get it. That is what a trade union leader does. He is not a philosopher or a socialist writer. I am a trade union negotiator and I am selling a product.

Alan Sapper,
leader of the ACTT, 1979

I don't see how we can talk to Mrs Thatcher. I will say to the lads, 'Come on, get your snouts in the trough.'

Sid Weighell,
leader of the National Union of Railwaymen, 1979

Nothing is illegal if one hundred businessmen decided to do it.

Andrew Young,
US ambassador to the United Nations

If we cannot be heard in Whitehall, then we shall be heard in Trafalgar Square.

David Basnett,
President of the General and Municipal Workers Union, advocating the TUC 'Day of Action' in the face of governmental refusal to consult the unions as they saw fit, 1980

In the first place trade unions are about individuals and the right to answer back to the boss.

Len Murray,
General Secretary of the TUC, 1980

FAIR COMMENT

The punishment which the wise suffer, who refuse to take part in the government, is to live under the government of worse men.

Plato,
Greek philosopher: *The Republic*, fourth century BC

It is evident that the state is a creation of nature and that man is by nature a political animal.

Aristotle,
Greek philosopher: *Politics*, fourth century BC

The first man to fence in a piece of land, saying 'This land is mine', and who found people simple enough to believe him, was the real founder of civil society.

Jean-Jacques Rousseau,
French politician, philosopher, educationist and essayist: *Discourse on the Origin and Bases of Inequality Among Men*, 1754

How pitiful in the eyes of reason is that false ambition which desolates the world with fire and the sword . . . when compared with the milder virtues of making our neighbours and our fellow men as happy as their frail conditions and perishable natures permit them to be.

George Washington,
1794

Whoever condemns the theatre is an enemy to his country.

Voltaire,
French philosopher and humanitarian

The less reasonable a cult is, the more men seek to establish it by force.

Jean-Jacques Rousseau,
French politician, philosopher, educationist and essayist

A whiff of grapeshot.

Napoleon Bonaparte
as an officer, ordering his troops to fire on the Parisian crowds who were attacking the Constitutional Convention, and subsequently killing one hundred of them with the fusillade, 1795

I can't tell a lie, Pa, you know I can't tell a lie. I did cut it with my hatchet.

George Washington
grooming himself for glory after chopping down a cherry tree, quoted by Mason Locke Weems: *Life of Washington*

Don't give up the ship!

Captain James Lawrence
of the USS *Chesapeake*, disabled by HMS *Shannon*. Allegedly Lawrence's last words, although the phrase may have been contrived by Benjamin Russell, editor of the Boston *Centinel*, 1813

FAIR COMMENT

Roll up that map. It will not be wanted these ten years.

William Pitt the Younger,
British prime minister, on the map of Europe after Napoleon's victory at Austerlitz, 1805

I view great cities as pestilential to the morals, the health and the liberties of man.

Thomas Jefferson

At the same pace that mankind masters nature, man seems to become enslaved to other men or to his own infamy. Even the pure light of science seems unable to shine, but on the dark background of ignorance. And our invention and progress seem to result in endowing material forces with intellectual life and in stultifying human life into a material force.

Karl Marx

Karl Marx/The Mansell Collection

BOOK OF POLITICAL QUOTES

The minds of some of our statesmen, like the pupil of the human eye, contract themselves the more the stronger light is shed upon them.

Thomas Moore,
Irish poet

The sickly, the weakly, the timid man fears the people and is a Tory by nature.

Thomas Jefferson,
former US president, 1823

I called the New World into existence to redress the balance of the old.

George Canning,
British head of Foreign Affairs, 1826

Democratic nations care but little for what has been, but they are haunted by visions of what will be.

Alexis de Tocqueville,
French political commentator, 1835

Education makes a people easy to lead, but difficult to drive; easy to govern, but impossible to enslave.

Lord Brougham of Vaux,
Scottish law reformer

If slavery must go by blood and war, let war come.

John Quincy Adams,
former US president, 1843

What has always made the state a hell on earth has been precisely that man has tried to make it his heaven.

Johann Friedrich Hölderlin,
German poet

The world will not know liberty until all that is religious, political, is transformed into something simple and human, is made susceptible to criticism and denial.

Alexander Herzen,
Russian political thinker and writer: *From the Other Shore,* 1847-50

Politics makes strange bedfellows.

Charles Dudley Warner,
US essayist: *My Summer in a Garden,* 1870

If I could save the Union without freeing *any* slave, I would do it, and if I could do it by freeing *all* the slaves, I would do it; and if I could do it by freeing some and leaving the others alone, I would also do that.

Abraham Lincoln,
US president: the Emancipation Proclamation, 1863

Assassination has never changed the history of the world.

Benjamin Disraeli,
British Chancellor of the Exchequer, on Lincoln's death, 1865

To scholars who become politicians, the comic role is usually assigned: they have to be the good conscience of state policy.

Friedrich Nietzsche,
German philosopher

We are not going to Canossa.

Otto von Bismarck,
German chancellor, launching the anti-papal *Kulturkampf,* referring to Emperor Henry IV's capitulation to Pope Gregory VII in 1077, 1872

A politician divides mankind into two classes: tools and enemies. That means he knows only one class — enemies.

Friedrich Nietzsche,
German philosopher

If we are to negotiate peace...I imagine an essentially modest role...that of an honest broker, who really intends to do business.

Otto von Bismarck,
German chancellor, on the Eastern Crisis, 1878

The Industrial Revolution.

Arnold J. Toynbee,
English historian; the phrase was first used in an Oxford University lecture, 1881, and published posthumously, 1884

No man is justified in doing evil on the grounds of expediency.

Theodore Roosevelt,
governor of New York State: *The Strenuous Life,* 'Latitude and Longitude Among Reformers', 1900

FAIR COMMENT

J'accuse.

Emile Zola,
French writer, headlining a letter in
***L'Aurore* attacking the French government**
during the Dreyfus Affair, 1894

It cannot in the opinion of HM Government be classified as slavery in the extreme acceptance of the word without some risk of terminological inexactitude.

Winston Churchill,
British statesman on the Chinese Labour
Contract, 1906

That a peasant may become king does not render the kingdom democratic.

Woodrow Wilson,
1910

The highest and best form of efficiency is the spontaneous co-operation of a free people.

Woodrow Wilson

The enemies of freedom do not argue, they shout and they shoot.

William R. Inge,
Dean of St Paul's: *The End of an Age*

In the construction of a country it is not the practical workers, but the planners and idealists that are difficult to find.

Sun Yat Sen,
Chinese republican leader

The lamps are going out all over Europe; we shall not see them lit again in our lifetime.

Sir Edward Grey,
British statesman, on the eve of the First
World War, 1914

There seems to be something wrong with our bloody ships today!

Vice-Admiral Beatty,
on the sinking of British battle-cruisers at
the battle of Jutland, 1916

If we are, in the end, forced to go, we shall slam the door behind us in such a way that the echo will be felt throughout the world.

Leon Trotsky,
Russian revolutionary leader, 1917

His Majesty's Government views with favour the establishment in Palestine of a national home for the Jewish people.

Arthur Balfour,
British Foreign Secretary, in a letter to
Lord Rothschild which became known as the
Balfour Declaration, 1917

Nothing was ever done so systematically as nothing is being done now.

Woodrow Wilson

The most popular mass insurrection in history.

Leon Trotsky
on the Russian Revolution

Mr Wilson bores me with his Fourteen Points. Why, God Almighty has only ten.

Georges Clemenceau,
French prime minister, at the Versailles
Peace Talks, 1919

Nationalization will be the Magna Carta of the twentieth century.

H. G. Wells,
English author, 1920

BOOK OF POLITICAL QUOTES

It is only by working with an energy that is almost superhuman and looks to uninterested spectators like insanity that we can accomplish anything worth the achievement.

Woodrow Wilson

First let me insist on what our opponents habitually ignore, and indeed what they seem intellectually incapable of understanding, namely the inevitable gradualness of our scheme of change.

Sidney Webb,
   British Labour Party president, 1920

Communism will pass away from Russia, but it will have lighted a torch for the world of workers not readily to be extinguished.

Maxim Gorki,
   Russian writer, 1921

If you ask yourself how Dostoyevsky's characters ought to be governed, you will understand.

Bertrand Russell,
   English philosopher, justifying the Russian Revolution to Lady Ottoline Morrell

Human history becomes more and more a race between education and catastrophe.

H. G. Wells,
   English author: *The Outline of History*, 1921

If it had not been for these things, I might have lived out my life talking at street corners to scorning men. I might have died unmarked, unknown, a failure. That is our career and our triumph. Never in our full life could we hope to do such work for tolerance, for justice, for man's understanding of man as we now do by accident. Our words, our lives, our pains, nothing. The taking of our lives — the lives of a good shoemaker and a poor fish pedlar — all! That last moment belongs to us, that agony is our triumph!

Bartolomeo Vanzetti,
   US anarchist, executed despite a massive public outcry, 1927

If communism achieves a certain success, it will achieve it not as an improved economic technique, but as a religion.

John Maynard Keynes,
   English economist, 1925

Free speech is about as good a cause as the world has ever known. But, like the poor, it is always with us and gets shoved aside in favour of things which seem at some given moment more vital.

Heywood Broun,
   US wit, 1926

The reason men oppose progress is not because they hate progress but because they love inertia.

Elbert Hubbard,
   US businessman: *The Notebooks,* 1927

Liberty don't work as good in practice as it does in speech.

Will Rogers,
   US humorist, 1927

A parliament elected by the universal suffrage of voters grouped according to geographical areas is about as truly representative as a bottle of Bovril is a true representative of an ox.

Eleanor Rathbone,
   British feminist MP, 1931

Gentlemen, in the little moment that remains to us between the crisis and the catastrophe, we may well drink a glass of champagne.

Paul Claudel,
   French ambassador to the USA, 1931

The fifth column.

General Emilio Mola,
   Franco's general in the Spanish Civil War, referring to four columns of troops attacking Madrid, and the 'fifth column' of sympathisers inside the town

We shall go down in history as the greatest statesmen of all time, or the greatest criminals.

Joseph Goebbels,
   Nazi Minister of Propaganda

FAIR COMMENT

The brains trust.

James M. Kieran, Jr
  on Franklin Roosevelt's team of advisers,
1932

I never vote *for* anyone, I always vote against.

W.C. Fields,
  Hollywood comedian

The radical invents the views. When he has worn them out the conservative adopts them.

Mark Twain,
  US writer: *Notebook*

The Labour Party should be something more than an alms house for retired agitators.

John Maynard Keynes,
  English economist, 1939

The meek do not inherit the earth unless they are prepared to fight for their meekness.

Harold Laski,
  English political scientist

In Germany democracy died by the headsman's axe. In Britain it can be by pernicious anaemia.

Aneurin Bevan,
  British Labour politician

Speak for England, Arthur!

Leo Amery and Robert Boothby,
  British MPs, shouting to Arthur Greenwood, who was rising to speak in the House of Commons, 2 September, 1939

Like an old man approaching a young bride — fascinated, sluggish and apprehensive.

Aneurin Bevan,
  British Labour politician, on the Allies' advance into Italy, 1943

Ignorance is an evil weed, which dictators may cultivate among their dupes, but which no democracy can afford amongst its citizens.

Sir William Beveridge,
  British economist, 1944

WINSTON IS BACK

Admiralty signal
  on the recall of Winston Churchill as First Lord of the Admiralty, 1939

You have sat here too long for any good you have been doing. Depart, I say, and have done with you. In the name of God, go!

Leo Amery,
  British Conservative politician, to Neville Chamberlain, quoting Oliver Cromwell's dismissal of the Long Parliament, 1940

Never in the field of human conflict was so much owed by so many to so few.

Winston Churchill,
  British prime minister, on the Battle of Britain, 1940

Victory at all costs, victory in spite of all terror, victory however long and hard the road may be, for without victory there is no survival.

Winston Churchill,
  1940

Give us the tools and we will finish the job.

Winston Churchill,
  1941

The century on which we are entering can be and must be the century of the common man.

Henry Wallace,
  US vice-president, 1942

The laws of nature are not suspended for a 'red' army any more than for a 'white' one. A louse is a louse and a bomb is a bomb, even though the cause you are fighting for happens to be just.

George Orwell:
  'Looking Back on the Spanish War', 1943

I do not see any way of realizing our hopes about world organization in five or six days. Even the Almighty took seven.

Winston Churchill,
  British prime minister, to Franklin Roosevelt, who was hoping to see the Yalta Conference last only a few days, 1945

BOOK OF POLITICAL QUOTES

Elections are won by men and women chiefly because most people vote against somebody rather than for somebody.

Franklin P. Adams,
  US columnist: *Nods and Becks,* **1944**

Hell no, I made it like that.

Harry S. Truman,
  US president, snapping his fingers and referring to the decision to drop atomic weapons on Japan, 1945

We must plan our civilization or we must perish.

Harold Laski,
  English political scientist, 1945

Last night the world fell on my shoulders.

Harry S. Truman
  on the death of Franklin Roosevelt and his own elevation to the presidency, 1945

From Stettin in the Baltic to Trieste in the Adriatic, an iron curtain has descended over the continent.

Winston Churchill,
  British opposition leader, coining a phrase to describe Russian encroachments in Europe, 1946

Dammit, they've shot my fox!

Nigel Birch,
  Tory MP, 1947. Birch pursued one favourite target: Chancellor of the Exchequer Hugh Dalton. When Dalton leaked his budget before showing it to the House and was forced to resign, Birch lost his opponent

Freedom cannot be trifled with. You cannot surrender it for security unless in a state of war, and then you must guard carefully the methods of so doing.

Arthur Hays Sulzberger,
  publisher of the *New York Times,* **1952**

Man can leave the earth and land on the moon, but cannot cross from East to West Berlin. Prometheus reaches for the stars with an insane grin on his face and a totem-symbol in his hand.

Arthur Koestler,
  Hungarian-born author and journalist:
Janus

We have grasped the mystery of the atom and rejected the sermon on the mount.

General Omar Bradley,
  US general, 1948

Here's a pretty prospect — an endless vista of false teeth with nothing to bite.

Robert Boothby,
  British MP, on the coincident phenomena of the UK welfare state and the policy of economic austerity, 1950

If we value the pursuit of knowledge, we must be free to follow wherever that search may lead us. The free mind is no barking dog, to be tethered on a ten-foot chain.

Adlai Stevenson,
  US presidential candidate, 1952

General, there comes a time when you have to piss or get off the pot!

Richard Nixon,
  US vice-president, calling President Eisenhower to demand his aid in refuting the charges that Nixon's campaigning had been corrupt, 1952

Nothing so dates a man as decrying the younger generation.

Adlai Stevenson,
  US presidential candidate, 1952

There is no evil in the atom, only in men's souls.

Adlai Stevenson,
  US presidential candidate, 1952

Those who wait for that must wait until a shrimp learns to whistle.

Nikita S. Khruschev
  on speculation that the USSR might abandon communism, 1955

There ain't gonna be no war.

Harold Macmillan,
  British Foreign Minister, returning from the Summit Conference, 1955

Introducing Super-Mac.

Vicky,
  cartoonist in the *Evening Standard,* **captioning a cartoon of Macmillan as Superman, 1958**

FAIR COMMENT

The city is the graveyard of the guerilla.

Fidel Castro

The cult of personality.

Nikita S. Khruschev,
attacking Stalin at the twentieth Party Congress, 1956

You call that statesmanship. I call it an emotional spasm.

Aneurin Bevan,
British Labour politician, decrying international thoughts of unilateral disarmament, 1957

I thought the best thing to do was to settle up these little local difficulties and then turn to the wider vision of the Commonwealth.

Harold Macmillan,
British prime minister, referring to the recent resignations by Treasury Ministers, as he left for a Commonwealth tour, 1958

Every snipe praises his own bog.

Nikita S. Khruschev,
after listening to his US chaperone, Henry Cabot Lodge, deliver a lengthy speech in favour of capitalism, 1959

One does not arrest Voltaire.

Charles de Gaulle,
French president, refusing to act against the philosopher Jean Paul Sartre, who was urging French troops to desert rather than serve in Algeria, 1960

The wind of change is blowing through the continent. Whether we like it or not, this growth of national consciousness is a political fact. We must all accept it as a fact.

Harold Macmillan,
British prime minister, referring to African independence movements in a speech to the South African parliament, 1960

Britain has lost an empire and not yet found a role.

Dean Acheson,
former US Secretary of State, 1962

I want to be the white man's brother, not his brother-in-law.

Martin Luther King Jr,
US civil rights leader, 1962

We stand today on the edge of a new frontier, the frontier of the 1960s.

John F. Kennedy
accepting nomination as the Democratic presidential candidate, 1960

It may not be a popular view, but I would dare to say that prisons are our most important and also our most deficient social service.

Enoch Powell,
British Minister of Health, 1961

Flattery is alright, if you don't inhale.

Adlai Stevenson,
US statesman, 1961

Adlai Stevenson/Popperfoto

Even then I knew that there was only one force with a greater potential for violence than the State of Mississippi and that was the US Government. The only way I was going to go to the University of Mississippi was to get a force on my side greater than the force opposed. The only real task was for me to get the US Government on my side, as simple as that. I tricked them, made them do on my behalf what I had not the power to do myself: exert more violent force than the State had the capacity to exert.

James Meredith,
first black student enrolled at the University of Mississippi

White men can't win this sort of a fight.

William P. Bundy,
US presidential adviser, on the escalating
US involvement in Vietnam, 1961

So I ask you tonight to join me and march along the road...that leads to the Great Society, where no child will go unfed... where every human being has dignity and every worker has a job; where education is blind to colour and employment is unaware of race.

Lyndon B. Johnson,
US president, 1964

I believe that this nation should commit itself to achieving the goal, before this decade is out, of landing a man on the moon and returning him safely to earth.

John F. Kennedy,
US president, 1961

The members of our Secret Service have apparently spent so much time looking under the bed for Communists, that they haven't had the time to look in the bed.

Michael Foot,
British Labour politician, on the Profumo
Affair, 1963

Lyndon B. Johnson/Popperfoto

FAIR COMMENT

Greater love hath no man than this, that he lay down his friends for his life.

Jeremy Thorpe,
British Liberal MP, on Macmillan's cabinet reshuffle, 1962

All free men, wherever they may live, are citizens of Berlin. And therefore, as a free man, I take pride in the words 'Ich bin ein Berliner.'

John F. Kennedy,
US president, 1963

What is objectionable, what is dangerous about extremists is not that they are extreme, but that they are intolerant. The evil is not what they say about their cause, but what they say about their opponents.

Robert Kennedy,
US Attorney General: *The Pursuit of Justice*, 1964

A week is a long time in politics.

Harold Wilson

It's easier to be a liberal a long way from home.

Don Price,
Dean of the Harvard Graduate School of Government

A Great Society...a place where the meaning of a man's life matches the marvels of man's labour.

Lyndon B. Johnson,
US president, 1964

Just being a negro doesn't qualify you to understand the race situation any more than being sick makes you an expert on medicine.

Dick Gregory,
US comedian and black activist: *Nigger*, 1964

Every society gets the kind of criminal it deserves. What is equally true is that every community gets the kind of law enforcement it insists on.

Robert Kennedy,
US Attorney-General, 1964

If they're determined to set up anarchy, we're determined to confront them with sufficient force to prevent it.

Sam Yorty,
mayor of Los Angeles, on the Watts riots, 1965

If being a communist, or being a capitalist or being a socialist is a crime, first you have to study which of these systems is more criminal. And then you'd be slow to say which one should be in jail.

Malcolm X,
US black activist, 1965

I learnt more about politics during one South Dakota dust storm than in seven years in the university.

Senator Hubert Humphrey

When you keep telling people they are unfairly treated and teach them disrespect for the law, you must expect this kind of thing sooner or later....One person threw a rock and, like monkeys in a zoo, others started throwing rocks.

William Parker,
Los Angeles Chief of Police, on the Watts riots, 1965

Your daddy may go down in history as the man who unleashed World War III.

Lyndon B. Johnson,
US president, to his daughter Luci, after ordering the bombing of Haiphong harbour, 1967

I think it is pleasant, though I do not think it was meant to be pleasant, that these allegations were brought out into the open.

John Gorton,
Australian prime minister, facing charges during the Hoffman Affair, 1969

Killing, rioting and looting are contrary to the best traditions of this country.

Lyndon B. Johnson,
US president, 1965

The present US objective in Vietnam is to avoid humiliation.

John McNaughton,
US Secretary of Defense, 1966

I have often thought of the parallel between Castro entering Havana and a new government entering power here...and had thought that the two events should be as similar as possible.

Anthony Wedgwood Benn,
    British Labour MP, 1966

The greatest achievement of the civil rights movement was that it restored the dignity of indignation.

Frederic Wertham,
    US psychologist: *A Sign For Cain,* 1966

What has violence ever accomplished? What has it ever created? No martyr's cause has ever been stilled by his assassin's bullet. No wrongs have ever been righted by riots and civil disorders. A sniper is only a coward, not a hero. And an uncontrollable mob is only the voice of madness and not the voice of the people.

Robert Kennedy,
    US presidential candidate, on the death of Martin Luther King Jr, 1968

They're young, they're idealistic and they don't like man's inhumanity to man. As they get older they will become wiser and more tolerant.

Colonel Joseph Bellas
    on US anti-war protesters, 1969

Think of it, a second chamber selected by the Whips — a seraglio of eunuchs.

Michael Foot,
    British Labour politician, on the House of Lords, 1969

I am fed up with a system that busts the pot-smoker and lets the big dope racketeers go free. I am sick of old men dreaming up wars for young men to die in.

George McGovern,
    US presidential candidate, 1972

In close-up the British revolutionary Left seethes with such repulsive, self-righteous dogmatists that it practically drives one to enlist as a deckhand on 'Morning Cloud'.

Richard Neville,
    Australian writer; the boat belonged to Edward Heath, 1972

The twentieth century may not be a very good thing, but it is the only century we have got.

Norman St John-Stevas,
    British Conservative MP, 1970

No normal parent will ever accept the judgement of a test, however apparently fair, that their child of eleven is a failure.

Edward Short,
    British MP, on the abolition of selective education, 1970

I don't think we will have achieved our objectives, but it was fair enough for us to seek them.

John Gorton,
    Australian prime minister, on his country's abortive involvement in Vietnam, 1971

This country seems to be passing a great kidney stone which will leave us completely changed.

Bill Moyers,
    former US presidential adviser, 1971

The era of low-cost energy is almost dead. Popeye is running out of spinach.

Peter Paterson,
    US Secretary of Commerce, 1972

Golf had long symbolized the Eisenhower years — played by soft, boring men with ample waistlines who went round rich men's country club courses in the company of wealthy businessmen and were tended by white-haired, dutiful negroes.

David Halberstam,
    US journalist: *The Best and the Brightest,* 1973

Once the toothpaste is out of the tube, it's hard to get it back in.

H.R. Haldeman,
    US presidential adviser, on the Watergate affair, 1973

We have a cancer within, close to the presidency, that is growing.

John Dean,
    special counsel to President Nixon, telling Nixon of the Watergate problems, 1973

FAIR COMMENT

It was just basic politics.

G. Gordon Liddy,
    White House 'plumber', on Watergate, 1973

Twelve years of formal education is twelve years of formal ignorance.

Huey P. Newton,
    black US militant, 1973

Never had so few lost so much so stupidly and so fast.

Dean Acheson,
    US lawyer and politician, on the Iranian nationalization of the oil companies, 1974

Politicians should not be preachers.

Enoch Powell,
    United Ulster Unionist MP, 1974

Looking around the House, one realizes that we are all minorities now. Indeed, some more than others.

Jeremy Thorpe,
    British Liberal leader, on the Labour Party's minority government and his own party's record showing at the polls, 1974

If you buy land on which is a slagheap 120 feet high and it costs £100,000 to remove it, that is not speculation but land reclamation

Harold Wilson,
    British prime minister, refuting charges of corruption, 1974

I'm not entirely upset by the Kennedy assassinations. In many ways, the two most dangerous men in the country were eliminated.

William Kunstler,
    US radical lawyer, 1976

I am not just a rose in my husband's lapel.

Margaret Trudeau,
    wife of Canadian prime minister, 1976

We believe that Americans should have the right to own guns because traditionally justice has always come from the ballot box, the jury box, but, if these failed, the cartridge box.

Congressman Steve Symms,
    leading lobbyist against gun control, 1975

The term 'democratic socialist' makes as much sense as 'pregnant virginity'.

Russell Prowse,
    Chief Manager of the Bank of New South Wales, 1976

Freedom under the law must never be taken for granted.

Margaret Thatcher,
    British opposition leader, 1975

To the right wing 'law and order' is often just a code phrase meaning 'Get the niggers.' To the left wing it often means political oppression.

Gore Vidal,
    US writer, 1975

The men of the IRA are to the men of the Easter Rising what Al Capone was to Garibaldi.

Harold Wilson,
    British prime minister, 1976

The price of championing human rights is a little inconsistency from time to time.

Dr David Owen,
    British Foreign Secretary, 1977

No word in the vocabulary has been so debased and abused as democracy.

Lord Shawcross,
    British Labour politician, 1977

I do not believe politicians should make artistic judgements.

Tony Staley,
    Australian Minister for the Arts, 1977

I am glad that justice was done.

Jeremy Thorpe,
    former British Liberal Party leader, after his Old Bailey acquittal on the charge of conspiracy to murder, 1979

It is an unfortunate fact that political theory, no matter how worthy or perceptive, is curiously disembodied; it gives no clues to the passions, the heroisms or the squalid conflicts that it inspired.

John Quail,
    British historian: *The Slow Burning Fuse*, 1978

Political morality is a long way from church morality.

Andrew Young,
  US ambassador to the United Nations, 1977

The Marxist analysis has nothing to do with what happened in Stalin's Russia. It's like blaming Jesus for the Inquisition in Spain.

Anthony Wedgwood Benn,
  British Labour politician, 1980

Law expands in proportion to the resources available for its enforcement. Bad law is more likely to be supplemented than repealed. Social legislation cannot repeal physical laws.

Dallin B. Oaks,
  president of Brigham Young University, 1978

Few politicians are masochists.

Sir Harold Wilson,
  former British prime minister, 1978

Harold Wilson in fine form/Publisher's files

RIOT AND REVOLT

Revolutions are not about trifles, but spring from trifles.

Aristotle,
Greek philosopher: *Politics*, fourth century BC

Make my skin into drumheads for the Bohemian cause!

John Ziska,
Czechoslovak patriot, last words, 1424

Rebellion to tyrants is obedience to God.

Anonymous
lines carved on a monument to John Bradshaw, president of the commission that tried Charles I

Rebellion to tyrants is obedience to God.

Motto
on Thomas Jefferson's personally designed coat of arms.

He that is taken and put into prison and chains is not conquered, though overcome, for he is still an enemy.

Thomas Hobbes,
English philosopher: *Leviathan,* 1651

The tree of liberty must be refreshed from time to time with the blood of patriots and tyrants. It is its natural manure.

Thomas Jefferson,
future US president, 1787

A little rebellion now and then is a good thing, and as necessary in the political world as storms are in the physical.

Thomas Jefferson,
1787

Is life so dear, or peace so sweet as to be purchased at the price of chains and slavery? Forbid it, almighty God! I know not what course others may take, but as for me, give me liberty or give me death!

Patrick Henry,
the 'Virginia Demosthenes', urging the American Revolution, 1775

Tyranny, like hell, is not easily conquered; yet we have this consolation with us, that the harder the conflict, the more glorious the triumph. What we obtain too cheap, we esteem too lightly.

Tom Paine,
English radical pamphleteer, 1776

Sire, it is not a revolt, it is a revolution!

Duc de Rochefoucauld-Liancourt
correcting Louis XVI who remarked on the fall of the Bastille, 'It is a revolt', 1789

The manna of liberty must be gathered afresh every day, otherwise it stinketh.

Tom Paine,
English radical pamphleteer

They have learnt nothing and forgotten nothing.

Charles Maurice de Talleyrand,
French statesman, on aristocratic emigrés, 1796

Ten persons who speak make more noise than ten thousand who are silent.

Napoleon Bonaparte:
***Maxims,* 1804-15**

Do you suppose then, that revolutions are made with rose-water?

Sebastien Chamfort,
    French writer, replying to those who condemned the violence of the French Revolution, 1793

Liberty, oh Liberty — what crimes are committed in thy name!

Marie Jeanne Roland,
    Girondist sympathiser, before her execution, 1793

All oppressed people are authorized, whenever they can, to rise and break their fetters.

Henry Clay,
    US politician, 1818

Oh, give me liberty or give me death!

James Ings,
    executed for the Cato Street Conspiracy, last words, 1820

Oh, to die for liberty is a pleasure and not a pain!

Marcos Bozzari,
    Greek freedom fighter, killed 1823

If we trace the history of most revolutions, we shall find that the first inroads upon the laws have been made by the governors as often as by the governed.

Charles Caleb Colton,
    British clergyman and writer, 1825

Every reform, however necessary, will by weak minds be carried to an excess which will itself need reforming.

Samuel Taylor Coleridge,
    English poet

Sometimes a scream is better than a thesis.

Ralph Waldo Emerson,
    US poet and essayist, 1836

It is not honest enquiry that makes anarchy, but it is error, insincerity, half belief and untruth that make it.

Thomas Carlyle,
    Scottish author: 'On Heroes and Hero-Worship', 1841

Beginning reform is beginning revolution.

Duke of Wellington,
    1830

On this subject I do not wish to think, or speak, or write with equivocation. . . . I will not equivocate, I will not excuse, I will not retreat a single inch and *I will be heard!*

William Lloyd Garrison,
    US abolitionist, 1831

Let the ruling classes tremble at a communist revolution. The proletarians have nothing to lose but their chains. They have a world to win. Workers of the world, unite!

Karl Marx:
    ***The Communist Manifesto*, 1848**

A man looks at something freely only when he does not bend it to his theory and does not himself bend before it; reverence before it, not free but enforced, limits a man, narrows his freedom.

Alexander Herzen,
    Russian political thinker and writer: 'Letter from France and Italy'

Every revolution was first a thought in one man's mind.

**Ralph Waldo Emerson,
US poet and essayist**

Philosophers have only *interpreted* the world, in various ways. The point is to *change* it.

**Karl Marx:
'Eleventh Thesis on Feuerbach', 1846**

The world is always childish, and with each new gewgaw of a revolution or a constitution that it finds, thinks it shall never cry any more.

**Ralph Waldo Emerson,
US poet and essayist: *Journals*, 1847**

Those who have served the cause of revolution have ploughed the sea.

**Simon Bolivar,
liberator of Venezuela**

It is essential to the triumph of reform that it should never succeed.

**William Hazlitt,
English essayist**

I know that compromises are often inevitable in practice, but I think they should be left to the enemy to propose. Reformers should assert principles and *accept* compromises.

**John Stuart Mill,
English philosopher, 1849**

With reasonable men I will reason, with humane men I will plead, but to tyrants I shall give no quarter, nor waste arguments where they will certainly be lost.

**William Lloyd Garrison,
US abolitionist**

If only people wanted, instead of saving the world, to save themselves; instead of saving humanity, to liberate humanity; they would do much for the salvation of the world and the liberation of man.

**Alexander Herzen,
Russian political thinker and writer: *From the Other Shore*, 1847-50**

When the people contend for their liberty, they seldom get anything by their victory but new masters.

**Lord Halifax,
English pamphleteer**

It implies a contradiction that a government could ever be called revolutionary, for the very simple reason that it is the government.

**Pierre-Joseph Proudhon,
French socialist**

It is better to abolish serfdom from above than to wait for it to abolish itself from below.

**Alexander II,
Russian tsar**

Men seldom, or never for any length of time and deliberately, rebel against anything that does not deserve rebelling against.

**Thomas Carlyle,
Scottish author and historian**

The social revolution...cannot draw its poetry from the past, but only from the future. It cannot begin with itself before it has stripped itself of all superstitions concerning the past.

Karl Marx

I do not want to be I. I want to be We.

**Mikhail Bakunin,
Russian anarchist**

Sic semper tyrannus! The South is avenged!

**John Wilkes Booth,
as he assassinated Abraham Lincoln, 1865**

A reform is a correction of abuses, a revolution is a transfer of power.

**Edward Bulwer-Lytton,
English historian, 1866**

Liberty, next to religion, has been the motive of good deeds and the common pretext of crime.

**Lord Acton,
English historian, 1877**

You have not converted a man because you have silenced him.

**Viscount Morley,
  English statesman, 1874**

This is the happiest day of my life!

**Adolf Fischer,
  executed for leading the Haymarket Riots in Chicago, last words, 1881**

The annihilation of the past is the procreation of the future.

**Alexander Herzen,
  Russian political thinker and writer, on nihilism**

There will come a time when our silence will be more power than the voices you strangle today.

**August Spies,
  executed for leading the Haymarket Riots in Chicago, last words, 1881**

Violence is the only way of ensuring a hearing for moderation.

**William O'Brien,
  Irish radical**

Let the voice of the people be heard!

**Albert Parsons,
  executed for leading the Haymarket Riots in Chicago, last words, 1881**

If bad institutions and bad men can be got rid of only by killing, then the killing must be done.

**William Randolph Hearst,
  US press magnate, 1900**

Reformatory measures are hailed as cure-alls by people who have a happy confidence in the perfectibility of human nature and no discouraging acquaintance with history to dim it.

**Agnes Repplier,
  US historian, 1900**

Revolutions have never lightened the burden of tyranny, they have only shifted it to another shoulder.

**George Bernard Shaw,
  Irish playwright, 1903**

I killed the President because he was the enemy of the good people, the good working people. I am not sorry for my crime.

**Leon Czogolsz,
  assassin of President McKinley, last words, 1901**

Women, children and revolutionaries hate irony.

**Joseph Conrad,
  Polish-born English author**

Everywhere revolutions are painful yet fruitful gestations of a people; they shed blood but create light, they eliminate men, but elaborate ideas.

**Manuel Gonzalez Prada,
  Peruvian writer, 1908**

It is to violence that socialism owed its high moral values, through which it brings salvation to the modern world.

**Georges Sorel,
  French syndicalist philosopher: *Reflections on Violence*, 1908**

If we believe a thing to be bad, and if we have a right to prevent it, it is our duty to try to prevent it and damn the consequences.

**Lord Milner,
  British statesman, opposing Lloyd George's finance bill, 1909**

Insurrection, n. An unsuccessful revolution.

**Ambrose Bierce,
  US journalist and author: *The Devil's Dictionary*, 1881-1911**

Assassination is the extreme form of censorship.

**George Bernard Shaw,
  Irish playwright, 1916**

Thinkers prepare the revolution, bandits carry it out.

**Mariano Azuela,
  Mexican novelist, 1918**

Doctrinaires are the vultures of principle. They feed upon principle after it is dead.

David Lloyd George

The revolutionary spirit is mightily convenient in this — that it frees one from all scruples as regards ideas.

Joseph Conrad,
   Polish-born English author: *A Personal Record,* 1912

The argument of the broken pane of glass is the most valuable argument in modern politics.

Emmeline Pankhurst,
   English suffragette, 1912

There is no need to carry me away to another prison. My life is already ebbing away. I suggest that you nail me to a cross and burn me alive. My flaming body will be a torch to light the people on their path to freedom.

Gavrilo Princip,
   assassin of Franz Joseph I of Austria's nephew Franz Ferdinand, 1914

Don't mourn for me — organize!

Joe Hill,
   US labour militant, last words, 1915

Rebel, n. A proponent of a new misrule who has failed to establish it.

Ambrose Bierce,
   US journalist and author: *The Devil's Dictionary,* 1881-1911

We are fighting for the gates of Heaven.

Karl Liebknecht,
   leader of German Spartacist revolutionaries, 1918

You cannot make a revolution with silk gloves.

Joseph Stalin

Every normal man must be tempted at times to spit on his hands, hoist the black flag and begin slitting throats.

H.L. Mencken,
   US philologist, editor and satirist

All movements go too far.

Bertrand Russell,
   English philosopher

They cannot put the Socialist movement in jail....I admit to being opposed to the present form of government; I admit being opposed to the present social system. I am doing what little I can to do away with the rule of the great body of people by a relatively small class and establish in this country industrial and social democracy.

Eugene V. Debs,
   US socialist, plea to the jury at his trial, 1913. He was jailed for ten years.

Revolutions are the locomotives of history. Drive them full speed ahead and keep them on the rails.

V.I. Lenin

The dictatorship of the Communist Party is maintained by recourse to every form of violence.

Leon Trotsky,
   founder of Russia's Red Army, 1924

A revolution only lasts fifteen years — a period which coincides with the effectiveness of a generation.

José Ortega y Gasset,
   Spanish philosopher and statesman, 1930

Men are not born equal and they are not born fraternal and I will ask any mother in the audience if she does not agree with me.

Stanley Baldwin,
   British prime minister, 1925

A continued progression to the left, a sort of inevitable landslide into the abyss, is the characteristic of all revolutions.

Winston Churchill,
   British Chancellor of the Exchequer, 1927

Revolutions are always verbose.

Leon Trotsky,
   exiled Russian revolutionary leader, 1929

A revolution is legality on holiday.

Léon Blum,
   French prime minister

To think is to say no.

Alain (Emile Chartier),
    French philosopher: 'Le citoyen contre les pouvoirs', 1925

Every revolution evaporates and leaves behind only the slime of a new bureaucracy.

Franz Kafka,
    Austrian novelist

A concern with the perfectibility of mankind is always a symptom of thwarted or perverted development.

Hugh Kingsmill,
    British author

Revolution is not the uprising against pre-existing order, but the setting up of a new order contradictory to the old one.

José Ortega y Gasset,
    Spanish philosopher and statesman: *The Revolt of the Masses,* 1930

All revolutions devour their own children.

Ernst Röhm,
    Nazi leader, who was duly purged by Hitler, 1934

It is better to die on your feet than to live on your knees.

Dolores Ibarruri
    (La Pasionara), 1936

I have never called for the police, but they have often called for me.

Emma Goldman,
    US anarchist, 1936

If you want to know the taste of a pear, you must change the pear by eating it yourself. ...If you want to know the theory and methods of revolution, you must take part in a revolution. All genuine knowledge originates in direct experience.

Mao Tse-tung,
    1937

A revolutionary must be able to do anything.

Joseph Goebbels,
    Nazi Minister of Propaganda

None will improve your lot/ If you yourselves do not.

Bertolt Brecht,
    German playwright: *Roundheads and Peakheads,* 1933

All reformers, however strict their social conscience, live in houses just as big as they can pay for.

Logan Pearsall Smith,
    US writer

Few revolutionists would be such if they were heirs to a baronetcy.

George Santayana,
    Spanish-born US philosopher, poet and novelist

Today, freedom has not many allies. I have been known to say that the real passion of the twentieth century was slavery.

Albert Camus,
    French author and philosopher

The moment the slave resolves that he will no longer be a slave, his fetters fall. He frees himself and shows the way to others. Freedom and slavery are mental states.

Mahatma Gandhi:
    Non-Violence in Peace and War, 1948

Most revolutionaries are potential Tories, because they imagine that everything can be put right by altering the shape of society. Once that change is effected — as it sometimes is — they see no need for any other.

George Orwell,
    English essayist and critic

The revolution as myth is the definitive revolution.

Albert Camus,
    French author and philosopher: *Notebooks,* 1942-51

The successful revolutionary is a statesman, the unsuccessful one is a criminal.

Erich Fromm,
    German-born US psychoanalyst: *The Fear of Freedom,* 1941

RIOT AND REVOLT

A great silence has fallen on the real soul of this nation.

W.E.B. Dubois,
   black US activist, on McCarthyism, 1951

The true revolutionary is guided by feelings of great love.

Che Guevara,
   Argentinian-born Communist revolutionary leader

All modern revolutions have ended in a reinforcement of the power of the State.

Albert Camus,
   French author and philosopher: *The Rebel*, 1951

The history of man, in one sense, is the sum total of his successive rebellions.

Albert Camus,
   French author and philosopher: *The Rebel*, 1951

Che Guevara/Popperfoto

An earthquake achieves what the law promises but does not in practice maintain — the equality of all men.

Ignazio Silone,
  Italian academic and radical: *Why I Became a Socialist*, 1949

The slave begins by demanding justice and ends by wanting to wear a crown. He must dominate in his turn.

Albert Camus,
  French author and philosopher: *The Rebel*, 1951

When hopes and dreams are loose in the streets it is well for the timid to lock the doors, shutter the windows and lie low until the wrath has passed.

Eric Hoffer,
  US philosopher: *The True Believer*, 1951

In a revolution one wins or dies.

Che Guevara,
  Argentinian-born Communist revolutionary leader

What is a rebel? A man who says no.

Albert Camus,
  French author and philosopher: opening line of *The Rebel*, 1951

If a man is willing and honest you can make a revolutionary out of him.

Che Guevara,
  Argentinian-born Communist revolutionary leader

One cannot be a part-time nihilist.

Albert Camus,
  French author and philosopher: *The Rebel*, 1951

Every revolutionary ends up by becoming either an oppressor or a heretic.

Albert Camus:
  ***The Rebel*, 1951**

The question is one of fighting the causes and not just being satisfied with getting rid of the effects.

Che Guevara,
  Argentinian-born Communist revolutionary leader, 1953

I cannot and will not cut my cloth to fit this year's fashions, even though I long ago came to the conclusion that I was not a political person and could have no comfortable place in any political group.

Lillian Hellman,
  US playwright, in a letter refusing to testify to the House Un-American Activities Committee, 1952

The time to stop a revolution is the beginning, not at the end.

Adlai Stevenson,
  US presidential candidate, 1952

Man is not just a stomach, above all he hungers for dignity.

Jacobo Arbenz,
  Guatemalan revolutionary, 1953

A revolution requires of its leaders a record of unbroken infallibility. If they do not possess it they are expected to invent it.

Murray Kempton,
  US journalist: *Part of Our Time*, 1955

You don't change the face of history by turning the faces of portraits to the wall.

Shri Jawaharlal Nehru,
  Indian prime minister

Revolutionary theory is not a collection of petrified dogmas and formulas, but the militant guide to action in transforming the world, in building Communism.

Nikita Khruschev,
  1956

A regime, an established order, is rarely overthrown by a revolutionary movement. Usually, a regime collapses of its own weakness and corruption, and then a revolutionary movement enters among the ruins and takes over the powers that have become vacant.

Walter Lippmann,
  US political commentator, 1958

Any movement in history which attempts to perpetuate itself becomes reactionary.

Josip Broz Tito,
  Yugoslav president

President Tito/Popperfoto

BOOK OF POLITICAL QUOTES

You cannot put theory into your soup or Marxism into your clothes. If, after forty years of Communism, a person cannot have a glass of milk or a pair of shoes, he will not believe that Communism is a good thing, no matter what you tell him.

Nikita Khruschev,
1958

A guerilla fighter is...a sort of guiding angel who has fallen into the area, always to help the poor and to bother the rich as little as possible.

Che Guevara,
   Argentinian-born Communist revolutionary leader, 1959

Each guerilla must be prepared to die. Not to defend an ideal, but to transform it into a reality.

Che Guevara:
   Guerilla Warfare, 1960

Freedom is not something that anybody can be given. Freedom is something people take, and people are as free as they want to be.

James Baldwin,
   US novelist: Nobody Knows My Name, 1961

Violence alone, violence committed by the people, violence organized and educated by its leaders, makes it possible for the masses to understand social truths and gives the key to them.

Frantz Fanon,
   French radical: The Wretched of the Earth, 1961

Inability of those in power to still the voices of their own consciences is the great force leading to desired changes.

Kenneth Kaunda,
   Zambian president, 1965

For a revolutionary, failure is a springboard. As a source of theory it is richer than victory. It accumulates experience and knowledge.

Regis Debray,
   French radical

Hatred as an element of the struggle, relentless hatred that impels us over and beyond the natural limitations of man and transforms us into effective, violent, selected and cold killing machines.

Che Guevara,
   Argentinian-born Communist revolutionary leader

Those who make peaceful revolution impossible, make violent revolution inevitable.

John F. Kennedy

I wonder what would happen if somebody was to stand up and say he was utterly opposed not only to the governments, but also to the people, to the entire land and complete foundations of his socially (sic).

Lee Harvey Oswald,
   alleged assassin of John F. Kennedy, in his diary, 1963

Revolutions are not made with literature. Revolutions equal gunfire.

François Duvalier (Papa Doc),
   dictator of Haiti, 1964

If we should promise people nothing better than only revolution, they would scratch their heads and say 'Isn't it better to have good goulash?'

Nikita Khruschev,
   1964

There's a time when the operation of the machine becomes so odious, makes you so sick at heart, that you cannot take part... and you've got to put your bodies upon the gears and upon the wheels and you've got to make it stop.

Mario Savio,
   leader of the Berkeley Free Speech Movement, 1964

Violence is American as cherry pie.

Stokely Carmichael,
   chairman of the Student Non-Violent Co-ordinating Committee

RIOT AND REVOLT

Everybody dances, or nobody dances.

Tupamaros,
  Uruguayan guerilla group, slogan

The negro revolt is not aimed at winning friends, but at winning freedom, not interpersonal warmth, but institutional justice.

Harvey Cox,
  US educator: *The Secular City*, 1966

A revolution is not a dinner party, or writing an essay, or painting a picture, or doing embroidery, it cannot be so refined.... A revolution is an insurrection, an act of violence by which one class overthrows another.

Mao Tse-tung: *Quotations from Chairman Mao*, 1966

Words divide us, action unites us.

Tupamaros,
  Uruguayan guerilla group, slogan

In order to get rid of the gun, it is necessary to take up the gun.

Mao Tse-tung:
  Quotations from Chairman Mao, 1966

Whoever hesitates while waiting for ideas to triumph among the masses before initiating revolutionary action will never be a revolutionary. Humanity will, of course, change. Human society will, of course, continue to develop — in spite of men and the errors of men. But that is not a revolutionary attitude.

Fidel Castro,
  Cuban president, 1967

I'm not a psychologist or a psychiatrist, I'm a political activist and I don't deal with the individual. I think it's a cop out when people talk about the individual. I want to talk about the system.

Stokely Carmichael,
  SUCC chairman, at the Dialectics of Liberation Conference, 1967

There are times when political documents, called Marxist, give the impression that someone has gone to an archive and asked for a form.... They are all alike, with the same empty words, in language incapable of expressing real situations. Very often... divorced from real life. And many people are told this is Marxism. In what way is this different from a catechism, from a rosary, and from a litany?

Fidel Castro,
  Cuban president, 1967

Wherever death may surprise us, let it be welcome, provided that this, our battle cry, may have reached some receptive ear, and another hand may be extended to wield our weapons, and other men be ready to intone the funeral dirge with the staccato chant of the machine gun and new battle cries of war and victory.

Che Guevara,
  Argentinian-born Communist revolutionary leader, 1967

The limitation of riots, moral questions aside, is that they cannot win and their participants know it. Hence, rioting is not revolutionary, but reactionary because it inspires defeat. It involves an emotional catharsis, but it must be followed by a sense of futility.

Martin Luther King,
  US civil rights leader

The gun in the hands of a guerilla is the seed of revolution.

Huey P. Newton,
  Black Panther Party chairman, 1968

Riots are the voices of the unheard.

Martin Luther King,
  US civil rights leader, 1968

A diplomat who can live with a dictatorship can live with us for three days.

Movimento Revolucionario do Outobro 8,
  Brazilian guerilla group, after capturing the US ambassador, 1969

A 'white radical' is three parts bullshit and one part hesitation. It is not revolutionary and should not be stockpiled at this time.

The Motherfuckers,
US urban guerilla group, 1969

You can jail a revolutionary, but you cannot jail the revolution.

Bobby Seale,
Black Panther leader, 1969

The urban guerilla's reason for existence, the basic action in which he survives and acts, is to shoot.

Carlos Marighella,
Brazilian author: *The Minimanual of the Urban Guerilla*

Those who set out to be their brother's keeper sometimes end up by becoming his jailer. Every emancipation has within it the seeds of a new slavery, and every truth can easily become a lie.

I.F. Stone,
US political commentator, 1969

Some of us do not accept the Establishment myth that bad laws must be obeyed.

Tom Driberg,
British MP, 1972

Pick up the gun? The Movement couldn't pick up lunch for two at Nedicks.

Dotson Rader,
US writer, on the decline of the New Left, 1972

The New Left started as a movement to force American institutions to live up to the revolutionary aspects of American ideology.

Jeremy Rifkin,
founder of the People's Bicentennial Commission, 1976

I will not resign. I declare my will to resist by every means, even at the cost of my life.

Salvador Allende,
president of Chile, 1973

Age has no real meaning in a revolutionary movement. I think it's something insurance companies dream up to balance their books. People don't seem to age who remain politically active.

Abbie Hoffman,
former Yippie! leader, 1975

Any essential reform must, like charity, begin at home.

John Macy,
US Secretary of the Treasury

Revolutionary violence is simply a response, an extreme measure to counter extreme conditions.

Emily Harris,
member of the Symbionese Liberation Army, a US urban guerilla group, 1976

1. You must answer in conformity with the questions I asked you. Don't try to turn away my questions.
2. Don't try to escape by making pretexts according to your hypocritical ideas. It is strictly forbidden to contest me.
3. Don't be a fool for you are a chap who dare to thwart the revolution.
4. You must immediately answer my questions without wasting the time to reflect.
5. Don't tell me about your little incidents committed against the propriety. Don't tell me either about the essence of the revolution.
6. During the bastinado or electrication you must not cry loudly.
7. Do sit down quietly. Wait for the orders. If there are no orders, do nothing. If I ask you to do something you must immediately do it without protesting.
8. Don't make protests about Kampuchea-Krom in order to hide your jaw of traitor.
9. If you disobey every point of my regulation you will get either ten strokes of whip or five shocks of electric discharge.

Regulations of Security Agents:
guidelines for prisoners in the Khmer Rouge's interrogation centre at Toul Sleng, established to discover counter-revolutionaries in Kampuchea

RIOT AND REVOLT

A coup that is known in advance is a coup that does not take place.

**William Colby,
CIA director**

The saddest illusion of revolutionary socialists is that revolution itself will transform the nature of human beings.

**Shirley Williams,
British Labour MP, 1977**

The romantic concept of the terrorist is an obstacle to his suppression.

**Conor Cruise O'Brien,
Irish journalist and statesman, 1976**

The most revolutionary statement in history is 'Love thine enemy'.

**Eldridge Cleaver,
former Black Panther leader, currently a Born Again Christian, 1980**

Revolutions need direction and exemplary leadership, but not heroes. Heroes subvert the fact that change comes about by lots of people taking action.

**Bill Harris,
member of the Symbionese Liberation Army, 1976**

Baader had the perfidy to shoot himself in the back of the head to make us look like murderers.

**Werner Maihofer,
West German Interior Minister, on the highly suspicious 'suicide' of urban guerilla Andreas Baader in his jail cell, 1977**

The reformer is an opportunist who will make it better now, but will also build an obstacle against future development. The revolutionist may appear the same, but he won't do anything to put up blocks or obstacles to future levels of development.

**Huey P. Newton,
Black Panther Party chairman, 1973**

LUNATIC FRINGE

I hate all Boets and Bainters.

George I,
English king

Are not the fine mixtures of red and white, the expressions of every passion by greater or less suffusions in the white race, preferable to that eternal monotony which reigns in the countenances, that immovable veil of black that covers all the emotions of the other race?

Thomas Jefferson,
future US president: 'Notes on Virginia',
1785

A bigot delights in public ridicule, for he begins to think he is a martyr.

Sydney Smith,
English journalist, clergyman and wit

Kill them while they're hot.

Porfirio Diaz,
Mexican president, governmental motto,
1850

I only know two tunes. One of them is Yankee Doodle and the other isn't.

Ulysses S. Grant,
US president

Bigot, n. One who is obstinately and zealously attached to an opinion that you do not entertain.

Ambrose Bierce,
US journalist and author: *The Devil's*
Dictionary, **1881-1911**

Personally I am a great believer in bed, in constantly keeping horizontal...the heart and everything else go slower and the whole system is refreshed.

Sir Henry Campbell-Bannerman,
British prime minister, 1906

Segregation is not humiliating, and ought to be so regarded by you gentlemen.

Woodrow Wilson,
US president, to assembled black leaders,
1913

Forget that I'm president of the United States. I'm Warren Harding, playing poker with friends, and I'm going to beat the hell out of them.

Warren G. Harding,
US president, at his twice weekly poker
nights with his Cabinet

Read the Bible, it teaches you how to act. Read the hymnbook. It contains the finest poetry ever written. Read the almanac. It shows you how to figure out what the weather will be. There isn't another book that is necessary for anyone to read and therefore I am opposed to all libraries.

Representative Hal Wimberly
of the Georgia State legislature,
successfully opposing a bill to introduce
public libraries to the State, 1925

LUNATIC FRINGE

Another pleasant thing about the President is his nice straight legs. Not a trace of curvature, of knocking of the knees, of bumps or hollows, mars his ambulatory equipment. He is straight and upright as a sapling, fashioned so slenderly young and so fair. His legs look best in black, his favourite hue. He is scrupulously pressed and valeted, just out of the bandbox effect. Gay tints in neckwear are not to the presidential taste. He likes black scarfs brocaded in white or silver, held fast by a modest little pearl or diamond, neat, but not gaudy.

Indianapolis *Star*
on Calvin Coolidge, 1925

Evolution means progress, but it does not mean that man, God's highest creation, is descended from a monkey or any other animal. I will not allow any such doctrine or intimation of such doctrine to be taught in our public schools.

Cameron Morrison,
Governor of Maryland, defying Darwin, 1925

Our country is filled with a socialistic, IWW, communistic, radical, lawless, anti-American, anti-Church, anti-God, anti-marriage gang and they are laying the eggs of rebellion and unrest in labour and capital and home; and we have some of them in the universities. I can take you back through the universities and pick out a lot of black-hearted communistic fellows who are teaching that to the boys and sending them out to undermine America. If this radical bunch could have their way, my friends, the laws of nature would be repealed, or they would reverse them. Oil and water would mix, the turtle dove would marry the turkey buzzard, the sun would rise in the west and set in the east, chickens would give milk and cows would lay eggs, the pigs would crow and the roosters would squeal, cats would bark and dogs would mew, the least would be the greatest, a part would be greater than the whole, yesterday would be today if that crowd were in control.

Billy Sunday,
US evangelist, preaching in Nashville, Tennessee, 1925

He said civilization today is merely working back to the heights reached by Babylon, Greece and Rome...the attention given to sanitation by these great cities of the past was the true index of their civilization. Babe Ruth and the American athletes who captured most of the honours in the Olympic Games were products of the American shower bath, he declared...the Russian Communist uprising would never have occurred if Russian homes had been equipped with bath tubs and other sanitary appliances.

St Louis *Globe Democrat*,
reporting a speech by Colonel W. C. Archer, 1925

I love to meet people. It is the most pleasant thing I do. It really is the only fun I have. It does not tax me and it seems to be a very great pleasure to them.

Warren G. Harding,
US president

President Harding/Popperfoto

BOOK OF POLITICAL QUOTES

President Harding was a thirty-third degree mason, and though he made some blunders in his appointments, he was awake to a large extent on the Roman Catholic question, and did not respond to their influence as readily as required. He...fell ill and passed away. He was not poisoned by food 'that disagreed with him' as the press related. He was poisoned mentally as a victim of the telepathic practises of Jesuit adepts.

Reverend Lewis C. Fowler,
editor of the *American Standard*, 1925

I think the American people wants a solemn ass as a president, and I think I'll go along with them.

Calvin Coolidge,
US president

I always think that one of the great charms of my sex is that the best of us remain boys to the end.

Stanley Baldwin,
British prime minister, 1925

When a great many people are unable to find work — unemployment results.

Calvin Coolidge,
former US president, 1930

It all seems like a fairy story.

Joseph Goebbels,
Nazi Minister of Propaganda, on Hitler's rise to power, 1932

For this reason the mothers in our homes must get used to porridge and be instructed to feed their children on it. Heil Hitler!

Heinrich Himmler,
head of the *Lebensborn* (Fount of Life) centres for breeding a Nazi elite, instructing his caterers to provide a diet of the favourite dish of the slim British aristocracy

Before the organization of the Blackshirt movement, free speech did not exist in this country.

Sir Oswald Mosley,
leader of the British Fascists

Gaiety is the most outstanding feature of the Soviet Union.

Joseph Stalin, 1935

It is very difficult to spend less than £200 in a morning when one goes out shopping.

Henry 'Chips' Channon,
English diarist, socialite and Conservative MP, 1935

Viva la Muerte!

Falangist Party,
right-wing faction in the Spanish Civil War, slogan

I often think how much easier the world would have been to manage if Herr Hitler and Signor Mussolini had been at Oxford.

Lord Halifax,
British Conservative statesman, 1937

If only Hitler and Mussolini could have a good game of bowls once a week at Geneva, I feel that Europe would not be as troubled as it is.

Captain R.G. Briscoe,
British MP

I am completely normal. Even when I was carrying out the task of extermination I led a normal family life and so on.

Rudolf Hoess,
commandant of Auschwitz

I still maintain that just as one prunes a tree — by removing old and undesirable branches in the spring — so for its own interest a certain hygienical supervision of the body of the people is necessary from time to time.

Dr Gustav Schubbe,
head of the Nazi Annihilation Institute, 1945

No Socialist system can be established without a political police...they would have to fall back on some form of Gestapo.

Winston Churchill,
British prime minister, in an election broadcast attacking the Labour Party, 1945

LUNATIC FRINGE

I Was a Sucker for a Left Hook.

**John Garfield,
erstwhile Hollywood proletarian pin-up,
writing the pamphlet of this name when he
died, a super-patriot, 1947**

I ain't gonna let no darkies and white folks segregate together in this town.

**Eugene 'Bull' Connor,
police commissioner of Birmingham,
Alabama, 1950**

Keep Britain White.

**Arnold Leese,
president of the Imperial Fascist League,
1952**

There is one thing about being president. Nobody can tell you when to sit down.

**Dwight D. Eisenhower,
US president, 1953**

We have a portrait of Nixon's mother, who was born Hannah Milhous. She looked Jewish, but of course we do not know what race she belonged to. Mr Nixon himself gives the impression of race chaos.

**Arnold Leese,
alerting the readers of his magazine *Gothic Ripples*, 1955**

It's a characteristic of all movements and crusades that the psychopathic element rises to the top.

**Robert Lindner,
US psychiatrist, *Must You Conform?*, 1956**

Hey Leander, what're you gonna do now the Feds have got the atom bomb?

**Earl Long,
Governor of Louisiana, to super-racist and
segregator Leander Perez**

If there is any danger of equality in the policy of the United Party, you will not find me in that party.

**Sir de Villiers Graaff,
leader of South Africa's United Party, 1958**

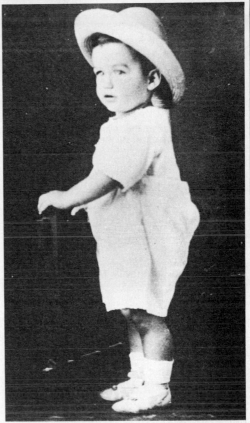

Barry Goldwater was cute at the age of two/Pepperfoto

Where fraternities are not allowed, Communism flourishes. Young men who are inexperienced but have faith are more useful than older, experienced men without faith. The fraternity system is a bastion of American strength.

**Barry Goldwater,
US senator, branding Harvard University as
a Communist cell, because it had no
fraternities, 1960**

Very powerful nuclear weapons can be used in such a manner that they have negligible effects on civilian populations.

**Dr Edward Teller,
military adviser to Nelson Rockefeller:
International Security: The Military Aspect,
1958**

There's nothing like fear to keep the niggers in line.

**Sheriff Z.T. Mathews,
after two of his deputies had beaten a
black, James Brazier, to death, 1958**

The National Assistance Board pays the children's allowances to the blacks for the coffee-coloured monstrosities they father....Material rewards are given to semi-savages to mate with the women of one of the leading civilized nations of the world.

Colin Jordan,
  British leader of the White Defence League, a forerunner of the National Front, 1958

I do not know how many we shot..., it all started when hordes of natives surrounded the police station. If they do these things they must learn their lesson the hard way.

Colonel Pienaar,
  area commander of the South African Police, on the Sharpeville Massacre, 1960

Liberalism or Bolshevism: whichever the people will follow, there is only one master — Judah, the all powerful.

John Tyndall,
  British National Front leader: *The Authoritarian State*, 1961

More and more people are opening their eyes and coming to see that Hitler was right....The people we should have fought were not Hitler and National Socialists in Germany, but world Jewry and its associates in this country.

Colin Jordan,
  leader of the British National Party, 1962

Hitler roped in the riff-raff and put them in camps. Some of them may have died from starvation, but there was a food shortage.

John Tyndall,
  British National Front leader, on Auschwitz, 1962

If I hit him, I don't know it. One of the first things I learnt was not to hit a nigger with your fist because his head is too hard. Of course, the camera might make me out a liar.

Sheriff James G. Clark,
  discussing his assault on a black marcher in Selma, Alabama, 1965

In every white land in the world, the Nazi movements have been formed and we join with them in the historic Nazi battlecry: Victory Hail! Sieg Heil!

Martin Webster,
  British National Front leader: 'Why I Am a Nazi', 1962

The Communists hate and fear the American motion picture. It is their number one hate.

Eric Johnston,
  president of the Motion Picture Producers' Association of America

People ask me who my heroes are. I have only one — Hitler. I admire Hitler because he pulled his country together when it was in a terrible state in the early thirties. But the situation here is so desperate now that one man would not be enough. We need four or five Hitlers in Vietnam.... I want to infuse in our youth the same fanaticism, the same dedication, the same fighting spirit that Hitler infused in his people.

Nguyen Cao Ky,
  South Vietnamese prime minister, 1965

One of the most alarming aspects of these student demonstrations is the ever-present evidence that the guiding hand of Communists and extreme leftists was involved.

The Police Chief,
  magazine of the International Association of Chiefs of Police, 1965

They are fine people, hard-working people. And they have no feelings whatsoever about all of this.

Richard Daley,
  mayor of Chicago, referring to white residents who were running vigilante raids on any black families who moved into their area, 1965

Pathological exhibits...human scum... paranoiacs, degenerates, morons, bludgers ...pack of dingoes...industrial outlaws and political lepers...ratbags. If these people went to Russia, Stalin wouldn't even use them for manure.

Arthur Calwell,
  Australian politician, on Communists

LUNATIC FRINGE

When you've got a problem with swine, you call in the pigs.

S.I. Hayakawa,
    president of San Francisco State College, using the police to deal with student demonstrators, 1967

If the House of Commons is representative of this country, there are at least thirty homosexuals in the house.

Sir Cyril Osborne,
    British MP, 1966

One of the swimmers forgot he was swimming and shouted 'Long live Chairman Mao!' He swallowed several mouthfuls of water, but it tasted especially sweet.

Radio Peking,
    reporting Mao Tse-tung's swims in the Yangtse, 1966

The only position for women in SNCC is prone.

Stokely Carmichael,
    chairman of the Student Non-Violent Co-ordinating Committee, 1966

Any student who waves a placard saying 'Get out of Vietnam' is the front man, whether he believes it or not, for a Communist organization or sympathiser somewhere up the line.

John Connally,
    governor of Texas

I wish I could be like an animal in the forest — go to sleep under a tree, eat when I feel like it, read a bit and after a while, do whatever I want to do.

Lyndon B. Johnson,
    US president, 1967

Only when we see our magic drugs as an ecstatic revolutionary implement, and feel our bodies as the cellular macrocosm and galactic microcosm will our spiral/life energy destroy everything dead as it races over the planet, leaving us alive, spinning at the pineal eye.

The Motherfuckers,
    US urban guerillas, 1968

Why would we have different races if God meant us to be alike and associate with each other?

Lester Maddox,
    governor of Georgia

It occurred to me that perhaps we would be able to identify the guerrilla — a farmer by day and a fighter by night — by the dark circles under his eyes.

General Kinnard,
    US 1st Cavalry, in Vietnam, 1967

I am interested in technology spiritually, because it liberates the mind.

Anthony Wedgwood Benn,
    British Minister of Technology, 1967

From Colonel and Mrs George S. Patton III
    Peace On Earth.

Colonel George S. Patton III,
    message on his Christmas card, beneath a picture of Viet Cong corpses, dismembered and piled neatly, 1968

As I look ahead I am filled with foreboding. Like the Roman, I seem to see the River Tiber foaming with much blood.

Enoch Powell,
    British politician, fuelling the immigration debate, 1968

I said: 'Ride over the bastards.' This comment made me quite popular with the President.

Robert Askin,
    New South Wales premier, instructing his chauffeur to drive through anti-war demonstrators who were awaiting the visiting Lyndon B. Johnson, 1968

Nice weather.

Sir Henry Bolte,
    premier of Victoria, greeting Haile Selassie at Melbourne airport, 1968

We could pave the whole country and put parking stripes on it and still be home for Christmas.

Ronald Reagan,
    on the problem of Vietnam

Policemen should   shoot arsonists and looters: arsonists to kill and looters to maim and detain. You wouldn't want to shoot children, but with mace you could detain youngsters.

Richard Daley,
**   mayor of Chicago, strategic instructions to**
his police during the riots that followed the
murder of Martin Luther King, 1968

I call it the 'Madman Theory', Bob. I want the North Vietnamese to believe I've reached the point where I might do *anything* to stop the war. We'll just slip the word to them that 'for God's sake, you know Nixon is obsessed about Communism. We can't restrain him when he's angry. And he has his hand on the nuclear button. . . .' And Ho Chi Minh will be in Paris in two days begging for peace.

Richard Nixon,
**   US president, expounding his foreign**
policy to H.R. 'Bob' Haldeman, 1969

The white honkie culture that has been handed to us on a platter is meaningless to us. We don't want it! Fuck God in the ass! Fuck your woman until she can't stand up! Fuck everybody you can get your hands on! Our programme of dope, rock and roll and fucking in the streets is a programme of total freedom for everyone!

John Sinclair,
**   White Panther Party chairman, 1969**

Get the thing straight once and for all. The policeman isn't there to create disorder. The policeman is there to preserve disorder.

Richard Daley,
**   mayor of Chicago, explaining the 'police**
riot' outside the Democratic Convention, 1968

Unless the courts stop their permissiveness, unless the people we work for are going to back us up, then the feeling of policemen is — maybe we had better resort to the old Mexican *deguello* — a shoot-out in which we take no prisoners.

Sergeant John Harrington
**   offering the view of the Fraternal Order of**
Police on campus riots, 1970

Anyone who wants to be president should have his head examined.

Averill Harriman,
**   US statesman, 1970**

There are a lot of mediocre judges and people and lawyers. They are entitled to a little representation.

Senator Roman Hruska
**   defending Supreme Court nominee Judge G.**
Harrold Carswell, who was generally seen as
mediocre

We do not condone this brutal act in any way and even though the Kennedy family may not deserve it (their works have brought it on themselves) they have our deepest sympathy. However, if it was God's will, who are we to argue.

Imperial Nighthawk,
**   Ku Klux Klan newspaper, in a requiem for**
Robert Kennedy, 1970

I'll tell you who's not informed. It's those stupid kids, why, they don't know the issues. . . . And the professors, they're just as bad, if not worse. They don't know anything. Nor do these stupid bastards who're ruining our educational institutions.

John Mitchell,
**   US Attorney-General, attacking anti-war**
protesters, 1970

You know what happens in the beehive. They kill all those drones. This is what happens in most primitive societies. Maybe we've just gotten too far away from the situation of primitive man.

Congressman W.R. Poage
**   on a solution for poverty, 1970**

If it takes a bloodbath, let's get it over with. No more appeasement.

Ronald Reagan,
**   governor of California, calling for a final**
solution to dealing with campus activists,
1970

Most of us have stopped using silver every day.

Margaret Thatcher,
**   British Minister of Education on the**
worsening economic situation, 1970

LUNATIC FRINGE

It needs to be said that the poor are poor because they don't have enough money.

Sir Keith Joseph,
    British Minister of Health, 1970

Contest Winners: We wish to thank all our good readers for their answers to the contest 'Which president did the most to help Communism?' Your response was overwhelming and there were so many excellent ones. There were more letters listing F.D. Roosevelt than all the others combined.

Imperial Nighthawk,
    Ku Klux Klan magazine, 1970

You see these bums, you know, blowing up the campuses. Listen, the boys on the college campuses today are the luckiest people in the world — going to the greatest universities — and there they are burning the books. I mean storming around about this issue. You name it. Get rid of this war, there'll be another one.

Richard Nixon,
    US president, complaining about the students, 1970

We do act as a screen, because there is a real danger of some advocate of an idea rushing in to see the President . . . if that person is actually allowed to do so, and actually managing to convince him in a burst of emotion or argument.

H.R. Haldeman,
    Nixon aide on making sure that no one sees President Nixon, 1971

We cannot judge it before it is concluded, and we cannot judge it even after it has been concluded.

Richard Nixon,
    US president, on the invasion of Laos, 1971

If they want to act like dogs, then they should be treated like dogs. I think they should issue every delegate and alternate a submachine gun next time.

LeRoy Stocks
    Whiteville, North Carolina's delegate to the Republican Party Convention, on the demonstrators outside the hall, 1972

I'll make Attila the Hun look like a faggot!

Frank Rizzo,
    former police commissioner, elected mayor of Philadelphia, 1971

Hijackers should be given a rapid trial with due process of law at the airport and then hanged.

Ed Davis,
    Los Angeles chief of police, 1972

If you don't mind smelling like a peanut for two or three days, peanut butter is darn good shaving cream.

Barry Goldwater,
    US senator, 1972

My favourite sandwich is peanut butter, bologna, cheddar cheese, lettuce and mayonnaise on toasted bread with lots of catsup on the side. Another favourite is toasted peanut butter, cheese and bacon, or, if I'm in a hurry, just peanut butter and jelly.

Hubert Humphrey,
    US senator, 1972

Everybody should rise up and say: 'Thank you Mr President, for bombing Haiphong.'

Martha Mitchell,
    wife of the US Attorney-General, 1972

It looks like a postcard.

Richard Nixon,
    US president, to Chou En Lai, admiring the Chinese landscape, 1972

I think it was sleeping pills. Sleeping pills and demons.

Billy Graham,
    US evangelist, on Nixon's involvement with Watergate, 1973

If the criminal wants to commit suicide then he should be allowed to do so. Something should be left in the cell. Perhaps a razor blade.

Jonathan Guinness,
    British Conservative MP, 1973

Expletive deleted.

**The Presidential transcripts
of the Nixon White House tapes, released
1973**

I read in the encyclopaedia that Ghana exports most of the world's cocoa. I just love chocolate.

**Shirley Temple Black,
former child star, taking up her
appointment as US ambassador to Ghana,
1974**

Every time there was a major crisis in the White House, President Nixon told us to read his book *Six Crises*. I read it fourteen times.

**Charles Colson,
former White House staffer, 1974**

Mr Nixon was the thirty-seventh president of the United States, he had been preceded by thirty-six others.

**Gerald Ford,
thirty-eighth US president, 1974**

I send out love waves to my enemies. They can't eat, they can't sleep, they hate so much. Love is the essence of success. I wouldn't kill a moth, a spider, anything. I don't believe in violence. I'm a spiritual man. I publish my own prayers to the people. I have been appointed to carry out a divine plan. It was all arranged long before I was born.

**Eric Gairy,
dictator of Grenada, 1974**

Don't confuse me with the facts.

**Senator Earl Landgrebe,
last of the die-hard supporters of Richard
Nixon, 1974**

Birth control is a plot to cut down the number of white people in America. Abortion and population control reduce the white population, but don't control the blacks or the Jews.

**Albert P. Lentz,
Imperial Wizard of the Ku Klux Klan, 1975**

I urge the Congress to join me in mounting a major new effort to replace the discredited President.

**Richard Nixon,
US president, a Freudian slip in the State
of the Union speech, 1974**

There is a sickness of Americans. They have to have intercourse. Virtue is self-discipline.

**Representative John M. Zwach,
in a debate on abortion, 1974**

In developing our industrial strategy for the period ahead we have the benefit of much experience: almost everything has been tried once.

**Anthony Wedgwood Benn,
British Labour politician, 1974**

I am the first Eagle Scout president of the US.

**Gerald Ford,
1974**

I think people of different races can work together, but that doesn't mean they have to socialize after work. The good Lord put us on the Earth the way He wanted us to be. If He'd wanted us to be mongrels, He'd have made us mongrels from the start.

**Albert P. Lentz,
Imperial Wizard of the Ku Klux Klan, 1975**

I thought it was a great pity that they were not taught to look after themselves and have their hair done nicely.

**Sonia McMahon,
wife of Australian prime minister William
McMahon, commenting on the Chinese
women she met on a trip to China with her
husband, 1975**

Some estimates have placed America's total investment requirement in the coming years at the astonishing figure of four trillion dollars. Even the figure is imposing — it's a four, followed by twelve zeros!

Gerald Ford

Vice-President Nixon looks on as Soviet Premier Kruschev quaffs a cup of Pepsi-Cola/Popperfoto

I would not like to be a Russian leader, they never know when they're being taped.

Richard Nixon,
  former US president, 1975

I am very happy to be here in Canada.

Shridath Surendranath Rhamphal,
  Secretary-General of the Commonwealth,
arriving in Australia, 1975

There are too many guns in the hands of people who don't know how to use them.

Hubert Humphrey,
  US senator, commenting on Sarah Moore's
bungled attempt to assassinate Gerald Ford,
when her gun jammed, 1975

I am convinced that UFOs exist, because I have seen one.

Jimmy Carter

The opportunity to sleep nine hours a night and really relax has been extremely good for me. I ask you to disabuse yourself of any idea that prison is harmful.

John Stonehouse,
  former British Cabinet minister, jailed for
corruption, 1975

The day that our followers lose their ability to hate will be the day they lose their power and their will to achieve anything worthwhile at all.

John Tyndall,
  British National Front leader, 1975

I captured some of the people who tried to assassinate me. I ate them before they ate me.

Idi Amin,
  Ugandan president

BOOK OF POLITICAL QUOTES

We won't be able to sit on uranium. Firstly because it will not be right, and secondly because it would be wrong as far as we are concerned.

Joh Bjelke-Petersen,
Queensland premier, 1976

Your experience will be a lesson to all us men not to marry ladies in very high positions.

Idi Amin,
Ugandan president, in a letter to Lord Snowdon after his divorce from Princess Margaret, 1976

When a man is asked to make a speech, the first thing he has to decide is what to say.

Gerald Ford

We say give us liberty and give them death. There's many times I've like picking up my gun and going to shoot a nigger. We've got a heritage to protect.

David E. Duke,
Grand Dragon of the Ku Klux Klan in Louisiana, campaigning for the State Senate, 1976

Black houseboys seeing scantily clad white women on the screen will feel an overwhelming urge to rush upstairs and rape the madam.

Dr Albert Hertzog
South African Minister for Broadcasting, on the introduction of television to his country, 1976

After a tour gets inside the camp, we'll have a recording broadcast a firefight — mortars exploding, bullets, flying, Vietnamese screaming — there's nothing offensive about it.

Reverend Carl McIntyre
on 'New Vietnam', his proposed tourist attraction, spreading over three hundred spare acres of Cape Canaveral, quoted in _Esquire,_ 1976

The member for Fuller is saying bullshit, which he is not allowed to say in this house.

Neville Wran,
New South Wales premier, 1976

Let's all take a deep breath and relax. We're wasting energy.

Jerry Brown,
Governor of California, at the start of his speeches, 1976

It is not accurate to believe that blacks were confined somehow to the lowest-paying jobs; rather, there was some tendency for blacks to be congregated in certain units which had a variety of characteristics, including, in some instances, a somewhat lower-than-average pay than some units where there might be a heavy concentration of white employees.

Ben Fisher,
special assistant to the president of the United Steelworkers of America, commenting on allegations of racial bias within the union, 1976

If you squawk like a crow, look like a crow and fly like a crow, you'll be shot like a crow.

Joh Bjelke-Petersen,
Queensland premier, asked by an ex Miss Australia why he branded any anti-uranium campaigner as a Communist, 1977

You can't explain a feeling like that. I decided right there and then that I was willing to die for the white race. It's like the first time you get a piece of ass.

Dennis Campbell,
Kligrapp in the Ku Klux Klan, on his first cross-burning, 1977

The more hold-up men shot and killed the better. It's far more economical to shoot them than to put them in prison. You kill a mad dog, so if a criminal holds you up and you shoot him down, there's no question of morality. Call it vigilantism, I don't give a damn what you call it. The criminal situation is so desperate that the citizens of this state and nation have got to start taking drastic steps.

Edwyn E. Mason,
New York State senator, 1977

Shoot people dead if they steal. There's too much freedom in our constitution.

Pita Lus,
Minister for Jails, Papua-New Guinea, 1977

If you back a horse against somebody, they move.

Vance Dickie,
Chief Secretary of Victoria, on allegations of police violence against protesters, 1977

Give the average tribal Rhodesian a ballot paper and he'll eat it.

Reverend Ralph Moss,
former Nixon adviser, 1977

I cannot say, and do not know whether the coming quota will be the same, more, or less than the previous one.. But the tonnage will definitely fall within one of these three options.

Yoshio Okawara,
Japanese ambassador to Australia, on the beef quota, 1977

He weighs 258 pounds. This is a sign of solidarity for Uganda.

Radio Uganda
announcing the carrying of President Amin on the shoulders of his British subjects, 1977

Were Hitler alive today, I like to think he'd be on tour in an American musical.

John Schlesinger,
British movie director, 1977

The world has missed a shining example of harmony and separate development by not recognizing the virtue of South Africa's apartheid policy.

Glenister Sheil,
Australian senator, 1977

I'm putting my head up, but if it's shot off, it's no skin off my back.

David Arblaster,
Australian politician, 1978

I say to people, 'Gee, if you're not satisfied with all the literature you see on the news-stands, for example, and what is available — goodness me! you're a glutton for punishment.'

Joh Bjelke-Petersen,
Queensland premier, defending his personal censorship of his state's literary tastes, 1978

We'll hang people. A few. We've still got a lot of chaps doing bad things.

General Zia ul-Haq,
Pakistani president, 1978

We are not just a bunch of illiterate Southern nigger-killers. We are good, white, Christian, hard-working people working for a white America. When one of your wives, or maybe one of your sisters, gets raped by a nigger, maybe you'll get smart and join the Klan.

Mary Bacon,
US jockey and Klan recruiter, 1979

You have to know a black. He wants someone to be his boss. They can't think quickly. You can take a baboon and learn him to play a tune on the piano, but it's impossible for himself to use his own mind to go on to the next step.

Arrie Paulus,
secretary of the all-white South African mine workers' union, 1979

One must avoid praying when one feels an urge to urinate or defecate or when one is wearing socks that are too tight.

Ayatollah Khomeini,
religious dictator of Iran: *Sayings*, 1980

First one up gets to fight the Russians in Ethiopia!

Zbigniew Brzezinski,
US National Security Adviser, racing up the Great Wall of China, to his Chinese guide, 1980

The word 'change' has become a political catchword for Communist propaganda.

Dr Andries Teurnicht,
South African hard-liner, 1980

We affirm that the ludicrous use of the Western hat stands in the way of our independence and is contrary to the will of God.

Ayatollah Khomeini,
religious dictator of Iran: *Sayings*, 1980

IF I RULED THE WORLD

A prince who desires to maintain his position must learn to be not always good, but to be so or not, as needs require.

Niccolò Machiavelli,
   Italian statesman: *The Prince,* 1513

Put not your trust in Princes.

Book of Psalms,
   146:3

Any excuse will serve a tyrant.

Aesop:
   Fables, sixth century BC

IF I RULED THE WORLD

In taking possession of a state the conqueror should well reflect as to the harsh measures that may be necessary and then execute them at a single blow....Cruelties should be committed all at once.

Niccolò Machiavelli:
The Prince, 1513

During the time that men live without a common power to keep them all in awe...the life of man is solitary, poor, nasty, brutish and short.

Thomas Hobbes,
English philosopher: _Leviathan,_ 1651

Tyrants commonly cut off the stairs by which they climb unto their thrones...for fear that, if they still be left standing, others will get up the same way.

Thomas Fuller,
English antiquarian and divine

There are few minds to which tyranny is not delightful.

Samuel Johnson,
English lexicographer and essayist

Dr Johnson and James Boswell enjoy a meal/Mary Evans Picture Library

BOOK OF POLITICAL QUOTES

So that in the first place I put for a general inclination of all mankind a perpetual and restless desire of power after power, that ceases only in death.

Thomas Hobbes,
English philosopher: *Leviathan,* **1651**

I am more and more convinced that man is a dangerous creature and that power, whether vested in many or a few, is ever grasping, and like the grave, cries, 'Give, give!'

Abigail Adams,
US letter-writer, 1775

My opinion is that power should always be distributed, in whatever hands it is placed.

Sir William Jones,
English jurist, 1782

Tyrants seldom want pretexts.

Edmund Burke,
British statesman

Necessity is the plea for every infringement of human freedom, it is the argument of tyrants, it is the creed of slaves.

William Pitt the Younger,
British Chancellor of the Exchequer, 1783

All oppressors...attribute the frustration of their desires to the want of sufficient rigour. Then they redouble the efforts of their impotent cruelty.

Edmund Burke,
British statesman, during the impeachment of Warren Hastings, 1788

They question my right to the title of philanthropist. Ah, what injustice! Who cannot see that I want to cut off a few heads to save a great number?

Jean-Paul Marat,
architect of the French Revolutionary 'Terror' in which — by his estimate — 263,000 were guillotined

Power is my mistress. I have worked too hard at her conquest to allow anyone to take her away from me, or even to covet her.

Napoleon Bonaparte,
1804

Republican despotism is more fertile in acts of tyranny, because everyone has a hand in it.

Napoleon Bonaparte

Whoever is foremost leads the herd.

Friedrich von Schiller,
German playwright

People who are masters in their own house are never tyrants.

Napoleon Bonaparte:
Maxims, **1804-15**

Despotism sits nowhere so secure as under the effigy and ensigns of freedom.

Walter Savage Landor,
English poet

Despots themselves do not deny the excellence of freedom, but they wish to keep it all to themselves.

Alexis de Tocqueville,
French political commentator

Tyrants never perish from tyranny, but always from folly — when their fantasies have built up a palace for which the earth has no foundation.

Walter Savage Landor,
English poet: *Imaginary Conversations,*
1824-29

The triumph of demagogues is short-lived, but the ruins are eternal.

Charles Péguy,
French poet and essayist

People demand freedom only when they have no power.

Friedrich Nietzsche,
German philosopher: *The Will to Power,*
1888

The worst form of tyranny the world has ever known is the tyranny of the weak over the strong, it is the only tyranny that lasts.

Oscar Wilde,
Irish poet, wit and dramatist

IF I RULED THE WORLD

Tyranny is always organised better than freedom.

**Charles Péguy,
  French poet and essayist**

Nothing should be left to an invaded people except their eyes for weeping.

**Otto von Bismarck,
  German statesman, 1862**

The way to power is to take it.

**William Marcy 'Boss' Tweed,
  Tammany Hall politician**

People will endure their tyrants for many years, but they tear their deliverers to pieces if a millennium is not created immediately.

Woodrow Wilson

We have arrived at a stage of political and social evolution in which a political party founded upon the individual interests of citizens and electors no longer has the right to exist. Isolated man is an abstraction — a fiction created under the dominating influence of the erroneous principles of the last century.

**Antonio de Salazar,
  Portuguese dictator, 1922**

The demagogue is one who preaches doctrines he knows to be untrue to men he knows to be idiots.

**H.L. Mencken,
  US philologist, editor and satirist**

The selfish wish to govern is often mistaken for a holy zeal in the cause of humanity.

**Elbert Hubbard,
  US businessman and writer**

Put pressure on your adversary with ice-cold determination. Probe him, search out his weak spot, deliberately and calculatingly sharpen the spear, hurl it with careful aim where the enemy is naked and vulnerable and then perhaps say with a friendly smile 'Sorry neighbour, I can't help it.' This is the dish of revenge that is enjoyed cold.

**Joseph Goebbels,
  Nazi Minister of Propaganda, 1929**

Not to aspire as a right, but to accept it and exercise it as a duty; to consider the state as God's ministry for the common good, and to obey from the heart those who are in authority; to command without forgetting the dues of justice, to obey without forgetting the sacred burden of those who command — what a tremendous social revolution this would be....It would mean power unhampered by ambitious greed, it would mean order ensured by obedience rooted in men's souls.

**Antonio de Salazar,
  Portuguese dictator, 1923**

The truth is that men are tired of liberty.

**Benito Mussolini,
  1923**

The efficiency of the truly national leader consists primarily of preventing the division of the attention of the people and always concentrating it on a single enemy.

**Adolf Hitler:
  Mein Kampf, 1924**

Dictators always look good until the last minutes.

**Thomas Masaryck,
  Czechoslovak president**

Perhaps the greatest consolation for the oppressed is to consider themselves superior to their tyrants.

**Julien Green,
  French novelist: Adrienne Mesurat, 1927**

Tyrants are always assassinated too late. That is their great excuse.

**Emile M. Cioran,
  Rumanian philosopher and essayist**

I do not believe that right alone is enough. One must also have might.

**Adolf Hitler,
  German presidential candidate, 1932**

When I hear anyone talk of culture, I usually reach for my revolver.

**Hanns Johst,
  German playwright, 1932**

BOOK OF POLITICAL QUOTES

If people say that here and there someone has been taken away and maltreated, then I can only reply, 'You can't make an omelette without breaking eggs.'

Hermann Goering,
   Nazi leader, 1933

Marching is the most meaningful form of our profession of faith.

Ernst Röhm,
   leader of the Nazi SA

What luck for the rulers that men do not think.

Adolf Hitler

I say who is a Jew!

Hermann Goering,
   Nazi leader, replying to critics who noted his Jewish friends

Strength Through Joy.

Robert Ley,
   head of the Nazi Labour Front: the movement's slogan, 1933

Dictatorship is a great adventure which crumbles in misery and blood.

Charles de Gaulle,
   1934

I was obliged to abandon that high calling of teaching and to tread a more difficult path with a heavier cross.

Antonio de Salazar,
   Portuguese dictator, on taking over power in Portugal

The undesirable classes never liquidate themselves.

Joseph Stalin
   to Lady Astor who had asked: 'When are you going to stop killing people?'

We have buried the putrid corpse of liberty.

Benito Mussolini,
   1934

Concentration camps cannot be sanatoriums.

Hermann Goering,
   Nazi leader 1934

It really makes no odds to us if we kill someone.

Hermann Goering,
   Nazi leader

Dictators ride to and fro upon tigers from which they dare not dismount.

Hindustani proverb
   quoted by Winston Churchill in *While England Slept*, 1936

The Chief of State is responsible before God and History.

Francisco Franco
   taking up supreme power and abolishing parties, 1937

As long as men worship the Caesars and Napoleons, Caesars and Napoleons will duly rise and make them miserable.

Aldous Huxley,
   English novelist and essayist: *Ends and Means*, 1937

All Spaniards may freely express their ideas, so long as these do not prejudice the fundamental principles of the state.

Francisco Franco:
   ***Charter of Spaniards*, 1945**

It is the curse of the great that they have to step over corpses to create new life.

Heinrich Himmler,
   Nazi leader

Power is not a means, it is an end. One does not establish a dictatorship in order to safeguard a revolution. One makes the revolution in order to establish the dictatorship.

George Orwell,
   English essayist and critic: *1984*

Power abdicates only under stress of counter power.

Martin Buber,
   Israeli philosopher, 1950

IF I RULED THE WORLD

If you really want to do something new, the good won't help you with it.... 'Let me have men about me that are fat.' An anointed king can say that, but not a leader who has made himself. Let me have men about me that are arrant knaves. The wicked, who have something on their conscience, are obliging, quick to hear threats, because they know how it's done, and for booty. You can offer them things, because they will take them. Because they have no hesitation. You can hang them if they get out of step. Let me have men about me that are utter villains — provided that I have the power, the absolute power, over life and death.

Hermann Goering,
Nazi leader explaining his philosophy to
his lawyer at the Nuremberg Tribunal, 1945

Absolute freedom mocks at justice. Absolute justice denies freedom.

Albert Camus:
***The Rebel,* 1951**

Our revolution...seeks to change the political system for the benefit of the people. It is therefore necessary to defend the revolution against those who try to deter it from its course and prevent it from attaining its ultimate goals.

Gamal Abdel Nasser,
Egyptian president, warning off any other
groups after his coup, 1953

The perfection preached in the Gospels never yet built up an Empire. Every man of action has a strong dose of egotism, pride, hardness and cunning. But all these things will be forgiven him, indeed they will be regarded as high qualities, if he can make them the means to achieve great ends.

Charles de Gaulle

Foreign papers say I am a dictator, a pharaoh. But a dictator is one who governs his country in spite of his people. It is up to you to find out if this is so in my case.

Gamal Abdel Nasser,
Egyptian president, 1956

The future is the only kind of property that the masters willingly concede to slaves.

Albert Camus,
French author and philosopher: *The Rebel,*
1951

My parliament is the army.

Gamal Abdel Nasser,
Egyptian president, 1957

Some people get crazy. They are not responsible. And I am a doctor.

François Duvalier (Papa Doc),
dictator of Haiti, explaining his repressive,
terror-wielding rule, 1959

A single death is a tragedy, a million deaths is a statistic.

Joseph Stalin,
1958

I am and I symbolize a historic moment in your history as a free and independent people. God and the people are the source of all power. I have twice been given the power. I have taken it and, damn it, I will keep it for ever.

François Duvalier (Papa Doc),
dictator of Haiti, 1963

Totalitarian movements...can remain in power only so long as they keep moving and set everything around them in motion.

Hannah Arendt,
US political philosopher: *Origins of*
Totalitarianism

Our Doc who art in the National Palace for life, hallowed be Thy name by present and future generations. Thy will be done at Port au Prince and in the provinces. Give us this day our new Haiti and never forgive the trespasses of the anti-patriots who spit every day on our country; let them succumb to temptation and under the weight of their venom, deliver them not from any evil.

François Duvalier (Papa Doc),
dictator of Haiti: *La Catechisme de la*
Revolution, 1964

Idealism is the noble toga that political gentlemen drape over their will to power.

Aldous Huxley,
   English novelist and essayist, 1963

Great citizens who lead their countries with firmness and all the necessary savagery know what they are doing. Duvalier...knew what he was doing.

François Duvalier (Papa Doc),
   dictator of Haiti, 1964

Absolute despotism equates itself with the belief in absolute human happines — though it is an all-inclusive and universal tyranny.

Milovan Djilas,
   Yugoslav politician

If anyone thinks he can turn his ass left or right, I will crush it into flour and pass it through a sieve.

François Duvalier (Papa Doc),
   dictator of Haiti, 1964

I have no objections to politicians being interested in personal power — I think they should be.

Michael Foot,
   British Labour MP, 1966

Of course, in my country, most political leaders are, well, not gangsters, but more or less the same kind of thing. No, I mean, people who go in for getting elected, what can you expect of men like that?

Jorge Luis Borges,
   Argentine writer, 1971

I don't think prime ministers go until they are pushed.

Jo Grimond,
   former British Liberal Party leader, 1973

Anybody that wants the presidency so much that he'll spend two years organizing and campaigning for it, is not to be trusted with the office.

David Broder,
   US political commentator, 1973

Papa Doc is not a dictator, he is a democrat. His own people in the country consider him a democrat, because he is the leader of the country.

François Duvalier (Papa Doc),
   dictator of Haiti

I would never accept a Communist to run in an election of Vietnam. When we say 'one man, one vote', we mean the vote to be given to Vietnamese citizens who deserve it.

Nguyen Van Thieu,
   South Vietnamese president, 1968

I do not want to be controlled by any superpower, I myself consider myself the most powerful figure in the world.

Idi Amin,
   Ugandan president

Jesus, Tip, do you realize how much my damn *pension* is going to be, now?

Gerald Ford,
   US president, telling Tip O'Neill, Speaker of the House of Representatives, of the benefits of power, 1974

Sometimes democracy must be bathed in blood.

Auguste Pinochet,
   dictator of Chile, 1979

In view of the success of my economic revolution in Uganda, I offer myself to be appointed head of the Commonwealth.

Idi Amin,
   Ugandan president, 1975

What's the man in the street got to do with it?

Joh Bjelke-Petersen,
   Queensland premier, asked whether he had considered the man in the street's attitude to his policies, 1976

Intelligence is not all that important in the exercise of power and is often, in point of fact, useless. Just as a leader doesn't need any intelligence, a man in my job doesn't need much of it either.

Henry Kissinger

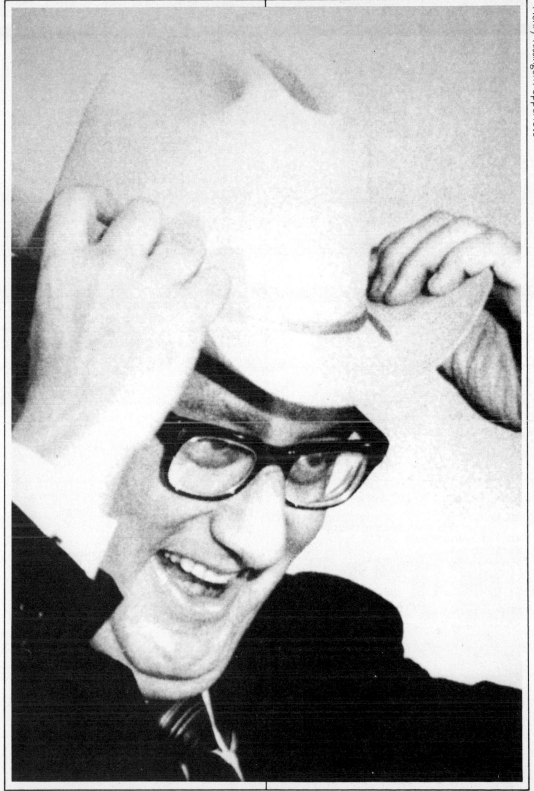

Henry Kissinger/Popperfoto

BOOK OF POLITICAL QUOTES

In any country there must be people who have to die. They are the sacrifices any nation has to make to achieve law and order.

Idi Amin,
Ugandan president, 1976

Power as an instrument in its own right has no fascination for me.

Henry Kissinger

Truth. This is all I ask from anyone in my country. That they tell the truth. If they don't they suffer and I feed them to the crocodiles and wild dogs.

Idi Amin,
Ugandan president, 1977

It is not our task as politicians to make out prescriptions for other people's happiness against their will. That would be the end of freedom.

Franz-Josef Strauss,
right-wing German politician, 1976

My people share their money with me and I share my heart with them. That is the right way.

Idi Amin,
Ugandan president, 1977

I have no mercy on evil-doers.

Idi Amin,
Ugandan president, sending two of his sons to reform school, 1976

Universities are funny places. They are the breeding grounds for all the political war-mongers who make life a misery...it is the same world over. Too many brains, too much intelligence and the mice want to play and tell the government what to do. It cannot be allowed.

Idi Amin,
1977

I have to keep law and order and it means that I have to kill my enemies before they kill me.

Idi Amin,
1977

We need a head of government who is not at the mercy of his lust and other temptations. We need someone to govern us for whom all are equal, for whom all enjoy the same rights and obligations; someone who doesn't indulge in favouritism, who regards his family in the same light as others, who will cut off his son's hands if he steals and execute his brothers and sisters if they sell heroin.

Ayatollah Khomeini,
religious dictator of Iran: *Sayings*, 1980

Oh boy! If I was down there in Canberra, there'd be change in a lot of things!

Joh Bjelke-Petersen,
Queensland premier, 1977

Idi Amin gets a warm welcome at Kampala/Publisher's files

134

THE CORRIDORS OF POWER

The people may be made to follow a path of action, but they may not be made to understand it.

Confucius,
   Chinese philosopher: *Analects,* sixth century BC

Nothing doeth more hurt in a state than that cunning men pass for wise.

Francis Bacon,
   English statesman: *Essays,* 1625

It is essential to banish pity when judging crimes against the State.

Cardinal Richelieu,
   French statesman, 1641

Secrecy is the first essential in affairs of state.

Cardinal Richelieu,
   1641

No government has ever been, or can ever be, wherein time-servers and blockheads will not be uppermost.

John Dryden,
   English poet

Nothing is as dangerous for the State as those who would govern kingdoms with maxims found in books.

Cardinal Richelieu,
   French statesman: *Political Testament,* 1687

Party loyalty lowers the greatest of men to the petty level of the masses.

Jean de la Bruyère,
   French writer: *Characters,* 1688

Party is the madness of many for the gain of a few.

Jonathan Swift,
   English satirist, 1711

Never needlessly disturb a thing at rest.

John Randolph,
   US statesman, on his craft

Nothing appears more surprising to those who consider human affairs with a philosophical eye, than the easiness with which the many are governed by the few.

David Hume,
   Scottish philosopher

To govern mankind one must not over-rate them.

Lord Chesterfield,
   English statesman and essayist, 1754

I would not give half a guinea to live under one form of government rather than another. It is of no moment to the happiness of an individual.

Samuel Johnson,
   English lexicographer, critic and poet, 1772

Those who would carry on great public schemes must be proof against the worst delays, the most mortifying disappointments, the most shocking insults, and what is worst, the presumptuous judgement of the ignorant upon their design.

Edmund Burke,
   British statesman

The pleasure of governing must certainly be exquisite if we may judge from the vast numbers who are eager to be concerned with it.

Voltaire,
  French author and humanitarian:
  Philosophical Dictionary, 1764

Government implies the power of making laws. It is essential to the idea of a law, that it be attended with the sanction, or in other words, a penalty of punishment for disobedience.

Alexander Hamilton,
  US statesman, 1787

All government — indeed, every human benefit and enjoyment and every prudent act — is founded on compromise and barter.

Edmund Burke,
British statesman, on the conciliation with the American colonies, 1775

In general, the art of government consists in taking as much money as possible from one party of the citizens to give to the other.

Voltaire,
French author and humanitarian

Kings govern by means of popular assemblies only when they cannot do without them.

Charles James Fox,
British politician, 1776

Between craft and credulity, the voice of reason is stifled.

Edmund Burke,
British statesman

When security and equality are in conflict, it will not do to hesitate a moment — equality must yield.

Jeremy Bentham,
English philosopher: Introduction to the Principles of Morals and Legislation, 1789

The essence of a free government consists in an effectual control of rivalries.

John Adams,
US vice-president, 1789

Constitutions are good only as we make progress under them.

Napoleon Bonaparte:
Maxims, 1804-15

When a man assumes a public trust, he should consider himself as a public property.

Thomas Jefferson,
US president, 1807

The art of governing consists in not letting men grow old in their jobs.

Napoleon Bonaparte:
Maxims, 1804-15

Which government is best? That which teaches us to govern ourselves.

Johann Wolfgang von Goethe,
German playwright

Every country has the government it deserves.

Joseph de Maistre,
French political philosopher, 1811

I am afraid the question of the Irish church can neither be avoided or postponed, it must therefore be attempted to be solved.

Lord Melbourne,
British statesman, on Catholic Emancipation

It is an easy and vulgar thing to please the mob, and not a very arduous task to astonish them; but essentially to benefit and improve them is a work fraught with difficult and teeming with danger.

Charles Caleb Colton,
British clergyman and writer, 1825

There are no necessary evils in government. Its evils exist only in its abuses.

Andrew Jackson,
US president, 1830

The Few assume to be the *deputies*, but they are often only the *despoilers* of the Many.

Georg Friedrich Hegel,
German philosopher, 1832

Mr Tierney, a great Whig authority, used always to say that the duty of an opposition was very simple — it was to oppose everything and to propose nothing.

Lord Stanley,
English historian and clergyman, 1841

In the long run every government is the exact symbol of its people, with their wisdom and unwisdom.

Thomas Carlyle,
Scottish author and historian: Past and Present, 1843

To govern men you must either excel them in their accomplishments or despise them. Affectation tells even better here than wit.

Benjamin Disraeli

That government is best which governs least.

Henry David Thoreau,
 US philosopher: *Civil Disobedience*, 1849

To be governed is to be watched, inspected, spied upon, directed, law-ridden, regulated, penned up, indoctrinated, preached at, checked, appraised, seized, censured, commanded by beings who have neither title, nor knowledge, nor virtue.

Pierre Joseph Proudhon,
 French socialist

I've got to follow them. I'm their leader.

Ledru-Rollin,
 French radical, watching the mob, 1848

Government is at best but an expedient, but most governments are usually, and all governments are sometimes, inexpedient.

Henry David Thoreau,
 US essayist: *Civil Disobedience*, 1849

I have a horror of losing my own individuality — which is to me as existence itself.

Richard Cobden,
 British statesman, refusing a Cabinet post, 1859

Laws are to govern all alike — those opposed as well as those who favour them. I know of no method to repeal of bad or obnoxious laws so effective as their stringent execution.

Ulysses S. Grant
 US president, 1869

Public men are bees working in a glass hive, and curious spectators enjoy themselves in watching every secret movement as if it were a study in natural history.

Henry Ward Beecher,
 US editor and clergyman, 1887

Let's not be too damn virtuous.

Thurlow Weed,
 US politician, 1850

One is never weaker than when one appears to be supported by everybody.

Emile Ollivier,
 French prime minister, 1870

The right of the minority is to draw its salaries and its function is to make a quorum.

Thomas Brackett Reed,
 US politician

Presidency, n. The greased pig in the field game of American politics.

Ambrose Bierce,
 US journalist and author: *The Devil's Dictionary*, 1881-1911

There are men who desire power simply for the sake of the happiness it will bring; these belong chiefly to political parties.

Friedrich Nietzsche,
 German philosopher: *The Will To Power*, 1888

They never open their mouths without subtracting from the sum of human knowledge.

Thomas Brackett Reed,
 US politician

Conservative, n: A statesman who is enamoured of existing evils, as distinguished from the Liberal who wishes to replace them with others.

Ambrose Bierce,
 US journalist and author: *The Devil's Dictionary*, 1881-1911

Fleas can be taught nearly everything a Congressman can.

Mark Twain,
 US author

The duty of an opposition is to oppose.

Lord Randolph Churchill,
 British statesman

THE CORRIDORS OF POWER

In statesmanship get the formalities right, never mind about the moralities.

Mark Twain,
   US author

Administration, n. An ingenious abstraction in politics, designed to receive the kicks and cuffs due to the premier or president.

Ambrose Bierce,
   US journalist and author: *The Devil's Dictionary*, 1881-1911

Our differences are policies, our agreements principles.

William McKinley,
   US president, 1901

It could probably be shown by facts and figures that there is no distinctively native American criminal class except Congress.

Mark Twain,
   US author

Consul, n. In American politics, a person who, having failed to secure an office from the people, is given one by the Administration, on condition that he leave the country.

Ambrose Bierce,
   US journalist and author: *The Devil's Dictionary*, 1881-1911

The art of government is the organization of idolatry. The bureaucracy consists of the functionaries; the aristocracy of idols; the democracy of idolators. The populace cannot understand the bureaucracy, it can only worship the national idols.

George Bernard Shaw,
   Irish playwright

The pleasure politicians take in their limelight pleases me with the sort of pleasure I get when I see a child's eyes gleam over a new toy.

Hilaire Belloc,
   Anglo-French writer

Practical politics consists in ignoring the facts.

Henry Brooks Adams,
   US historian, 1907

The White House is a bully pulpit.

Theodore Roosevelt

You mean it is Mr Balfour's poodle! It fetches and carries for him. It barks for him. It bites anybody he sets it on to.

David Lloyd George,
   president of the British Board of Trade, replying to a speech that characterized the House of Lords as the 'Watchdog of the Constitution', 1907

Reader, suppose you were an idiot, and suppose you were a member of Congress — but I repeat myself.

Mark Twain,
   US author

Wait and see.

H.H. Asquith,
   British prime minister, admonishing Opposition ministers who were demanding a statement on the Parliamentary Procedure Act, 1910

Opposition, n. In politics, the party that prevents the government from running amuck by hamstringing it.

Ambrose Bierce,
   US journalist and author: *The Devil's Dictionary*, 1881-1911

No party commands the services of more than half a dozen first-rate men, and it has to depend for the filling up of all the other posts in government on the services of men of second or even third-rate capacity.

David Lloyd George,
   British Chancellor of the Exchequer, advocating a coalition in a letter to Asquith, 1910

The first basis of government is justice, not pity.

Woodrow Wilson,
   US president, 1912

I am afraid I shall have to show myself very vicious, Mr Asquith, this session. I hope you will understand.

Andrew Bonar Law,
   leader of the British House of Commons, 1912

BOOK OF POLITICAL QUOTES

Political institutions are a superstructure voting on an economic foundation.

V.I. Lenin,
  1913

Unless the reformer can invent something which substitutes attractive virtues for attractive vices, he will fail.

Walter Lippmann,
  US political commentator: *A Preface to Politics*, 1914

It is perfectly true that that government is best which governs least. It is equally true that that government is best which provides most.

Walter Lippmann: *A Preface to Politics*, 1914

There are three golden rules for parliamentary speakers: stand up, speak up and shut up.

J. W. Lowther,
  Speaker of the British House of Commons, 1919

English experience indicates that when the two great political parties agree about something it is generally wrong.

G.K. Chesterton
  English critic, novelist and poet, 1919

All governments are pretty much alike, with a tendency on the part of the last to be the worst.

Sir Austen Chamberlain,
  British politician, 1919

The art of government wants more character than brains.

T.E. Lawrence (Lawrence of Arabia),
  1920

Nothing beyond the State, above the State, against the State. Everything to the State, for the State, in the State.

Benito Mussolini

Nine tenths of the activities of a modern government are harmful. Therefore the worse they are performed the better.

Bertrand Russell,
  English philosopher, 1922

A good government remains the greatest of human blessings and no nation has ever enjoyed it.

William R. Inge,
  Dean of St Pauls: *Outspoken Essays*, 1922

We will be fools unless we *immediately* and forcibly send him to a sanatorium.

V.I. Lenin
  setting an ideological precedent for 'punitive psychiatry' in his treatment of his 'deviationist' foreign minister, Chicherin

All political power claiming to act effectively in the real interests of the nation must be based on an organization not exclusively political, but social, of professions and classes.

Antonio de Salazar,
  Portuguese dictator, 1922

The more you read and observe about this Politics thing, the more you've got to admit that each party's worse than the other. The one that's out always looks the best.

Will Rogers,
  US humorist: *The Illiterate Digest*, 1924

You cannot govern nations without a mailed fist and an iron will.

Benito Mussolini,
  1924

There is just as much security in a political agreement as in a regiment of soldiers or a fleet of battleships.

Ramsay MacDonald,
  British prime minister, 1929

Just as every conviction begins as a whim, so does every emancipator serve his apprenticeship as a crank. A fanatic is a great leader who is just entering the room.

Heywood Broun,
  US critic and wit, 1928

THE CORRIDORS OF POWER

Too often the strong silent man is silent only because he does not know what to say and is reputed strong only because he has remained silent.

Winston Churchill,
   British Chancellor of the Exchequer, 1924

It is no use having a thermometer which is near the radiator — and that is the trouble with all these political and industrial thermometers in London.

David Lloyd George,
   British statesman, advocating greater regional powers, 1926

In a political fight, when you've got nothing in favour of your side, start a row in the opposition camp.

Huey P. Long,
   governor of Louisiana

Our government is the potent, the omnipresent teacher. For good or ill it teaches the whole people by its example.

Louis D. Brandeis,
   US jurist, 1928

The final test of a leader is that he leaves behind in other men the conviction and the will to carry on.

Walter Lippmann,
   US political commentator

To rule is not so much a question of the heavy hand as the firm seat.

José Ortega y Gasset,
   Spanish philosopher: *The Revolt of the Masses,* **1930**

A leader gets up a programme, and then he goes out and explains it patiently and more patiently until they get it. He asks for a mandate and if they give it to him he goes ahead with the programme in spite of hell and high water. He don't tolerate no opposition from the old gang of politicians, the legislature and the courts, the corporations, or anybody.

Huey P. Long,
   governor of Louisiana, his political credo

We had to divert the attention of the masses from material to moral values. It is more important to feed the souls of men than their stomachs.

Robert Ley,
   head of the Nazi Labour Front

When we get sick, we want an uncommon doctor; if we have a construction job we want an uncommon engineer; when we get into a war we dreadfully want an uncommon general and an uncommon admiral. Only when we get into politics are we satisfied with the common man.

Herbert Hoover

One thing is sure: we have to do something. We have to do the best we know how at the moment. If it doesn't turn out right, we can modify it as we go along.

Franklin D. Roosevelt,
   US president, 1932

Government defines the physical aspects of man by means of the printed form, so that for every man in the flesh, there is an exactly corresponding man on paper.

Jean Giraudoux,
   French playwright: *The Enchanted,* **1933**

If from any speech in the House one begins to see any results within five to ten years after it has been delivered, one will have done very well indeed.

Robert Boothby,
   British MP, 1936

Let us never forget that government is *ourselves* and not an alien power over us. The ultimate rulers of our democracy are not a president and senators and congressmen and government officials but the voters of this country.

Franklin D. Roosevelt,
   US president, 1938

BIG BROTHER IS WATCHING YOU

George Orwell,
   English author and critic: *1984,* **1948**

BOOK OF POLITICAL QUOTES

A certain amount of patting on the back for workers is desirable, if a form can be found free of patronage.

Sir Kenneth Clark,
   head of the Home Morale Emergency Committee, 1940

The excitement of politics got into my veins. . . .I knew how to say 'no', but seldom could I bring myself to say it. A woman and a politician must say that word often and mean it, or else.

James J. Walker,
   mayor of New York City

The first star a child gets in school for the mere performance of a needful task is its first lesson in graft.

Philip Wylie,
   US writer: *Generation of Vipers*, 1942

People on the whole are very simple-minded in whatever country one finds them. They are so simple as to take literally, more often than not, the things their leaders tell them.

Pearl S. Buck,
   US novelist: *What America Means to Me*, 1943

I learned that a great leader is a man who has the ability to get other people to do what they don't want to do and like it.

Harry S. Truman

Politics, and the fate of mankind, are shaped by men without ideals and without greatness.

Albert Camus,
   French author and philosopher: *Notebooks*

No government can remain stable in an unstable society and an unstable world.

Léon Blum,
   French politician, 1945

A great many persons are able to become members of this House without losing their insignificance.

Beverley Baxter,
   British MP, 1946

All the president is, is a glorified public relations man who spends his time flattering, kissing and kicking people to get them to do what they are supposed to do anyway.

Harry S. Truman,
   US president, in a letter to his sister, 1947

For, in the case of nutrition and health, just as in the case of education, the gentleman in Whitehall really does know better what is good for people than the people know themselves.

Douglas Jay,
   British Labour politician: *The Socialist Case*, 1947

Government can easily exist without laws, but law cannot exist without government.

Bertrand Russell,
   English philosopher: *Unpopular Essays*, 1950

Government is only as good as the men in it.

Drew Pearson,
   US journalist

Nobody outside of a baby-carriage or a judge's chamber can believe in an unprejudiced point of view.

Lillian Hellman,
   US writer

There is no nonsense so arrant that it cannot be made the creed of the vast majority by adequate governmental action.

Bertrand Russell,
   English philosopher: *Unpopular Essays*, 1950

Let's talk sense to the American people. Let's tell them the truth. That there are no gains without pains.

Adlai Stevenson,
   US presidential candidate, 1952

A thick skin is a gift from God.

Konrad Adenauer,
   West German Chancellor

THE CORRIDORS OF POWER

The Pentagon, that immense monument to modern man's subservience to the desk.

Sir Oliver Frank,
 1952

Government cannot be stronger or more tough-minded than its people. It cannot be more inflexibly committed to the task than they. It cannot be wiser than the people.

Adlai Stevenson,
 US presidential candidate, 1952

To leave positions of great responsibility and authority is to die a little.

Dean Acheson,
 US Secretary of State, quitting office after the election of 1952

Being a president is like riding a tiger. A man has to keep riding it or be swallowed. ...A president is either constantly on top of events or, if he hesitates, events will soon be on top of him.

Harry S. Truman

Always take the job, but not yourself, seriously.

Dwight D. Eisenhower

Self-criticism is the secret weapon of democracy — and candour and confession are good for the political soul.

Adlai Stevenson

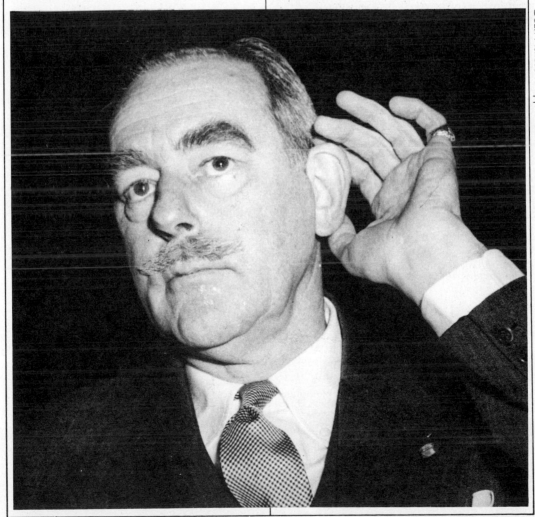

Dean Acheson/Popperfoto

Bureaucracy is the antithesis of democracy.

Jo Grimond,
British Liberal Party leader

Sometimes in politics one must duel with skunks, but no one should be fool enough to allow the skunks to choose the weapons.

Joe Cannon,
Speaker of the US House of Representatives

If you want to get along, go along.

Sam Rayburn,
Speaker of the US House of Representatives

No government could survive without champagne. Champagne in the throats of our diplomatic people is like oil in the wheels of an engine.

Joseph Dargent,
French vintner, 1955

A government is the only known vessel that leaks from the top.

James Reston,
US political commentator

Popular government has not yet been proved to guarantee always and everywhere, good government.

Walter Lippmann,
US political commentator: *The Public Philosophy*, 1955

Under democracy one party always devotes its chief energies to trying to prove that the other party is unfit to rule — and both commonly succeed, and are right.

H.L. Mencken,
US philologist, editor and satirist: *Minority Report*, 1956

When everything is going badly and you are trying to make up your mind, look towards the heights, no complications there.

Charles de Gaulle,
French president, 1958

Liberals must give up being so excessively respectable. We must have some bloody noses in the party.

Jo Grimond,
British Liberal Party leader, 1958

Every government is a device by which a few control the actions of the many.... On both sides at the moment, complex human societies depend for the final decisions of war and peace on a group of elderly men any sensible plant personnel manager, whether under capitalism or Communism, would hesitate to hire.

I.F. Stone,
US political commentator, during the Berlin crisis, 1959

Social justice is imposed with love, yet with a firm, hard hand.

Francisco Franco,
1960

What is a committee? A group of the unwilling, picked from the unfit, to do the unnecessary.

Richard Harkness,
US radio and TV commentator, 1960

No government is better than the men who compose it.

John F. Kennedy,
US president, 1960

The longer the title the less important the job.

Senator George McGovern,
1960

Your public serves you right.

Adlai Stevenson

The politician must have that instinctive sense of occasion which is also the actor's art. To the right challenge he must have the right response. He is, in the purest sense, an opportunist.

Gore Vidal,
US author, 1961

THE CORRIDORS OF POWER

President Truman keeps fit/Popperfoto

Whenever you have efficient government, you have a dictatorship.

Harry S. Truman,
    former US president, 1959

Exhortation of other people to do something is the last resort of politicians who are at a loss to know what to do themselves.

Paul Chambers,
    1961

Congress — these, for the most part illiterate hacks whose fancy vests are spotted with gravy and whose speeches, hypocritical, unctuous and slovenly, are spotted also with the gravy of political patronage.

Mary McCarthy,
    US writer: 'On the Contrary', 1961

The plea for security could well become a cloak for errors, misjudgements and other failings of government.

Richard Nixon,
    US statesman, 1961

Ask not what your country can do for you, but what you can do for your country.

John F. Kennedy,
    US president, 1961

The British, being brought up on team games, enter their House of Commons in the spirit of those who would rather be doing something else. If they cannot be playing golf or tennis, they can at least pretend that politics is a game with very similar rules.

C. Northcote Parkinson,
    British political scientist: *Parkinson's Law*, 1962

It is a function of government to invent philosophies to explain the demands of its own convenience.

Murray Kempton,
    US journalist: *America Comes of Middle Age*, 1963

I do not want to force anyone to his knees. Nor will I let anyone force me to kneel.

**Willy Brandt,
West German Chancellor**

We all know why 'Blue Streak' was kept on although it was an obvious failure. It was to save the Minister of Defence's face. We are, in fact, looking at the most expensive face in history. Helen of Troy's face, it is true, may only have launched a thousand ships, but at least they were operational.

**Harold Wilson,
British opposition leader, on the cancellation of Britain's expensive 'Blue Steak' missile**

Don't take a nickel, just hand them your business card.

**Richard Daley,
Mayor of Chicago, advice on enjoying graft**

Extremism in the defence of liberty is no vice. Moderation in the pursuit of justice is no virtue.

**Barry Goldwater,
US presidential candidate, 1964**

Extremism in the pursuit of the presidency is an unpardonable vice. Moderation in the affairs of the nation is the highest virtue.

**Lyndon B. Johnson,
US president, 1964**

In a secret department the greatest temptation in the world is to use secrecy not in the national interest, but in the departmental interest — to cover up.

**Richard Crossman,
British politician**

A government that is big enough to give you all you want is big enough to take it all away.

**Barry Goldwater,
US presidential candidate, 1964. Also attributed to Gerald Ford, 1974**

The Labour Party is a moral crusade or it is nothing.

**Harold Wilson,
British prime minister, 1964**

A political leader must keep looking over his shoulder all the time to see if the boys are still there. If they aren't still there, he's no longer a political leader.

**Bernard Baruch,
US financier and statesman, 1965**

In so far as it represents a genuine reconciliation of differences, a consensus is a fine thing. In so far as it represents a concealment of differences, it is a miscarriage of democratic procedure.

**Senator William Fulbright,
1965**

A president's hardest task is not to do what is right, but to know what is right.

**Lyndon B. Johnson,
1965**

These presidential ninnies should stick to throwing out baseballs and leave the important matters to serious people.

**Gore Vidal,
US author**

People, like sheep, tend to follow a leader, occasionally in the right direction.

**Alexander Chase,
US journalist, 1966**

Not only do most people accept violence if it is perpetrated by legitimate authority, they also regard violence against certain kinds of people as inherently legitimate, no matter who commits it.

**Edgar Z. Friedenberg,
US sociologist, 1966**

When the majority of the people have clear-cut criteria to go by, criticism and self-criticism can be conducted along proper lines, and these criteria can be applied to people's words and actions to determine whether they are fragrant flowers or poisonous weeds.

Mao Tse-tung

THE CORRIDORS OF POWER

I'm against any deal I'm not in on.

Tip O'Neill,
Speaker of the US House of
Representatives

The true statesman is one who is willing to take risks.

Charles de Gaulle,
French president, 1967

It is the anonymous 'they', the enigmatic 'they' who are in charge. Who is 'they'? I don't know. Nobody knows. Not even 'they' themselves.

Joseph Heller,
US novelist

The speed of exit of a civil servant is directly proportional to the quality of his service.

Ralph Nader,
US consumer campaigner: The Spoiled
System

Governments tend not to solve problems, only to rearrange them.

Ronald Reagan,
governor of California

A government deals with problems, it doesn't solve them.

Abbie Hoffman,
former Yippie! leader: Revolution for the
Hell of It, 1968

There are times in politics when you must be on the right side and lose.

John Kenneth Galbraith,
Canadian-born US economist, 1968

Politics demands a certain rhetoric. It does not demand moral action to fit the rhetoric. Instead politics demands political action.

Julius Lester,
US black activist: Look Out Whitey!, 1968

Government expands to absorb revenues, and then some.

Tom Wicker,
US journalist, 1968

The House Agriculture Committee has not been able to find a single instance of starvation in the US, it reported today. There are many reports of malnutrition, it conceded. But these were attributed to local custom and ignorance.

Joseph A. Loftus
writing in the New York Times, 1968

The two party system . . . is a triumph of the dialectic. It showed that two could be one and one could be two and had probably been fabricated by Hegel for the American market on a subcontract from General Dynamics.

I.F. Stone,
US political commentator, 1968

The two-party system is like those black and white squares which look like a staircase at one moment and a checkerboard the next.

I.F. Stone:
Who are the Democrats?, 1968

Whatever happens in government could have happened differently and it usually would have been better if it had.

Professor Charles Frankel,
US political philosopher: High on Foggy
Bottom, 1969

I did not desire to fire Mr Fitzgerald. I prefer to use the correct term: which is to abolish his job.

Robert C. Seamons,
US Secretary of the Air Force, on the
dismissal of efficiency expert Ernest
Fitzgerald, who had revealed massive
overspending on the Air Force, 1969

Politics is not the art of the possible. It consists of choosing between the disastrous and the unpalatable.

John Kenneth Galbraith,
Canadian-born US economist, 1969

In quantitative terms, which are reliable, the negro is making extraordinary progress . . . The time may have come when the issue of race could benefit from a period of benign neglect.

Daniel Patrick Moynihan,
counsellor to President Nixon, 1970

BOOK OF POLITICAL QUOTES

Always stay in with the outs.

David Halberstam,
US journalist, on political success

I have an absolute rule. I refuse to make a decision that somebody else can make. The first rule of leadership is to save yourself for the big decision. Don't allow your mind to become cluttered with the trivia. Don't let yourself become the issue.

Richard Nixon

Where you stand depends on where you sit.

Rufus Miles,
administrator at the US Department of Health, Education and Welfare

No, we don't stop and figure, we don't think about history or theories or none of that. We just go ahead.

George Wallace,
governor of Alabama, 1972

If you want democracy, a little bit of inefficiency must be accepted.

Hugh Cubitt,
leader of the Westminster City Council, 1972

We believe in what works.

Ron Ziegler,
press secretary for President Nixon

Truth is the glue that holds governments together. Compromise is the oil that makes governments go.

Gerald Ford,
US vice-president, 1973

Too often I find that the volume of paper expands to fill the available briefcases.

Jerry Brown,
governor of California, 1973

Throughout history rulers have invoked secrecy regarding their actions in order to enslave citizens.

Senator Sam Ervin,
chairman of the Congressional Hearings on the Watergate Affair, 1973

If politicians lived on praise and thanks, they'd be forced into some other line of business.

Edward Heath,
British prime minister, 1973

At Harvard it took me ten years to develop a relationship of total hostility with my environment. I want you to know that here I have done it in eighteen months.

Henry Kissinger,
National Security Adviser, on his relationship with the White House

Better a three-day week than a no-day week.

Edward Heath,
British prime minister, during the economic crisis of 1974

Running a country is like playing the organ. You have to use all the stops, pull out one, push back the other. It is not like playing the penny whistle.

Harold Macmillan,
British Conservative elder statesman, 1974

Call it porridge then. You like porridge, don't you.

Dave Barratt,
British Columbian socialist premier, to a lawyer who claimed to admire his policies but loathe their 'socialist' label, 1974

A bronco is something that kicks and bucks, twists and turns, and very seldom goes in one direction. We have one of those things here in Washington — it's called the Congress.

Gerald Ford

As I learned very early on in my life in Whitehall, the acid test of any political question is: what is the alternative?

Lord Trend,
Secretary to the Cabinet, 1975

Flexibility in pursuit of the nation's interests must never be allowed to degenerate into expediency.

Malcolm Fraser,
Australian prime minister, 1976

THE CORRIDORS OF POWER

Today, if you invent a better mousetrap, the government comes along with a better mouse.

Ronald Reagan,
   US presidential candidate, campaigning, 1976

Perhaps you'll be interested in what we're going to do. We're having the President of Mexico here for a state dinner in a few days and Rosalynn and I have never been to a state dinner, so we're going to look at movies of past state dinners to see how it's done.

Jimmy Carter,
   US president, excusing himself after dining with the Supreme Court justices, 1977

Self criticism is a luxury all politicians should indulge in, but it is best done in private.

Malcolm Fraser,
   Australian prime minister, 1977

In a bureaucratic system, useless work drives out useful work.

Milton Friedman,
   monetarist guru of Chile, Israel and UK, 1977

It is not the business of politicians to please everyone.

Margaret Thatcher,
   British opposition leader, 1978

People will tear each other apart if given half a chance. Politics is a jungle and it's getting worse. People want a dictator these days, a man on a white horse. They're looking for a man on a white horse to ride in and tell them what to do. A politician can do anything as long as he manipulates the right symbols.

Jerry Brown,
   governor of California, 1978

Society today is so organized that every individual group has the power to disrupt it. How is their power to be channelled into constructive channels?

James Callaghan,
   British prime minister, 1978

When it is not necessary to make a decision, it is necessary not to make a decision.

Lord Falkland,
   quoted by Paul Dickson: *The Official Rules*, 1978

The quality of legislation passed to deal with a problem is inversely proportional to the volume of media clamour that brought it on.

G. Ray Funkhouser,
   quoted by Paul Dickson: *The Official Rules*, 1978

I was not elected to shut up.

Emma Bonino,
   Italian member of the European Parliament, on disrupting a session, 1979

I can get up at nine and be rested, or I can get up at six and be President.

Jimmy Carter,
   1977

There are two ways of making a Cabinet. One way is to have in it people representing the different points of view within the party, within the broad philosophy. The other way is to have in it only the people who want to go in the direction which every instinct tells me we have to go: clearly, steadily, firmly, with resolution. As Prime Minister, I could not waste my time having internal arguments.

Margaret Thatcher,
   British prime minister, 1979

Take our politicians: they're a bunch of yo-yos. . . . The Presidency is now a cross between a popularity contest and a high-school debate, with an encyclopedia of clichés as the first prize.

Saul Bellow,
   US novelist, 1980

What do we need political trials for if we have psychiatric hospitals?

Dr Georgy Morozov,
   head of the Serbsky Institute of Forensic Psychiatry, Moscow, quoted by A. Podrabinek: *Punitive Medicine*, 1980

I don't mind how much my ministers talk — as long as they do what I say.

Margaret Thatcher,
   British prime minister, 1980

DECLARATIONS OF WAR

It is always easy to begin a war, but very difficult to stop one, since its beginning and end are not under the control of the same man. Anyone, even a coward, can commence a war, but it can be brought to an end only with the consent of the victors.

Sallust,
Roman historian: *Jugurtha*, **first century BC**

To those for whom war is necessary, it is just; and resort to arms is righteous for those to whom no further hope remains.

Livy,
Roman historian: *History*

War is delightful for those who have had no experience of it.

Erasmus,
Dutch scholar

War should be the only study of a prince. He should consider peace only as a breathing time, which gives him leisure to contrive, and furnishes ability to execute military plans.

Niccolò Machiavelli,
Italian statesman: *The Prince*, **1513**

The last argument of kings.

Louis XV,
French king, the motto engraved on his cannon

The horsemen withheld the use of their pistols until they could see the whites of their eyes.

Pietro Duodo,
Venetian ambassador to France, describing the 'pistolade', a new style of cavalry charge

I hate war, for it spoils conversation.

Bernard le Fontenelle,
French scholar

Force and fraud are in war the two cardinal virtues.

Thomas Hobbes,
English philosopher: *Leviathan*, **1651**

Every bullet has its billet.

William III,
English king, 1688

An army, like a serpent, travels on its belly

Frederick the Great,
Prussian king

No soldier can properly fight unless he is fed on beef and beer.

Duke of Marlborough

Silent, till you see the whites of their eyes.

Prince Charles of Prussia,
1745

If he is mad, I wish he would bite my other generals.

George II,
English king, on hearing the comment that General James Wolfe (victor at Quebec) was mad

I have heard the bullets whistle, and believe me, there is something charming in the sound.

George Washington,
future US president, 1754

DECLARATIONS OF WAR

By the push of bayonets. No firing until you see the whites of their eyes.

Frederick the Great,
Prussian king, 1755

Don't fire until you see the whites of their eyes.

Colonel William Prescott
at the Battle of Bunker Hill, 1775

To be prepared for war is one of the most effectual ways of preserving peace.

George Washington,
US president, 1790

War is the faro table of governments, and nations the dupes of the game.

Tom Paine,
English radical pamphleteer: *The Rights of Man*, 1791

My first wish is to see this plague of mankind — war — banished from the earth.

George Washington,
US president, in his farewell address, 1796

The greatest general is he who makes fewest mistakes.

Napoleon Bonaparte

I always say that next to a battle lost, the greatest misery is a battle gained.

Duke of Wellington,
1815

I love a brave soldier who has undergone the baptism of fire.

Napoleon Bonaparte,
1817

War educates the senses, calls into action the will, perfects the physical constitution, brings men into such swift and close collision in critical moments that man measures man.

Ralph Waldo Emerson,
US poet and philosopher

War is nothing but a duel on a larger scale.

Karl von Clausewitz,
Prussian general: *On War*

War belongs not to the arts and sciences, but to the province of social life.

Karl von Clausewitz,
1832

There are no manifestos like cannon and musketry.

Duke of Wellington

War is not merely a political act, but also a political instrument, a continuation of political relations, a carrying out of the same by other means.

Karl von Clausewitz,
Prussian general

The existence of the soldier, next to capital punishment, is the most grievous vestige of barbarism which survives amongst men.

Alfred de Vigny,
French poet, 1835

Is not life miserable enough, comes not death soon enough, without resort to the hideous enginery of War?

Horace Greeley,
US editor, 1846

Military glory, that attractive rainbow that rises in showers of blood, that serpent's eye that charms to destroy.

Abraham Lincoln,
US statesman, opposing war with Mexico, 1848

Better pointed bullets than pointed speeches.

Otto von Bismarck,
German statesman, 1850

It is magnificent, but it is not war.

General Pierre Bosquet,
watching the Charge of the Light Brigade, 1854

They were learning the reality of war, these youngsters, getting face to face with the sickening realization that men get killed uselessly because their generals are stupid, so that desperate encounters, where the last drop of courage has been given, serve the country not at all, and make a patriot look a fool.

Bruce Catton,
US historian: *Mr Lincoln's Army*

My duty is to obey orders.

**Thomas 'Stonewall' Jackson,
  US Civil War general**

It is well that war is so terrible, or we should get too fond of it.

**Robert E. Lee,
  US Civil War general**

It is not by speeches and resolutions that the great questions of the time are decided...but by iron and blood.

**Otto von Bismarck,
  German statesman, 1862**

We have met on a great battlefield of that war. We have come to dedicate a portion of that field as a final resting place for those who here gave their lives that the nation might live. It is altogether fitting and proper that we should do this. But in a larger sense, we cannot dedicate, we cannot consecrate, we cannot hallow this ground. The brave men, living and dead, who struggled here, have consecrated it far above our poor power to add or detract. The world will little note, nor long remember, what we say here. But it can never forget what they did here.

**Abraham Lincoln,
  US president, 'the Gettysburg Address',
1863**

The art of war is simple enough. Find out where your enemy is. Get at him as soon as you can. Strike at him as hard as you can, and keep moving on

**Ulysses S. Grant,
  US president**

Anyone who has ever looked into the glazed eyes of a soldier dying on a battlefield will think before starting a war.

**Otto von Bismarck,
  German statesman, 1867**

In the time of war, the loudest patriots are the greatest profiteers.

**August Bebel,
  German socialist, 1870**

We are so well equipped that if war were to last ten years, we should not have to buy the button of a soldier's gaiter.

**Marshall Edmond Leboeuf
  prior to the French defeat by Germany,
1870**

War is, in a sense, one condition of progress — the whipcut preventing a country from going to sleep. And forcing satisfied mediocrity to shake off its apathy.

**Ernest Renan,
  French critic, 1871**

A war, even the most victorious, is a national misfortune.

**Helmuth von Moltke,
  German general, 1880**

There is many a boy here today who looks on war as all glory, but boys, it is all hell. You can bear this warning voice to generations yet to come. I look upon war with horror.

**William Tecumseh Sherman,
  US Civil War general, 1880**

War is hell when you're getting licked.

**William Tecumseh Sherman,
  his actual words, according to Brigadier-
General Henry J. O'Reilly, 1931**

Hold the fort, for I am coming!

**William Tecumseh Sherman;
  what he actually said was 'Relief is
coming!', but the message has been thus
sanctified since 1864**

As long as war is regarded as wicked it will always have its fascination. When it is looked upon as vulgar, it will cease to be popular.

**Oscar Wilde,
  Irish poet, wit and dramatist: 'Intentions',
1891**

Perhaps my dynamite plants will put an end to war sooner than your congresses. On the day two army corps can annihilate each other in one second, all civilized nations will recoil from war in horror.

**Alfred Nobel,
  Swedish armaments manufacturer,
speaking at a pacifist meeting, 1892**

DECLARATIONS OF WAR

Battle, n. A method of untying with the teeth a political knot that would not yield to the tongue.

Ambrose Bierce,
  US journalist and author: *The Devil's Dictionary,* **1881-1911**

When was a war not a war? When it was carried out by methods of barbarism in South Africa.

Sir Henry Campbell-Bannerman,
  British Liberal Party leader, on the Boer War, 1901

When the military man approaches, the world locks up its spoons and packs off its womankind.

George Bernard Shaw,
  Irish playwright

Capitalism carries in itself war, like the clouds carry rain.

Jean Jaurès,
  French prime minister, 1902

No triumph of peace is quite so great as the supreme triumph of war.

Theodore Roosevelt,
  US president, Nobel Peace Prize winner, 1906

Military service produces moral imbecility, ferocity and cowardice, and defence of nations must be undertaken by the civil enterprise of men enjoying all the rights and liberties of citizenship.

George Bernard Shaw,
  Irish playwright: *John Bull's Other Island,* **1907**

War is a biological necessity of the first importance, a regulative element in the life of mankind which cannot be dispensed with...but it is not only a biological law, but a moral obligation and, as such, an indispensable factor in civilization.

Friedrich von Bernhardi,
  German general: *Germany and the Next War,* **1912**

Just for a word, 'neutrality', a word which in wartime has so often been disregarded, just for a scrap of paper, Great Britain is going to make war.

Theobald von Bethmann-Hollweg,
  German statesman, to Sir Edward Goschen, 1914

YOUR COUNTRY NEEDS YOU

London Opinion,
  front cover, 1914

It is a great opportunity, an opportunity which comes once in many centuries to the children of men. For most generations sacrifice comes in drab guise and weariness of spirit. It comes to you today as to all of us, in the form of the glow and thrill of a great movement for liberty that impels millions throughout Europe to the same noble end.

David Lloyd George,
  British Chancellor of the Exchequer, on the outbreak of the Great War, 1914

My right has been rolled up; my left has been driven back; my centre has been smashed. I have ordered an advance from all directions.

General Ferdinand Foch,
  in a message to Marshall Joffre during the First Battle of the Marne, 1914

Blood alone moves the wheels of history.

Benito Mussolini,
  1914

War is too important to be left to the generals.

Georges Clemenceau,
  French prime minister

They shall not pass.

General Pétain
  at Verdun, 1916

We have to make war as we must, and not as we would like to.

Lord Kitchener,
  British general

WOMEN OF BRITAIN SAY GO!

Propaganda slogan,
  during the Great War

Soldiers are citizens of death's grey land.

Siegfried Sassoon,
  English poet: 'Dreamers'

BOOK OF POLITICAL QUOTES

War is a series of catastrophes which result in a victory.

Georges Clemenceau,
   French prime minister

The world must be made safe for democracy. . . . We shall fight for the things which we have always carried nearest our hearts, for democracy.

Woodrow Wilson,
   US president, taking America into the Great War, 1917

Every position must be held to the last man. There must be no retirement. With our backs to the wall and believing in the justice of our cause, each one of us must fight to the end.

Field Marshal Sir Douglas Haig,
   Order of the Day opposing the major German offensive of April 1918

Come on you sons of bitches! Do you want to live for ever!

Gunnery Sergeant Daniel Daly,
   US Marine Corps, at Belleau Wood, 1918

As long as there is mankind there will be wars. Only dreamers believe otherwise.

Field Marshal Hindenburg,
   1919

The professional military mind is by necessity an inferior and unimaginative mind; no man of high intellectual quality would willingly imprison his gifts in such a calling.

H.G. Wells,
   English author: *The Outline of History*, 1920

The Italian proletariat needs a bloodbath for its force to be renewed.

Benito Mussolini,
   1920

There is no record in history of a nation that ever gained anything valuable by being unable to defend itself.

H.L. Mencken,
   US philologist, editor and satirist

There is nothing that war has achieved that we could not better achieve without it.

Havelock Ellis,
   English psychologist

When the leaders speak of peace/The common folk know/That war is coming./When the leaders curse war/The mobilization order is already written out.

Bertolt Brecht,
   German playwright

We hear war called murder. It is not. It is suicide.

Ramsay MacDonald,
   British prime minister, 1930

The bomber will always get through. The only defence is offence, which means that you have to kill more women and children more quickly than the enemy if you want to save yourselves.

Stanley Baldwin,
   Lord President of the Council during the MacDonald coalition, 1932

That this House will in no circumstance fight for its King and Country.

Oxford Union Society:
   a successfully carried debate motion, 1933

War alone brings up to its highest tension all human energy and puts the stamp of nobility upon the peoples who have the courage to face it.

Benito Mussolini,
   1935

War is a contagion.

Franklin D. Roosevelt,
   US president, 1935

There will be no mediation. Criminals and their victims cannot live together.

Francisco Franco
   condoning his terror-tactics during the Spanish Civil War, 1937

Guns will make us powerful, butter will only make us fat.

Hermann Goering,
   Nazi leader, 1936

Adolf Hitler and Eva Raf . . . in the style of Tristram and Isolde/Popperfoto

The one means to win the easiest victory over reason — terror and force.

Adolf Hitler:
    Mein Kampf, **1924**

Sometime they'll give a war and nobody will come.

Carl Sandburg,
    US poet: *The People, Yes*, **1936**

There is some mysterious cycle in human events. To some generations much is given; of other generations much is expected. This generation of Americans has a rendezvous with destiny.... We are fighting to save a great and precious form of government for ourselves and for the world.

Franklin D. Roosevelt,
    US president, 1936

The most shocking fact about war is that its victims and its instruments are individual human beings and that these individual beings are condemned by the monstrous conventions of politics to murder or be murdered in quarrels not their own.

Aldous Huxley,
    English novelist and essayist: 'The Olive Tree', 1937

On the wall in chalk is written/They want war/He who wrote it/Is already dead.

Bertolt Brecht,
    German playwright: *Songs, Poems and Choruses*, 1934

In war, whichever side may call itself the victor, there are no winners, but all are losers.

Neville Chamberlain,
    British prime minister, 1938

The truth is that any real advance, let alone any genuinely revolutionary change, can only begin when the mass of the people definitely refuse capitalist-imperialist war.... So long as they show themselves willing to fight 'in defence of democracy' or 'against fascism', or for any other fly-blown slogan, the same tricks will be played on them again and again.

George Orwell,
    English author and critic, 1938

War cannot be divorced from politics for a single moment.

Mao Tse-tung,
    1938

War is like love — it always finds a way.

Bertolt Brecht,
    German playwright: *Mother Courage*, 1939

I shall give a propagandist reason for starting this war, no matter whether it is plausible or not. The victor will not be asked afterwards whether he told the truth or not. When starting and waging war it is not right that matters, but victory.

Adolf Hitler,
    German führer, briefing his generals, 1939

We shall not flag or fail. We shall fight in France, we shall fight on the seas and oceans, we shall fight with growing strength in the air. We shall defend our island, whatever the cost may be, we shall fight on the beaches, we shall fight on the landing grounds, we shall fight in the fields and in the streets, we shall fight in the hills; we shall never surrender.

Winston Churchill,
    British prime minister, 1940

To make a people great it is necessary to send them into battle, even if you have to kick them in the pants.

Benito Mussolini,
    1940

I wouldn't tell the people anything till the war was over, and then I'd tell them who won.

Anonymous US military censor,
    1941

Everlasting peace will come to the world when the last man has slain the last but one.

Adolf Hitler,
    German führer, 1942

Battle is the most magnificent competition in which a human being can indulge. It brings out all that is best. It removes all that is base.

General George S. Patton

Look at an infantryman's eyes and you can tell how much war he has seen.

William H. Mauldin,
    US cartoonist, 1944

DECLARATIONS OF WAR

The idea of treating wars as other than the harshest means of settling questions of very existence is ridiculous. Every war costs blood, and the smell of blood arouses in man all the instincts which have lain within us since the beginning of the world: deeds of violence, the intoxication of murder and many other things. Everything else is empty babble. A human war exists only in human brains.

Adolf Hitler,
German führer, 1942

I love war and responsibility and excitement. Peace is going to be hell on me.

General George S. Patton

We must not be squeamish when we hear the figure of seventeen thousand shot.

Hans Frank,
Nazi governor of Poland

NUTS!

Anthony McAuliffe,
US commander, replying to the German demand for a surrender at Bastogne, 1944

But then, that's what young men are there for.

Adolf Hitler
commenting on the especially heavy casualty lists among junior officers

War would always exist, because there will always be boys of twenty to bring it into existence by dint of love.

Henri de Montherlant,
French poet and essayist

An army without culture is a dull-witted army. And a dull-witted army cannot defeat the enemy.

Mao Tse-tung,
1944

We want to get this thing over and then get the hell out of here and get at those purple-pissing Japs!! The shortest road home is through Berlin and Tokyo. We'll win this war, but we'll win it only by showing the enemy we have more guts than they have or ever will have.

General George S. Patton,
in his D-Day pep talk, 1944

Only one thing is valid: orders!

Theodor Eicke,
commandant of Dachau, motto on his writing paper

A weapon of unparalleled power is being created. Unless, indeed, some international agreement about the control of the use of the new active materials can be obtained, any temporary advantage, however great, may be outweighed by a perpetual menace to human society.

Niels Bohr,
Danish physicist, warning Churchill and Roosevelt of the dangers of developing nuclear weapons, 1944

You can thank God that twenty years from now, with your grandson on your knee, and he asks you 'What did you do in the war?', you won't have to shift him to the other knee, cough, and say 'I shovelled shit in Louisiana.'

General George S. Patton
in his D-Day pep talk, 1944

My God, what have we done?

Robert Lewis,
US Air Force captain, after his plane *Enola Gay* destroyed Hiroshima with a nuclear bomb, 1945

The atomic bomb is another powerful weapon in the arsenal of righteousness.

Harry S. Truman,
US president, 1945

We live under a system by which the many are exploited by the few, and war is the ultimate sanction of that exploitation.

Harold Laski,
English political scientist, 1945

Oh, you know, one became such a blackguard.

General Wilhelm Keitel,
on trial at Nuremberg, 1946

I have never met anybody who wasn't against war. Even Hitler and Mussolini were, according to themselves.

David Low,
English political cartoonist, 1946

That a man can take pleasure in marching in fours to the strains of a band is enough to make me despise him.

Albert Einstein,
  German-born physicist

What difference does it make to the dead, the orphans and the homeless, whether the mad destruction is wrought under the name of totalitarianism or the holy name of liberty and democracy?

Mahatma Gandhi:
  ***Non-Violence in Peace and War*, 1948**

The people are like water and the army is like fish.

Mao Tse-tung

The idea that every nation ought to have an atomic bomb, like every woman of fashion ought to have a mink coat, is deplorable.

Clement Attlee

In war there is no second prize for the runner-up.

Omar Bradley,
  US general, 1950

Mahatma Gandhi as a young man/Popperfoto

DECLARATIONS OF WAR

People who are vigorous and brutal often find war enjoyable, provided that it is a victorious war, and there is not too much interference with rape and plunder. This is a great help in persuading people that wars are righteous.

Bertrand Russell,
English philosopher: *Unpopular Essays,*
1950

Whose finger on the trigger?

Daily Mirror
headline on the eve of the 1951 General Election

The wrong war, at the wrong place, at the wrong time, with the wrong enemy.

Omar Bradley,
US general, on the Korean War, 1951

My policy? Sir, I am a soldier. I do not have a policy.

Colonel Henri Girard
to pressmen on being appointed governor of Algeria

In war there is no substitute for victory.

General Douglas MacArthur

After each war there is a little less democracy to save.

Brooks Atkinson,
US critic: *Once Around the Sun,* **1951**

A prisoner of war is a man who tries to kill you and fails, and then asks you not to kill him.

Winston Churchill,
British prime minister, 1952

The way to win an atomic war is to make certain it never starts.

General Omar Bradley,
1952

In the final choice the soldier's pack is not so heavy as the prisoner's chains.

Dwight D. Eisenhower,
US president, 1953

When it's a question of peace, one must talk to the Devil himself.

Edouard Herriot,
French Radical-Socialist statesman, 1953

It is important when you haven't any ammunition to have a butt on your rifle.

Winston Churchill,
British prime minister, 1954

The Zef-Zef incident was an isolated case that will not recur, an unfortunate consequence of warfare.

French Foreign Ministry
commenting on the Zef-Zef massacre in Algeria, in which hundreds of non-combatants were murdered by French troops, 1955

War is a very rough game, but I think politics is worse.

Field Marshal Lord Montgomery,
1956

I hate war only as a soldier who has lived it can, only as one who has seen its brutality, its futility, its stupidity.

Dwight D. Eisenhower

How vile and despicable war seems to me. I would rather be hacked to pieces than take part in such an abominable business.

Albert Einstein

We are not at war with Egypt. We are in an armed conflict.

Anthony Eden,
British prime minister, on the Suez Crisis, 1956

It is an unfortunate fact that we can only secure peace by preparing for war.

John F. Kennedy,
US president, 1960

Wars are always popular for the first thirty days.

Arthur Schlesinger Jr,
US presidential adviser

Mankind must put an end to war, or war will put an end to mankind.

John F. Kennedy,
US president, 1961

BOOK OF POLITICAL QUOTES

I fired MacArthur because he wouldn't respect the authority of a president. I didn't fire him because he was a dumb son of a bitch, although he was, but that's not against the law for generals. If it was, half to three quarters of them would be in jail.

Harry S. Truman,
 former US president, 1961

Only when arms are sufficient beyond doubt can we be certain without doubt that they will never be employed.

John F. Kennedy,
 US president, 1961

People live in constant fear lest the storm that every moment threatens them should break upon them with dreadful violence.

Pope John XXIII
 in his encyclical 'Pacem in Terris', 1963

The end move in politics is always to pick up a gun.

R. Buckminster Fuller,
 US inventor and engineer

We are the unwilling, led by the unqualified, doing the unnecessary for the ungrateful.

Graffito
 on GI helmets during the Vietnam War

If you've got 'em by the balls, their hearts and minds will follow.

The Green Berets'
 (special forces) motto

The subjects of interrogation so often die under questioning that intelligence seems to be a secondary matter.

Malcolm W. Browne,
 US journalist, on torture in Vietnam: *The New Face of War,* **1965**

The guns, the bombs, the rockets and the warships are all symbols of human failure. They are necessary symbols. They protect what we cherish. But they are witness to human folly.

Lyndon B. Johnson,
 US president, 1965

Hell, Vietnam is just like the Alamo. Hell, it's just like if you were down at that gate and you were surrounded and you damn well needed somebody. Well, by God, I'm going to go. And I thank the Lord that I've got men who want to go with me, from Macnamara right down to the littlest private who's carrying a gun.

Lyndon B. Johnson
 addressing the National Security Council, 1965

No Viet Cong ever called me nigger.

Muhammad Ali,
 world heavyweight boxing champion, refusing to serve in Vietnam, 1966

There's no better way to fight than goin' out to shoot VC. An' there's nothing I like better than killin' Cong.

General James F. Hollingsworth
 who took out his personal helicopter and M-16 machine gun to hunt the guerillas, 1966

The atom bomb is a paper tiger which the US reactionaries use to scare people. It looks terrible, but in fact it isn't.

Mao Tse-tung:
 Quotations from Chairman Mao, **1966**

British defence policy is like a sacred cow. We are neither feeding it nor killing it.

Christopher Mayhew,
 British MP, 1966

People who dismiss the domino theory are all wet.

General William Westmoreland,
 Commander in Chief US troops in Vietnam

Warfare is a means and not an end. Warfare is the tool of revolutionaries. The important thing is the revolution, the revolutionary ideas, the revolutionary cause, revolutionary objectives, revolutionary sentiments and revolutionary virtues.

Fidel Castro,
 Cuban president, in his eulogy to Che Guevara, 1967

DECLARATIONS OF WAR

You've got to forget about this civilian stuff. Whenever you drop bombs you're going to hit civilians.

Senator Barry Goldwater,
  pooh-poohing anti-war protesters, 1967

Tell the Vietnamese they've got to draw in their horns and stop aggression or we're going to bomb them back to the Stone Age.

General Curtis LeMay,
  US Air Force, 1967

History is littered with wars which everybody knew would never happen.

Enoch Powell,
  British Conservative MP, 1967

We must be willing to continue our bombing until we have destroyed every work of man in North Vietnam if this is what it takes to win the war.

General Curtis LeMay,
  US Air Force, 1967

BOMBS AWAY WITH CURT LEMAY!

Slogan,
  1967

They were just like regular punishment cells — isolation cells like in every prison. I had it all investigated. For that climate things were a great deal more humane, they were open to the air and sea breezes.

Robert Komer,
  CIA agent in charge of the 'tiger cages',
nine-foot-deep pits covered with iron gratings
for the detention of alleged Viet Cong

Congratulations. You have been killed through the courtesy of the 361st. Yours truly, Pink Panther 20. [On the reverse side] Call us for death and destruction night and day.

Captain Lynn A. Carlson:
  'visiting cards' dropped from his helicopter
gunship after attacks in Vietnam, 1968

We have not sought to impose a military solution. Regrettably wars have their built-in escalation.

Senator Hubert Humphrey,
  1968

We lost sight of one of the cardinal maxims of guerilla war — the guerilla wins if he does not lose, the conventional army loses if it does not win.

Henry Kissinger,
  Director of Defense Studies, Harvard
University, on US errors in Vietnam, in
Foreign Affairs **magazine, 1968**

Highly intelligent citizens with a broad grasp of our military potential and future needs...well equipped to make meaningful recommendations for policy.

Melvin Laird,
  US Secretary of Defense, on the military
leadership, 1968

I sincerely believe that any arms race with the Soviet Union would act to our benefit. I believe that we can out-invent, out-research, out-engineer and out-produce the USSR in any area from sling-shots to space weapons and in doing so become more prosperous while the Soviets become progressively poorer. That is the faith I have in the free enterprise system.

General Curtis LeMay,
  US Air Force: *Is America in Danger?*, **1968**

The present ratio of about ninety per cent killing to ten per cent pacification is just about right.

Colonel George S. Patton III,
  1968

It became necessary to destroy the town to save it.

US Army dispatch
  on the razing of Ben Tre, 1968

The American attitude towards the war is wholesome.

General William Westmoreland,
  C in C US troops in Vietnam, 1968

For a second I said to myself, maybe I screwed up in basic training, missed a couple of days, and maybe this is what war is all about.

Michael Bernhardt,
  US soldier at the My Lai massacre, 1969

Thank heavens for the military-industrial complex: its ultimate aim is peace in our time, regardless of the aggressive militaristic image that the left wing is attempting to give it.

**Senator Barry Goldwater,
1969**

Sir, we will go waltzing Matilda with you.

**John Gorton,
Australian prime minister, committing
Australians to Vietnam, 1969**

Deterrence is our primary mission, and peace is our profession. We have a mixed force of bombers and missiles to carry out this mission.

**General Bruce C. Halloway,
C in C Strategic Air Command, 1969**

The suggestion that Australian troops in Vietnam are breaking off contact with the enemy to avoid casualties is anathema to the traditions of our army.

**Phillip Lynch,
Australian Minister for the Army, 1969**

There were about forty or forty-five people that were gathered in the centre of the village — men, women, children, babies — Lieutenant Calley...started shooting them. And he told me to start shooting. I poured about four clips into the group....I fired them on automatic....I might have killed fourteen or fifteen of them....So we started to gather them up, more people. We put them in the hootch and we dropped a hand grenade in there with them....They had about seventy or seventy-five people all gathered up...so we threw ours in with them and Lieutenant Calley started pushing them off...into the ravine...and just started using automatics on them...men, women, children and babies....It just seemed like it was the natural thing to do at the time.

**Private Paul Meadlo,
interviewed on CBS-TV about the My Lai
massacre, 1969**

I consider the Department of Defense to be a Department of Peace.

**Richard Nixon,
US president, 1969**

I don't hate the North Vietnamese, but I do like to see the arms and legs fly.

**Colonel George S. Patton III,
1969**

This is the only war in history where the fighting man can sleep in a warm bed, eat a good breakfast, take a helicopter ride to battle, pause for a lunch break and return to base in time for supper and a look at the day's fighting on the evening's telecast. Vietnam is the first commuter war.

**Colonel James Rivers,
1969**

The arms race is based on an optimistic view of technology and a pessimistic view of man. It assumes that there is no limit to the ingenuity of science and no limit to the deviltry of human beings.

**I.F. Stone,
US political commentator: *Nixon and the
Arms Race,* 1969**

We maintain our strength, but we maintain it for peace.

**Richard Nixon,
US president, 1969**

I may have a lack of imagination, but I fail to see a moral issue involved.

**Henry Kissinger,
US National Security Adviser, on the illegal
bombing of Cambodia, 1970**

You always write it's bombing, bombing, bombing. It's not bombing — it's air support!

**Colonel H.E. Opfer,
US air attaché in Phnom Penh, to reporters**

This is not an invasion of Cambodia....We take this action not for the purpose of expanding the war into Cambodia, but for the purpose of ending the war in Vietnam and winning the just peace we all desire.

**Richard Nixon,
US president, addressing America on TV,
1970**

DECLARATIONS OF WAR

We weren't in My Lai to kill human beings, really. We were there to kill *ideology* that is carried by—I don't know—pawns, blobs, pieces of flesh....And I wasn't in My Lai to destroy intelligent men. I was there to destroy an intangible idea.

Lieutenant William Calley,
instigator of the My Lai massacre, 1971

Maybe if I were president, I could change things. Till then I'm like anybody else. I'll carry America's orders out. For that's what the army is—a chisel. It has to keep sharp and let the American people use it.

Lieutenant William Calley

War is the most exciting and dramatic thing in life. In fighting to the death you feel terribly relaxed when you manage to come through.

General Moshe Dayan,
Israeli soldier and politician, 1972

I could have ended the war in a month. I could have made North Vietnam look like a mud puddle.

Senator Barry Goldwater,
1972

It was not a bombing of Cambodia. It was a bombing of North Vietnamese in Cambodia.

Henry Kissinger,
US National Security Adviser, 1973

You can't win through negotiations what you can't win on the battlefield.

Henry Kissinger,
1973

Those who note, those who have the courage to admit that the Third World War has already happened, that it is almost something of the past, that it ended this very year and that the free world has irretrievably lost it, are very few.

Alexander Solzhenitsyn,
Russian dissident author, 1975

The justification for the war is the re-election of the President.

William C. Sullivan,
US politician, justifying the continued US involvement in South-East Asia, 1972

When you are at war you don't call in the Salvation Army.

Joshua Nkomo,
Popular Front leader in Zimbabwe-Rhodesia, 1977

The history of warfare over the past couple of centuries can be thought of in terms of soldiers lowering themselves closer and closer to the ground and then deeper and deeper into it.

Len Deighton,
English writer: *Fighter*, 1977

We are living in a pre-war and not a post-war world.

Eugene Rostow,
US academic and strategian, 1977

The arms business is founded on human folly. That is why its depths will never be plumbed and why it will go on forever. All weapons are defensive, and all spare parts non-lethal. The plainest print cannot be read through a solid gold sovereign, or a rouble or a golden eagle.

Sam Cummings,
international arms dealer, 1978

I question whether God himself would wish me to hide behind the principles of non-violence while innocent persons were being slaughtered.

Bishop Abel Muzorewa,
Zimbabwean leader, 1978

The most persistent sound reverberating through man's history is the beating of war drums.

Arthur Koestler,
Hungarian-born author and journalist, 1978

I HAVE A DREAM

Nothing is so firmly believed as what we least know.

Michel de Montaigne,
French moralist

No man who knows aught, can be so stupid to deny that all men naturally were born free.

John Milton,
English poet and author: *The Tenure of Kings and Magistrates*, 1649

Where the annual elections end, there slavery begins.

John Adams,
US statesman, 1776

Those who expect to reap the blessings of freedom must, like men, undergo the fatigue of supporting it.

Tom Paine,
English radical pamphleteer: 'The American Crisis' 1776

'Tom Paine's nightly rest'/Mary Evans Picture Library

I HAVE A DREAM

Necessity hath no law.

Oliver Cromwell,
Protector of the commonwealth of England
Scotland and Ireland, 1654

In this world nothing is certain but death and taxes.

Benjamin Franklin,
US statesman, 1789

The only thing necessary for the triumph of evil is that good men do nothing.

Edmund Burke,
British statesman

All stones are cut to build the structure of freedom. You can build a palace or a tomb of the same stones.

Louis Antoine de Saint Just,
French revolutionary, 1794

Let the human mind loose. It must be loosed. It will be loose. Superstition and despotism cannot confine it.

John Adams,
US president, 1797

To innovate is not to reform.

Edmund Burke,
British statesman

Nothing is more difficult, and therefore more precious, that to be able to decide.

Napoleon Bonaparte:
Maxims, 1804-15

It is error alone which needs support of government. Truth can stand by itself.

Thomas Jefferson,
US president, 1804

The poor man commands respect, the beggar must always command anger.

Napoleon Bonaparte:
Maxims, 1804-15

Throw theory into the fire. It only spoils life.

Mikhail Bakunin,
Russian anarchist

One never climbs so high as when he knows not where he is going.

Napoleon Bonaparte.
Also attributed to Oliver Cromwell

My maxim was: 'La carrière est ouverte aux talents', without distinction of birth or fortune.

Napoleon Bonaparte,
1817

Man exists for his own sake and not to add a labourer to the State.

Ralph Waldo Emerson,
US poet and philosopher, 1839

Youth is a blunder; Manhood a struggle; Old Age a regret.

Benjamin Disraeli,
British statesman: Coningsby, 1844

He who anticipates his century is generally persecuted when living and is always pilfered when dead.

Benjamin Disraeli

It is harder to preserve than to obtain liberty.

John C. Calhoun,
US politician, 1848

Better that the whole world should be destroyed and perish utterly than that a free man should refrain from one act to which his nature moves him.

Karl Marx

A majority is always the best repartee.

Benjamin Disraeli,
British statesman: Tancred, 1847

The State is not armed with superior wit or honesty, but with superior physical strength. I was not born to be forced, I will breathe after my own fashion Let us see who is the strongest.

Henry David Thoreau,
US philosopher: On the Duty of Civil Disobedience, 1848

BOOK OF POLITICAL QUOTES

Do not look for solutions in this book — there are none. In general, modern man has no solutions.

Alexander Herzen,
   Russian political thinker and writer: *From the Other Shore,* **1847-50**

A just cause is not ruined by a few mistakes.

Feodor Dostoyevsky,
   Russian author

Greater than the tread of mighty armies is an idea whose time has come.

Victor Hugo,
   French author, 1852

One has to arrange life as best one can, because there is no libretto...History is all improvisation, all will, all extempore — there are no frontiers, no intineraries.

Alexander Herzen,
   Russian political writer and thinker: *From the Other Shore,* **1847-50**

What kills a skunk is the publicity it gives itself.

Abraham Lincoln
   on slavery

The end of generations is itself. Not only does Nature never make one generation the means for the attainment of some future goal, but she doesn't concern herself with the future at all; like Cleopatra she is ready to dissolve the pearl in wine for a moment's pleasure.

Alexander Herzen,
   Russian political writer and thinker: *From the Other Shore,* **1847-50**

If all mankind, minus one, were of one opinion, and only one person were of the contrary opinion, mankind would be no more justified in silencing that one person, than he, if he had the power, would be justified in silencing mankind.

John Stuart Mill,
   English philosopher: 'On Liberty', 1859

It is easier to be critical than to be correct.

Benjamin Disraeli,
   British statesman, 1860

Among free men there can be no successful appeal from the ballot to the bullet, and those who take such appeal are sure to lose their cause and pay the costs.

Abraham Lincoln,
   US president, 1865

Apologies only account for that which they do not alter.

Benjamin Disraeli,
   British statesman, 1871

We cannot safely leave politics to politicians or political economy to college professors.

Henry George,
   US sociologist, 1879

To get rid of an enemy one must love him.

Leo Tolstoy,
   Russian author

When a nation's young men are conservative, its funeral bell is already rung.

Henry Ward Beecher,
   US editor and clergyman, 1887

Nothing so needs reforming as other people's habits.

Mark Twain,
   US author, 1894

A thing is not necessarily true because a man dies for it.

Oscar Wilde,
   Irish poet, wit and dramatist

There is a homely adage which runs 'Speak softly and carry a big stick and you will go far.'

Theodore Roosevelt,
   US president, 1901

Don't let good fellowship get the least hold of you.

John D. Rockefeller,
   US millionaire: his advice to young men

I HAVE A DREAM

Stand the gaff, play fair, and be a good man to camp out with.

Theodore Roosevelt:
   his personal philosophy

A right is only worth fighting for when it can be put into operation.

Woodrow Wilson

Those who cannot remember the past are condemned to repeat it.

George Santayana,
   Spanish-born US philosopher, poet and novelist: *The Life of Reason,* **1905-06**

Great things are achieved by guessing the direction of one's century.

Giuseppe Mazzini,
   Italian patriot, 1910

Martyrdom is the only way in which a man can become famous without ability.

George Bernard Shaw,
   Irish playwright: *Fabian Essays*

While the State exists there is no freedom; when there is freedom there will be no State.

V.I. Lenin:
   The State and Revolution, **1917**

When great changes occur in history, when great principles are involved, as a rule the majority are wrong.

Eugene V. Debs,
   US socialist, 1918

Nothing matters very much, and few things matter at all.

Arthur Balfour,
   British statesman

Nothing great can be achieved without faith.

Antonio de Salazar,
   Portuguese dictator, 1921

Punctuality, regularity, discipline, industry, thoroughness are a set of 'slave' virtues.

G.D.H. Cole,
   English Fabian, 1922

Morality is that which serves to destroy the old, exploiting society.

V.I. Lenin

Fact is all.

Benito Mussolini

You would not enjoy Nietzsche, sir. He is fundamentally unsound.

P.G. Wodehouse,
   English novelist: *Carry On, Jeeves,* **1925**

To die for an idea — it is unquestionably noble. But how much nobler it would be if men died for ideas that were true.

H.L. Mencken,
   US philosopher, editor and satirist

A platitude is simply a truth repeated till people get tired of hearing it.

Stanley Baldwin,
   British prime minister, 1924

One must do the greatest good for one's friends and the utmost harm to one's enemies.

Benito Mussolini,
   1925

Gods and beasts, that is what our world is made of.

Adolf Hitler

EVERY MAN A KING, BUT NO MAN WEARS A CROWN.

Huey P. Long,
   governor of Louisiana, campaign slogan, 1928

Biography should be written by an acute enemy.

Arthur Balfour,
   former British prime minister, 1927

Let us have a dagger between our teeth, a bomb in our hands and an infinite scorn in our hearts.

Benito Mussolini,
   1928

BOOK OF POLITICAL QUOTES

The earth is the heritage of the strong, and the future belongs to the victorious people who have a right to life. The struggle for existence, that is, is also one for domination.

**Ahmad Hussein,
   founder of the Young Egypt movement,
1928**

On the whole women think of love and men of gold braid or something of that nature. Beyond that, people think only of happiness — which doesn't exist.

Charles de Gaulle

It ain't enough to get the breaks, you got to know how to use them.

**Huey P. Long,
   governor of Louisiana**

Men are freest when they are most unconscious of freedom. The shout is a rattling of chains and always was.

**D.H. Lawrence,
   English author**

There is more to life than increasing its speed.

Mahatma Gandhi

General Charles de Gaulle/Publisher's files

I HAVE A DREAM

The State is made for man, not man for the State.

Albert Einstein,
German-born physicist: _The World as I See It,_ 1934

Destroy him as you will, the bourgeois always bounces up. Execute him, expropriate him, starve him out _en masse_, and he reappears in your children.

Cyril Connolly,
English critic and essayist, 1937

Man is not the sum of what he has, but the totality of what he does not yet have, of what he might have.

Jean-Paul Sartre,
French existentialist philosopher: _Situations,_ 1939

Modern collectivism is the last barrier raised by man against a meeting with himself.

Martin Buber,
Israeli philosopher

De mortuis nil nisi bunkum.

Harold Laski,
English political scientist

Truth never damages a cause that is just.

Mahatma Gandhi

We must be aware of needless innovations, especially when guided by logic.

Winston Churchill,
British prime minister, 1942

The higher a monkey climbs, the more you see of his behind.

General Joseph 'Vinegar Joe' Stilwell

You are noticed more if you stand on your head than you are if you are the right way up.

George Orwell,
English essayist and critic, quoted in the _New Statesman,_ 1974

Eternal truths will neither be true nor eternal unless they have fresh meaning for every new social situation.

Franklin D. Roosevelt,
US president, 1940

The dagger plunged in the name of Freedom is plunged into the breast of Freedom.

Jose Marti,
Cuban patriot, 1942

Take calculated risks, that is quite different from being rash.

General George S. Patton,
1944

Man's capacity for justice makes democracy possible, but man's inclination to injustice makes democracy necessary.

Reinhold Niebuhr,
US theologian, 1944

But you know, don't you, that in my dictionary 'duty' is written in capitals.

Martin Bormann,
Nazi leader

You can't repeal human nature by an Act of Congress.

Bernard Baruch,
US financier and statesman

No good deed goes unpunished.

Clare Booth Luce,
US diplomat

A pint of sweat will save a gallon of blood.

General George S. Patton,
1947

It is better for a man to go wrong in freedom than to go right in chains.

T.H. Huxley,
English biologist and writer

And in the last analysis, success is what matters.

Adolf Hitler

No matter what you have, you're missing your purpose unless your purpose is integrated into what you call your recreation.

Huey P. Newton,
  1973

For evil to triumph, it is only necessary for good men to do nothing.

Frank Chapple,
  General Secretary of EEPTU, 1974

Always give your best. Never get discouraged. Never be petty. Always remember, others may hate you. Those who hate you don't win unless you hate them. And then you destroy yourself.

Richard Nixon,
  US president, in his farewell speech to the White House staff, 1974

You cannot oppose violence with anything but violence.

Juan Peròn,
  exiled Argentinian president, 1974

There are hazards in anything one does, but there are greater hazards in doing nothing.

Shirley Williams,
  British politician, 1974

The key to not getting caught is to change your class and your culture.

Abbie Hoffman,
  Yippie! leader, 1975

Mercy is not what every criminal is entitled to. What he is entitled to is justice.

Lord Hailsham,
  English jurist, 1975

This is the only way of life in which you can indulge in total vanity without a sense of guilt. Your looks are your passport.

Abbie Hoffman,
  Yippie! leader, on living underground, 1975

A little uncertainty is good for everyone.

Henry Kissinger,
  1976

Greatness is a road leading towards the unknown.

Charles de Gaulle

We must learn to distinguish morality from moralizing.

Henry Kissinger,
  adviser to the Rockefeller family, 1976

I would define morality as enlightened self-interest. That old Platonic ideal that there are certain pure moral forms just isn't where we are.

Andrew Young,
  US ambassador to the United Nations

To deal with individual human needs at the small, everyday level can actually be noble sometimes.

Jimmy Carter

Life is like ice cream: there's thirty-eight flavours out there and you just choose the flavour you want.

Bob Kunst,
  US gay rights activist, 1977

Who wouldn't eat caviar if it was offered?

Reginald Maudling,
  British Conservative politician, 1977

The shortest way to get someplace is not a straight line.

Jerry Brown,
  governor of California, 1978

You can never reach the promised land. You can march towards it.

James Callaghan,
  British prime minister, 1978

We do not believe that bread and liberty are incompatible.

Morarji Desai,
  Indian prime minister, 1978

I HAVE A DREAM

To paper over cracks can cause them to become chasms.

Jack Lynch,
 Irish prime minister, 1978

My father always said: 'If it is on the table, eat it.'

Senator Edward Kennedy,
 1979

You cannot shake hands with a clenched fist.

Indira Gandhi,
 Indian prime minister

Old age is like a plane flying through a storm. Once you're aboard there's nothing you can do.

Golda Meir,
 Israeli prime minister

Golda Meir during the time she was prime minister of Israel. Publisher's files

If blood be shed, let it be our blood. Cultivate the quiet courage of dying without killing. For man lives freely only by his readiness to die, if need be, at the hands of his brother, never by killing him.

Mahatma Gandhi

Governments never learn. Only people learn.

Milton Friedman,
  monetarist guru of Chile, Israel and the UK, 1980

Non-violence is not a garment to be put on and off at will. Its seat is in the heart and it must be an inseparable part of our very being.

Mahatma Gandhi,
  1948

Call it paramountcy or what you will, it is still domination. I am being as blunt as I can. I am making no excuses. Either the white man dominates or the black man takes over.

Johannes Strijdom,
  South African prime minister, 1949

Prestige . . . the shadow cast by power.

Dean Acheson,
  US Secretary of State, 1950

Men don't change. The only thing new in the world is the history you don't know.

Harry S. Truman

Man is a clever animal who behaves like an imbecile.

Albert Schweitzer,
  German medical missionary, on politics

Society . . . prepares crimes. Criminals are only the instruments necessary for executing them.

L.A.J. Quételet,
  Belgian statistician

History will absolve me!

Fidel Castro,
  Cuban revolutionary, on trial after his guerilla attack on the Moncada barracks, 1953

We know what happens to people who stay in the middle of the road — they get run over.

Aneurin Bevan,
  British Labour politician, 1953

The only acceptable authority is morality, events, necessity.

Gamal Abdel Nasser,
  Egyptian president, 1954

It has been said that there is no fool like an old fool, except a young fool. But the young fool has first to grow up to be an old fool to realise what a damn fool he was when he was a young fool.

Harold Macmillan

Power corrupts the few, while weakness corrupts the many.

Eric Hoffer,
  US philosopher: *The Passionate State of Mind,* 1954

Righteous people terrify me. . . . Virtue is its own punishment.

Aneurin Bevan,
  British Labour politician

Let one hundred flowers blossom and let one hundred schools of thought contend.

Mao Tse-tung,
  1957

Life is short, live it up.

Nikita Khruschev,
  1958

It seems to be the fate of idealists to obtain what they have struggled for in a form which destroys their ideals.

Bertrand Russell,
  English philosopher: *Marriage and Morals,* 1929

When written in Chinese, the word 'crisis' is composed of two characters: one represents danger and the other represents opportunity.

John F. Kennedy,
  US senator, 1959

I HAVE A DREAM

Freedom is not worth having if it does not connote freedom to err.

Mahatma Gandhi,
  quoted posthumously, 1959

If you cannot catch a bird of paradise, better take a wet hen.

Nikita Khruschev

When it is not necessary to change, it is necessary not to change.

John F. Kennedy

Injustice anywhere is a threat to justice everywhere.

Martin Luther King,
  US civil rights leader

Failure has no friends.

John F. Kennedy

No member of our generation who wasn't a communist or a drop-out in the thirties is worth a damn.

Lyndon B. Johnson,
  US vice-president, 1960

In a fight you don't stop to choose your cudgels.

Nikita Khruschev

If you can't cry a little bit in politics, the only other thing you'll have is hate.

Senator Hubert Humphrey,
  1960

The best way I know to win an argument is to start by being in the right.

Lord Hailsham,
  English jurist, 1960

It is one of the ironies of our time that the techniques of a harsh and repressive system should be able to instill discipline and ardour in its servants, while the blessings of liberty have too often stood for privilege, materialism and a life of ease.

John F. Kennedy,
  US president, 1961

Man is born to seek power, yet his actual condition makes him a slave to the power of others.

Hans J. Morgenthau,
  US political scientist and historian

Conformity is the jailer of freedom and the enemy of growth.

John F. Kennedy,
  US president, 1961

In bygone days commanders were taught that, when in doubt, they should march their troops towards the sound of gunfire. I intend to march my troops towards the sound of gunfire.

Jo Grimond,
  British Liberal Party leader, 1962

Whoever undertakes to set himself up as a judge in the field of truth and knowledge is shipwrecked by the laughter of the Gods.

Albert Einstein

The moment you have protected an individual, you have protected society.

Kenneth Kaunda,
  Zambian president, 1962

The one unchangeable certainty is that nothing is certain or unchangeable.

John F. Kennedy,
  US president, 1962

Never respond to criticism or you'll be doing everybody else's thing but your own.

Saul Alinsky,
  US radical

Don't get mad, get even.

Senator Everett Dirksen

Success, recognition and conformity are the by-words of the modern world, where everyone seems to crave the anesthetizing security of being indentified with the majority.

Martin Luther King,
  US civil rights leader: *Success to Love*, 1963

BOOK OF POLITICAL QUOTES

Freedom is indivisible, and when one man is enslaved, all are not free.

John F. Kennedy,
  US president, 1963

Nothing in the world is more dangerous than sincere ignorance and conscientious stupidity.

Martin Luther King,
  US civil rights leader

The ultimate measure of a man is not where he stands in moments of comfort and convenience, but where he stands at times of challenge and controversy.

Martin Luther King

Our defence is not in armaments, nor in science, nor in going underground. Our defence is in law and order.

Albert Einstein,
  German-born physicist, 1964

I've got on my watch the Golden Rule: do unto others as you would have them do unto you.

Lyndon B. Johnson,
  US president, 1964

There is no force so powerful as an idea whose time has come.

Senator Everett Dirksen,
  nominating Barry Goldwater for the presidency, 1964

The price of eternal vigilance is indifference.

Marshall McLuhan,
  US communications specialist:
Understanding Media, **1964**

Never trust a man whose eyes are too close to his nose.

Lyndon B. Johnson

The right to be heard does not automatically include the right to be taken seriously.

Hubert Humphrey,
  US vice-president, 1965

You can't separate peace from freedom, because no one can be at peace unless he has his freedom.

Malcolm X,
  US black activist, 1965

While you're saving your face, you're losing your ass.

Lyndon B. Johnson

I would rather be killed by a man, than kill a man myself. I believe that any time you muster an army together that is willing to die for what is right, you frighten the death out of armies that are willing to kill for what is wrong.

Dick Gregory,
  US comedian and black activist

Be peaceful, be courteous, obey the law, respect everyone; but if someone puts his hand on you — send him to the cemetery.

Malcolm X,
  US black activist

In politics, as in womanizing, failure is decisive. It sheds its retrospective gloom on earlier endeavours which at the time seemed full of promise.

Malcolm Muggeridge,
  English journalist: *Boring for England,* **1966**

Complacency is the enemy of study. We cannot really learn anything until we rid ourselves of complacency.

Mao Tse-tung:
  Quotations from Chairman Mao, **1966**

Idealism is fine, but as it approaches reality the cost becomes prohibitive.

William F. Buckley Jr,
  US editor and critic

I never trust a man unless I've got his pecker in my pocket.

Lyndon B. Johnson

To betray, you must first belong.

Harold 'Kim' Philby,
  British diplomat and Russian spy, 1967

I HAVE A DREAM

To give up the task of reforming society is to give up one's responsibility as a free man.

Alan Paton,
   South African writer, 1967

So long as you place your final reliance on armed struggle, controlled and led by a military or quasi-military organization, you have little incentive to develop the power of a self-reliant, unarmed people.

David Dellinger,
   US militant pacifist

The first duty of a revolutionary is to get away with it.

Abbie Hoffman,
   Yippie! leader

When eating an elephant, take one bite at a time.

General Creighton W. Abrams,
   US commander in Vietnam

It is better to be defeated on principle than to win on lies.

Arthur Calwell,
   Australian politician, 1968

Non-violence is the only weapon that is compassionate and recognizes each man's value.

Cesar Chavez,
   US labour leader

The passion for destruction is a creative joy.

Graffito
   during the Paris student demonstrations, 1968

For an extraordinary situation, extraordinary measures and sacrifices in proportion.

Graffito
   during the Paris student demonstrations, 1968

He who is conceived in a cage yearns for the cage.

Yevgeny Yevtushenko,
   Russian poet, 1968

All life is essentially the contributions that come from compromise.

Spiro T. Agnew,
   US vice-president, 1969

You're either part of the solution or part of the problem.

Eldridge Cleaver,
   Black Panther leader

The real distinction is between those who adapt their purposes to reality and those who seek to mould reality in the light of their purposes.

Henry Kissinger,
   US National Security Adviser: *The Necessity for Choice*

History teaches us that men and nations behave wisely once they have exhausted all other alternatives.

Abba Eban,
   Israeli politician, 1970

I try to operate on two unconnected levels. One is the practical level of action in which I am extremely cautious and conservative. The second is the realm of ideas where I try to be very free.

Anthony Wedgwood Benn,
   British Labour politician, 1971

If what I had done had not carried hope within itself, how could I have done it? Action and hope are inseparable. It certainly seems that only human beings are capable of hope. And remember, that in the individual, the end of hope is the beginning of death.

Charles de Gaulle

There's no such thing as a free lunch.

Milton Friedman,
   monetarist guru of Chile, Israel and the UK

I am a student of the universe and never really the master. Once you think you can't lose an argument, once you think you can't be corrected, then you are a fool.

Huey P. Newton,
   chairman of the Black Panther party, 1973

BEHIND CLOSED DOORS

We treat women too well and in this way we have spoiled everything. We have done everything wrong in raising them to our level. Truly, the oriental nations have more mind and sense than we in declaring the wife to be the property of the husband. In fact, nature has made woman our slave.

Napoleon Bonaparte

The tender breasts of ladies were not formed for political convulsions.

Thomas Jefferson

Man cannot fulfil his destiny alone, he cannot redeem his race unaided. . . . The world has never yet seen a truly great and virtuous nation, because in the degradation of woman the very fountains of life are poisoned at their source.

Lucretia Mott,
** US feminist, in an address to the first**
Woman's Rights Convention, 1848

Palmerston is now seventy. If he could provide evidence of his potency in his electoral address, he would sweep the country.

Benjamin Disraeli,
** on being offered evidence of Palmerston's alleged philandering, carried on despite his age**

There is no greater stupidity than for people of general aspirations to marry and so surrender themselves to the small miseries of domestic and private life.

Karl Marx,
** in a letter to Engels, 1856**

I have always thought that every woman should marry and no man.

Benjamin Disraeli,
** British prime minister: *Lothair,* 1870**

No man is regular in his attendance at the House of Commons until he is married.

Benjamin Disraeli

No public character has ever stood the revelation of private utterance and correspondence.

Lord Acton,
** English historian, 1887**

We in the Suffragette Army have a great mission: the greatest mission the world has ever known — the freeing of one half of the human race and through that freedom the saving of the other half. I incite this meeting to rebellion!

Emmeline Pankhurst,
** English suffragette, 1912**

Every woman attracts me like blazes. I prowl around like a ravening wolf, yet I'm as bashful as a boy. I can hardly understand myself sometimes. I ought to get married and become a solid citizen — then hang myself after a week.

Joseph Goebbels,
** Nazi Minister of Propaganda: diary entry**

Bunnies *can* and *will* go to France. Yours affectionately, Jeremy

Jeremy Thorpe,
** English Liberal politician, ending a letter to his friend Norman Scott, 1961**

Jeremy Thorpe/Popperfoto

No one wants me as a Cabinet minister and they are perfectly right. I am an agitator, not an administrator.

Nancy Astor,
  the first woman MP, 1919

I would warn the wives of eminent men to treat their husbands as if they were not eminent.

A. Clutton Brock,
  British essayist and critic, 1919

Marriage is the waste-paper basket of the emotions.

Sidney Webb,
  English Fabian socialist

Never become ladies. Remain German girls and women!

Julius Streicher,
  Nazi editor, exhortation to the faithful

IT IS A MORAL ISSUE

The Times,
  heading of a first leader on the Profumo Affair, 1963

The only problem with women is men.

Kathie Sarachild,
  US feminist

Women's Liberation is just a lot of foolishness. It's the men who are discriminated against — they can't bear children. And no one's likely to do anything about that.

Golda Meir,
  Israeli prime minister

One perhaps, two conceivably. But eight — I just can't believe it.

Harold Macmillan,
  on hearing from Iain Macleod the rumours of an orgy involving eight High Court judges, 1963

Women are capable of the best and of the worst, therefore they never should be shot.

Charles de Gaulle,
  on automatically commuting the death sentences of any female killers to life terms

Of course, I may go into a strange bedroom now and then. *That* I don't want you to write about, but otherwise you can write everything.

Lyndon B. Johnson,
  US president, to reporters, 1964

To me women are no more than a pastime, a hobby. Nobody devotes too much time to a hobby. Moreover my engagement book is there to show that I only devote a limited amount of my time to them.

Henry Kissinger

Honey, whatever women do, they do best after dark.

John V. Lindsay,
  mayor of New York City

Women do the lickin' and the stickin'.

Moon Landrieu,
  mayor of New Orleans, on the woman's role in politics

Power is the ultimate aphrodisiac.

Henry Kissinger

Women are on the outside when the door to the smoke-filled room is closed.

Millicent Fenwick,
  US politician, 1973

I'm the only one amongst you who has the balls to run for president.

Shirley Chisholm,
  black, feminist presidential candidate to the Black Democratic caucus, 1972

I didn't think New York could handle two sex symbols in one go.

Henry Kissinger,
  claiming in fun that he had turned down an offer from the New York Jets to succeed 'Broadway' Joe Namath

I am notorious. I will go down in history as another Lady Hamilton.

Mandy Rice Davies,
  recalling her role in the Profumo Affair, 1963

BEHIND CLOSED DOORS

They relate to us sexually. They assume that the reason you're in politics is for sex.

Esther Newberg,
   executive director of the New York Democratic committee, 1973

A few years ago designers decided that women shouldn't have busts. Well, God gave me a bust. What am I supposed to do with it?

Martha Mitchell,
   wife of Attorney-General John Mitchell, 1971

Of course I'm bisexual. We all are. This is the revolution. The women's movement has always had lesbians at its vanguard.... The lesbian is the archetypal feminist, because she's not into men — she's the independent woman par excellence.

Kate Millett,
   US feminist, 1973

Norma was not interested in such subjects as defence.

Lord Lambton,
   Minister for the Air Force, explaining that his liaison with prostitute Norma Levy had not threatened the nation's security, 1973

If there's a kind of semi-attractive woman around a candidate, the assumption is that she's there to sleep with him.

Richard Reeves,
   US journalist, 1973

I'd rather be regarded as a figure of fun than not at all.

Margaret Whitlam,
   wife of Australian prime minister, Gough Whitlam, 1973

I was never worried about any sex investigation in Washington. All the men on my staff can type.

Bella Abzug,
   US politician, 1974

She's my little Argentine hillbilly and I've come to see her dance.

Wilbur Mills,
   erstwhile chairman of the House Ways and Means Committee, appearing on stage with his mistress Fanne Fox, a burlesque stripper, shortly before retiring from politics, 1974

I owe nothing to women's lib.

Margaret Thatcher,
   the first woman to lead a British political party, 1974

I've looked on a lot of women with lust. I've committed adultery in my heart many times. This is something God recognizes I will do — and I have done it — and God forgives me for it.

Jimmy Carter,
   US president, in an interview in *Playboy*, 1976

If men could get pregnant, abortion would be a sacrament.

Flo Kennedy,
   US feminist, 1976

Women really do tend to be more snobbish creatures than men.

Margaret Whitlam,
   wife of Australian prime minister Gough Whitlam, 1976

The conventional wisdom is that power is the ultimate aphrodisiac. In truth, it's exhausting.

Dom Bonafede,
   US author: *Surviving in Washington*, 1977

Basically public officials are human beings. They spend as much time thinking about whether they'll have a woman companion for the evening as your average Pittsburgh steelworker. Or your average newspaper reporter for that matter. Gossip is part of a gradual trend to humanize the newsmakers, which I think is healthy.

Rudy Maxa,
   pioneer of 'hard gossip' in the *Washington Post*, 1979

Margaret Trudeau — the picture of smiling motherhood/Publisher's files

Deep down, one is aware that prostitution is degrading to women.

Frank Walker,
    Attorney General of New South Wales, 1977

I'd like to think that he's a friend, but after all, I'm a married lady.

Margaret Trudeau,
    wife of Canadian prime minister Pierre Trudeau, on her friend Mick Jagger, 1977

If God had meant us to have homosexuals, he would have created Adam and Bruce.

Anita Bryant,
    US politician and campaigner against gay liberation

Women are important in a man's life only if they are beautiful and charming and keep their femininity. . . . What do these feminists want? What do you want? You say equality. . . . You are equal in the eyes of the law but not, excuse my saying so, in ability.

Mohammad Reza Pahlevi,
    Shah of Iran

I wrote out a little list of questions for Pierre to put to the Pope about our marriage problems.

Margaret Trudeau,
    wife of Canadian prime minister Pierre Trudeau, 1979

I'm kept very busy just keeping up with my little man.

Tamara Fraser,
    wife of Australian prime minister Malcolm Fraser, 1977

Even though the labels 'stripper' and 'congressman' are completely incongruous, there was never anything but harmony in our hearts.

Fanne Fox,
    stripper and mistress of Wilbur Mills, chairman of the House Ways and Means Committee

THE SLIPPERY POLE

It is as hard and severe a thing to be a true politician as to be truly moral.

Francis Bacon,
English philosopher and statesman, 1625

I need pity. I know what I feel. Great place and business in the world is not worth looking for.

Oliver Cromwell,
protector of the commonwealth of England, Scotland and Ireland, 1650

Royalty is but a feather in a man's cap. Let children enjoy their prattle.

Oliver Cromwell,
protector of the commonwealth of England, Scotland and Ireland, rejecting plans to have him crowned king, 1658

The people would be just as noisy if they were going to see me hanged.

Oliver Cromwell
replying to a friend who pointed out the cheering crowds

I gave you all, and you have rewarded me with confiscation, disgrace and a life of impeachment.

Warren Hastings,
first Governor-General of India, impeached 1788

Vanity, I am sensible, is my cardinal vice and cardinal folly.

John Adams

Give me the avowed, the erect, the manly foe/ Bold I can meet, perhaps may turn his blow./ But of all plagues, good Heaven, thy wrath can send,/ Save me, oh save me from the candid friend.

George Canning,
British statesman: *New Morality,* 1823.
Later used by Peel to defend himself from attacks by Disraeli

No man who ever held the office of president would ever congratulate a friend on obtaining it. He will make one man ungrateful and a hundred men his enemies, for every office he can bestow.

John Adams

My movements to the chair of government will be accompanied by feelings not unlike those of a culprit who is going to the place of his execution.

George Washington,
US president, 1789

I do not say when I became a politician, for that I never was.

John Adams

I am a man of cold, reserved, austere and forbidding manners. My political adversaries say a gloomy misanthropist and my personal enemies, an unsocial savage.

John Quincy Adams,
US Secretary of State, diary entry, 1819

THE SLIPPERY POLE

Science is my passion, politics my duty.

Thomas Jefferson

Do they think I am such a damned fool as to think myself fit for president of the United States? No sir, I know what I am fit for. I can command a body of men in a rough way, but I am not fit for president.

Andrew Jackson,
seven years before his election, 1821

I have only two regrets: that I have not shot Henry Clay or hanged John C. Calhoun.

Andrew Jackson,
US president, on his retirement, 1837

As to the presidency, the two happiest days of my life were those of my entry upon the office and those of my surrender of it.

Martin Van Buren

The idea that I should become president seems to me too visionary to require a serious answer. It has never entered my head, nor is it likely to enter the head of any sane person.

Zachary Taylor
before he was elected US president

I am fully persuaded that I am worth inconceivably more to hang than for any other purpose.

John Brown,
US abolitionist, 1859

I claim not to have controlled events, but confess plainly that events have controlled me.

Abraham Lincoln

If you are as happy, my dear sir, on entering this house as I am in leaving it and returning home, you are the happiest man in the country.

James Buchanan,
US president, turning over the White House to his successor, Abraham Lincoln, 1861

At the top of the greasy pole.

Benjamin Disraeli
describing his position as prime minister, 1868

Nobody ever left the presidency with less regret, less disappointment, fewer heart-burnings or any general discontent with the result of his term (in his own heart, I mean) than I do.

Rutherford B. Hayes,
US president, 1881

My God! What is there in this place that a man should ever want to get into it?

James Garfield,
US president

The President is the last person in the world to know what the people really want and think.

James Garfield

All great men make mistakes. Napoleon forgot Blücher. I forgot Goschen.

Lord Randolph Churchill,
British Chancellor of the Exchequer, on finding that after resigning tactically from his post, Lord Salisbury actually accepted his resignation and replaced him with G.J. Goschen, 1886

I am honest and sincere in my desire to do well, but the question is whether I know enough to accomplish what I desire.

Grover Cleveland,
US president, 1886

If I am a great man, then a good many of the great men of history are frauds.

Andrew Bonar Law,
British prime minister, during the Ulster crisis

I understand what Christ suffered in Gethsemane as well as any man living.

James Keir Hardie,
British Labour Party pioneer, 1914

I work for a government I despise for ends I think criminal.

John Maynard Keynes,
   English economist, 1917

I must follow them, I am their leader.

Andrew Bonar Law

I am of that unfortunate class who never knew what it was to be a child in spirit. Even the memories of boyhood and young manhood are gloomy.

James Keir Hardie,
   British Labour Party pioneer

I am signing my death warrant.

Michael Collins,
   Irish patriot, signing the unpopular Irish Treaty which indeed led to his assassination, 1921

I don't know what to do or where to turn on this taxation matter. Somewhere there must be a book that tells all about it, where I could go to straighten it out in my mind. But I don't know where the book is, and maybe I couldn't read it if I found it. My God, this is a hell of a place for a man like me to be!

Warren G. Harding,
   US president, who solved his problem by ensuring that only the rich and corrupt benefited from his various budgets

My God! This is a hell of a job! I can take care of my enemies all right. But my friends, my goddamn friends, they're the ones that keep me walking the floor nights.

Warren G. Harding

I speak not as the man in the street even, but as a man in a fieldpath, a much simpler person, steeped in tradition and impervious to new ideas.

Stanley Baldwin

I am not fit for this office and never should have been here.

Warren G. Harding,
   US president

I have not had your advantages, gentlemen. What poor education I have received has been gained in the University of Life.

Horatio Bottomley,
   English financier and fraud, addressing the Oxford Union, 1921

I can't listen to music too often. It affects your nerves, makes you want to say stupid, naïve things and stroke the heads of people who could create such beauty while living in this vile hell. And now you mustn't stroke anyone's head, you might get your hand bitten off.

V.I. Lenin

There are three classes which need sanctuary more than others: birds, wild flowers and prime ministers.

Stanley Baldwin,
   British prime minister, 1925

The vice-presidency ain't worth a pitcher of warm spit.

John Nance Garner,
   US vice-president

The young man today is compelled by circumstances beyond his control to become a robot in a fatalistic scheme of things which must cause him to believe that he counts for very little.

Ernest Bevin,
   British Labour politician, 1934

I wonder why he shot me?...God, don't let me die. I have so much to do.

Huey Long,
   governor of Louisiana, dying words, 1935

It was, of course, a grievous disappointment that peace could not be saved, but I know that my persistent efforts have convinced the world that no part of the blame can lie here. That consciousness of moral right, which it is impossible for the Germans to feel, must be a tremendous force on our side.

Neville Chamberlain,
   British prime minister, 1939

THE SLIPPERY POLE

I was such an outcast I could have had a meeting of all my friends and supporters in a telephone booth.

Arthur Fadden,
  Australian prime minister, 1941

Believe me, it wasn't always a pleasure to see those mountains of corpses and to smell the perpetual burning.

Rudolf Hoess,
  commandant of Auschwitz

Why in hell does anybody want to be a head of state? Damned if I know.

Harry S. Truman,
  US president, 1945

I am a very diffident man. I find it hard to carry on a conversation. But if any of you wish to come and see me, I will welcome you.

Clement Attlee,
  British prime minister, to his junior ministers, 1945

Kissing babies gives me asthma.

John F. Kennedy,
  during his campaign for Congress, 1946

Everything is going nowadays. Before long I shall also have to go.

George VI,
  King of England, living under a Labour government, 1948

The White House is the finest jail in the world.

Harry S. Truman,
  US president, 1949

No attempt at ethical or social education can eradicate from my heart a deep, burning hatred for the Tory Party....So far as I am concerned, they are lower than vermin.

Aneurin Bevan,
  British Labour politician, 1949

I have none of the qualities which create publicity.

Clement Attlee,
  British prime minister, 1949

I can think of nothing more boring for the American public than to have to sit in their living rooms for a whole half hour looking at my face on their television screens.

Dwight D. Eisenhower

We need supermen to rule us — the job is so vast and the need for wise judgement so urgent. But, alas, there are no supermen.

Brooks Atkinson,
  US critic, 1951

We are innocent. This is the whole truth. To forsake this truth is to pay too high a price even for the priceless gift of life, for life thus purchased we could not live out in dignity and self-respect.

Ethel and Julius Rosenberg,
  alleged atom spies, in an open letter to President Eisenhower, 1953

We are the first victims of American fascism!

Ethel Rosenberg,
  last words in the electric chair, 1953

During the last few weeks I have felt that the Suez Canal was flowing through my drawing room.

Lady Clarissa Eden,
  wife of British prime minister Anthony Eden, during the Suez Crisis, 1956

I have been a conspirator for so long that I mistrust all around me.

Gamal Abdel Nasser,
  Egyptian president, 1958

You're right, I can't read a speech worth a shit.

John F. Kennedy
  to newsman Tom Wicker who commented on his stiffness on the podium

My daddy always told me that if I brushed up against the grindstone of life I'd come away with far more polish than I could ever get at Harvard and Yale. I wanted to believe him, but somehow I never could.

Lyndon B. Johnson

BOOK OF POLITICAL QUOTES

I have regret and condemnation for the extermination of the Jewish people which was ordered by the German rulers, but I myself could not have done anything to prevent it. I was a tool in the hands of the strong and the powerful and in the hands of fate itself.

Adolf Eichmann,
 former Nazi, on trial for war crimes, 1961

The doctor unfortunately said I was fit.

Sir Alec Douglas-Home,
 after a medical prior to his taking office as British prime minister, 1964

I'm not sure I've even got the brains to be president.

Senator Barry Goldwater,
 US presidential candidate, 1964

There are two problems in my life. The political ones are insoluble, and the economic ones are incomprehensible.

Sir Alec Douglas-Home,
 British prime minister, 1964

I simply can't stand Washington. It's impossible to think or breathe in the place.

Walter Lippmann,
 US political commentator, 1965

If you are black, the only roads into the mainland of American life are through subservience, cowardice and loss of manhood. These are the white man's roads.

LeRoi Jones,
 US writer: *Home,* 1966

I wake up at five a.m. some mornings and hear the planes coming in at National Airport and I think they're bombing me.

Lyndon B. Johnson

I just don't understand these young people. Don't they realize I'm really one of them. I always hated cops when I was a kid, and just like them I dropped out of school, and took off for California. I'm not some conformist middle-class personality.

Lyndon B. Johnson,
  former US president, 1970

My experience is that the political season in this country is never closed.

Harold Holt,
 Australian prime minister, 1966

If they come for me in the morning, they will come for you at night.

Angela Davis,
 US black activist, 1971

I can't trust anybody. What are you trying to do to me? Everybody is trying to cut me down.

Lyndon B. Johnson,
 US president, 1967

People do not respect you if you drink yourselves into monkeys.

Hastings Banda,
 president of Malawi, 1969

During the second semester of my freshman year I made a mistake. . . . I arranged for a fellow freshman friend of mine to take the examination for me. What I did was wrong. I have regretted it ever since.

Edward Kennedy

Everyone seemed to want an election.

Harold Wilson,
 British opposition leader, after Labour's surprise defeat in the General Election, 1970

I was overcome . . . by a jumble of emotions: grief, fear, doubt, exhaustion, panic, confusion and shock.

Senator Edward Kennedy
 explaining on television why he took so long to report his accident on the bridge at Chappaquiddick, 1969

Certain things happened during the Second World War for which I feel personally sorry.

Hirohito,
 Japanese Emperor, 1971

If the American people don't love me, then their descendants will.

Lyndon B. Johnson,
 former US president, shortly before his death, 1972

THE SLIPPERY POLE

I wanted to be an up-to-date king, but I didn't have much time.

Duke of Windsor,
   formerly Edward VIII, 1972

I'm not bitter. Hell, we could say it was the cheapest campaign I've run. Think of it. All that publicity and I didn't have to spend a cent.

Thomas Eagleton,
   after being dropped from the McGovern ticket when investigative journalists revealed his record of mental instability, 1972

The thought of being president frightens me and I do not think I want the job.

Ronald Reagan,
   governor of California, 1973

I refuse to lead a nation of drunkards. I would sooner die.

Kenneth Kaunda,
   Zambian president, 1973

I'm a Ford, not a Lincoln.

Gerald Ford,
   US president, on assuming office, 1974

I feel that in some way fate is placing its future in my hands. But I'm not sure I'm worthy of it.

Elliot Richardson,
   former US Attorney General, on his country's future, 1974

I think I'm going to the moon. That's the best place.

John Mitchell,
   former US attorney, after his conviction for his part in the Watergate Affair, 1975

I ask pardon from all, as with all my heart I forgive those who declared themselves my enemies — not that I considered them such.

Francisco Franco,
   his final public message to Spain, 1975

Sometimes I feel like a goddamned pinball machine.

Jerry Brown,
   governor of California, on campaigning, 1976

I don't claim to know all the answers.

Jimmy Carter,
   US president, 1976

I gave them a sword. And they stuck it in and they twisted it with relish. And I guess if I'd been in their position I'd have done the same thing.

Richard Nixon,
   former US president, talking on television to David Frost, 1977

You lose touch with what it's like out there. You come to believe that you really *are* better than the people who sent you here.

James Abourezk,
   US senator, 1977

I let down my friends. I let down the country. I let down our system of government. I brought myself down.

Richard Nixon,
   former US president, 1977

I went to the House of Lords because I had nowhere else to go.

Lord Shinwell,
   British socialist peer, 1977

Maybe it picks you up a little bit, but it sure lets you down in a hurry.

Betty Ford,
   wife of US president Gerald Ford, on her alcohol problem, 1979

I have got to admit that things haven't gone quite the way I wanted.

Ian Smith,
   last head of white Rhodesia, 1979

All I want if someone's going to blow my head off, I just want one swing at him first. I don't want to get it from behind.

Edward Kennedy,
   US senator, 1979

When I did not pay attention to matters of state I was called a playboy. When I began to deal with these matters I was called dictatorial.

Mohammad Reza Pahlevi,
   former Shah of Iran, 1980

THE LAST LAUGH

We, my lords, may thank Heaven that we have something better than our brains to depend on.

Lord Chesterfield,
   British statesman, to his fellow peers

That will depend, my Lord, on whether I embrace your principles or your mistress.

John Wilkes,
   British radical politician, replying to the Earl of Sandwich's comment: 'Egad, sir, I do not know whether you will die on the gallows or of the pox!'

The atrocious crime of being a young man...I shall attempt neither to palliate nor to deny.

William Pitt, Earl Chatham,
   British statesman replying to an attack by Robert Walpole, 1741

And if your friend is not standing?

John Wilkes,
   British radical politician, replying to a heckler who said he would rather vote for the devil than for Wilkes

You should treat a cigar like a mistress and put it away before you are sick of it.

Benjamin Disraeli

Mr Kremlin himself was distinguished for ignorance — for he had only one idea, and that was wrong.

Benjamin Disraeli,
   British prime minister: *Lothair*, 1870

One good turn deserves another.

Punch,
   caption for a cartoon referring to Disraeli's elevation to the peerage shortly after his having Queen Victoria declared Empress of India, 1876

Heckler:
   I'm a democrat!

Theodore Roosevelt.
   May I ask the gentleman why he is a Democrat?

Heckler:
   My grandfather was a Democrat, my father was a Democrat and I am a Democrat!

Theodore Roosevelt:
   My friend, suppose your grandfather had been a jackass and your father was a jackass, what would you be?

Heckler:
A Republican!

Why should it be my fate to have as my Minister of Finance the only Jew in France who knows nothing about finance?

Georges Clemenceau,
   French prime minister

When I was a boy I was told that anybody could become president. I'm beginning to believe it.

Clarence Darrow,
   US lawyer

THE LAST LAUGH

The healthy stomach is nothing if not conservative. Few radicals have good digestions.

Samuel Butler,
English writer: _Notebooks,_ 1912

It is one of the consolations of middle-aged reformers that the good they inculcate must live after them if it is to live at all.

Saki,
British author: _Beasts and Superbeasts,_ 1914

You can make prostitution illegal in Louisiana, but you can't make it unpopular.

Martin Behrman,
political boss of Louisiana, 1920

Heckler:
Go ahead, Al. Tell 'em all you know. It won't take long.

Al Smith,
US presidential candidate: If I tell 'em all we both know, it won't take me any longer.

The intelligent are to the intelligentsia what a man is to a gent.

Stanley Baldwin

There may be said to be two classes of people in the world: those who constantly divide the people of the world into two classes and those who do not.

Robert Benchley,
US wit

Everybody favours free speech in the slack moments when no axes are being ground.

Heywood Broun,
US wit

Lady Astor:
If I were your wife, I should flavour your coffee with poison!

Winston Churchill:
And if I were your husband, madam, I should drink it.

I don't make jokes; I just watch the government and report the facts.

Will Rogers,
US humorist

A sense of humour always withers in the presence of the messianic delusion, like justice and truth in front of patriotic passion.

H.L. Mencken,
US philologist, editor and satirist:
Prejudices

Animals, I hope.

Sir Eric Phipps,
British diplomat, to Hermann Goering who explained his late arrival at a dinner by his attendance at a shooting party, 1934

The only recorded instance in history of a rat swimming _towards_ a sinking ship.

Winston Churchill,
commenting on a failed Tory candidate who then attempted to stand as a Liberal

We can't always cross a bridge until we come to it, but I always like to lay down a pontoon ahead of time.

Bernard Baruch,
US statesman and financier

Yes my friend, we are both Marxists. You in your way and I in Marx's.

Harold Laski,
English political scientist and socialist, crushing a heckler

Replacement does not arise. I cannot help thinking that anything like a serious invasion would be bound to leak out.

Winston Churchill,
British prime minister, refusing to consider any plans other than the ringing of bells to announce an invasion, 1943

Always remember that I have taken more out of alcohol than alcohol has taken out of me.

Winston Churchill

The House of Lords is like a glass of champagne that has stood for five days.

Clement Attlee,
former British prime minister, elevated to the Lords

Heckler:
    If you were the Archangel Gabriel I wouldn't vote for you!

Sir Robert Menzies,
    Australian prime minister: If I were the Archangel Gabriel, madam, I'm afraid you would not be in my constituency.

The human brain starts working the moment you are born and never stops until you stand up to speak in public.

Sir George Jessel,
    1949

That's not enough, I'm going to need a majority.

Adlai Stevenson,
    US Presidential candidate, on seeing a placard offering 'The support of all thinking Americans', 1952

Earl Warren,
    US jurist: I'm pleased to see such a dense crowd here tonight.

Heckler:
    Don't be too pleased, Governor, we ain't all dense.

I will undoubtedly have to seek what is happily known as gainful employment, which I am glad to say does not describe holding public office.

Dean Acheson,
    on resigning as US Secretary of State with the change of government, 1952

Old age is always fifteen years older than I am.

Bernard Baruch,
    US financier and statesman, 1955

What counts is not necessarily the size of the dog in the fight — it's the size of the fight in the dog.

Dwight D. Eisenhower,
    US president, 1958

It would have been twice as bad if they'd sent the dog.

Harold Macmillan,
    British prime minister, referring to the deceased space dog Little Laika as he watched crowds cheer the world's first cosmonaut, Yuri Gagarin

Why, I've been retired for twelve years and they still call me 'General'.

Argentinian general
    to Evita Peron who complained when the crowds called her *puta* (whore) in the streets

I have been accused of being ungenerous to this government. Generosity is part of my character and I therefore hasten to assure this government that I will never make an allegation of dishonesty against it wherever a simple explanation of stupidity will suffice.

Leslie Lever,
    British MP

It was involuntary, they sank my boat.

John F. Kennedy,
    US president, asked how he became the hero of PT-109 — his motor torpedo boat which was sunk by the Japanese

I regret that I have but one law firm to give to this country.

Adlai Stevenson
    on Kennedy's wholesale use of his law firm for his Administration

I'd like that translated, if I may.

Harold Macmillan,
    British prime minister, after watching Khruschev pound his shoe at the United Nations, 1960

Beware of Greeks bearing gifts, coloured men looking for a loan and whites who understand the negro.

Adam Clayton Powell,
    US politician

I had announced earlier this year that, if successful, I would not consider campaign contributions as a substitute in appointing ambassadors. Ever since that statement I have not received one single cent from my father.

John F. Kennedy,
    countering rumours that his father Joseph had bought him the presidency and recalling the elder Kennedy's notorious performance as US ambassador to the UK in the 1930s, 1960

Bessie Braddock,
  British MP: Winston, you're drunk!

Winston Churchill:
  Bessie, you're ugly; and tomorrow I shall
be sober.

As usual the Liberals offer a mixture of
sound and original ideas. Unfortunately,
none of the sound ideas is original and none
of the original ideas is sound.

Harold Macmillan,
  British prime minister, 1961

I'm too young to retire and too old to go
back to work.

Senator Barry Goldwater,
  explaining his presidential candidacy, 1964

How can anyone govern a country that has
246 different kinds of cheese?

Charles de Gaulle

Too bad all the people who know how to
run the country are busy driving taxi-cabs
and cutting hair.

George Burns,
  US comedian

A memorandum is written not to inform
the reader but to protect the writer.

Dean Acheson,
  US lawyer and politician

They want me not only to bare my breast,
but to go in for indecent exposure.

Senator Eugene McCarthy,
  **facing ultra-liberal attacks on his
campaign, 1968**

The illegal we do immediately, the unconstitutional takes a little longer.

Henry Kissinger

The first requirement of a statesman is that he be dull. This is not always easy to achieve.

Dean Acheson,
   US lawyer and politician

I am a fan of President Nixon. I worship the quicksand he walks on.

Art Buchwald,
   US humorist. Also used by Buchwald with Jimmy Carter as its butt

Since I'm only half Jewish, can I join if I only play nine holes?

Senator Barry Goldwater,
   attributed rejoinder on being blackballed by an anti-semitic Phoenix, Arizona golf club

There cannot be a crisis next week — my schedule is already full.

Henry Kissinger

There are two ways to indicate a horse: one is to draw a picture that is a great likeness. And the other is to draw a picture that is a great likeness and write underneath it 'This is a horse'. We just drew the picture.

Senator Sam Ervin,
   chairman of the Congressional Committee on the Watergate Affair, after releasing a report that made no specific statement as to President Nixon's involvement, 1973

A group of politicians deciding to dump a president because his morals are bad is like the Mafia getting together to bump off the Godfather for not going to church on Sunday.

Russell Baker,
   US humorist, 1974

As President Nixon said: 'Presidents can do almost anything.' And President Nixon has done many things no one would have thought of doing.

Golda Meir,
   Israeli prime minister, 1974

Washington is a much better place if you are asking questions rather than answering them.

John Dean,
   star Watergate witness, launching his syndicated radio talk show

I will consider selling off the Crown Jewels, but I am not absolutely sure that they are the property of Her Majesty's government.

Denis Healey,
   British Chancellor of the Exchequer, on the economic crisis, 1976

The cupboard is not only bare, it has holes in it.

Joh Bjelke-Petersen,
   Queensland premier, on the Australian economy, 1976

I have no intention, no *present* intention, of standing for parliament.

Harold Macmillan,
   British Conservative elder statesman, 1979

I have a criminal record and I felt I could gain more acceptance among the Republicans because of it.

Margo St James,
   US prostitute activist and Republican candidate, 1980

Like buttered bread, state ministers usually fall on the good side.

Ludwig Börne,
   German political writer and satirist

Hell hath no fury like a liberal scorned.

Dick Gregory,
   US comedian and black activist

Golda Meir speaks to the press/Publisher's files

GOD ON OUR SIDE

God is generally for the big squadrons against the little ones.

Roger, Comte de Bussy-Rabutin,
1677

It is said that God is always on the side of the heaviest battalions.

Voltaire,
French author and humanitarian, 1770

I tremble for my country when I reflect that God is just.

Thomas Jefferson,
future US president, 1784

Society cannot exist without inequality, an inequality which cannot be maintained without religion...it must be possible to tell the poor 'It is God's will!...Religion introduces into the thought of Heaven an idea of equalization which saves the rich from being massacred by the poor.

Napoleon Bonaparte

The existence of religion is the existence of a defect....Religion for us no longer has the force of a basis for secular deficiencies, but only that of a phenomenon. We do not change secular questions into theological ones. We change theological questions into secular ones. History has for long enough been resolved into superstition. We now resolve superstition into history.

Karl Marx:
On the Jewish Question, 1843

Yes, I am a Jew, and when the ancestors of the Right Honourable Gentleman were brutal savages in an unknown island, mine were priests in the Temple of Solomon.

Benjamin Disraeli,
British parliamentary candidate, answering
a critical speech from Daniel O'Connell by a
letter in _The Times_, 1835

The Lord prefers common-looking people. That is the reason he makes so many of them.

Abraham Lincoln

Religion is the sigh of the oppressed creature, the feeling of a heartless world and the soul of soulless circumstances. It is the opium of the people.

Karl Marx,
1843

Mr Dean — no dogmas, no Deans.

Benjamin Disraeli,
admonishing Dean Stanley who suggested
removing the Athanasian creed from the
Book of Common Prayer

So long as there are earnest believers in the world, they will always wish to punish opinions, even when their judgement tells them that it is unwise and their conscience that it is wrong.

Walter Bagehot,
British economist and journalist

GOD ON OUR SIDE

One on God's side is a majority.

Wendell Phillips,
 US abolitionist, 1859

It is more important to know that we are on God's side.

Abraham Lincoln,
 on hearing the hope that God was on his side

God will see to it that war always recurs as a drastic medicine for the human race.

Heinrich von Treitschke,
 German historian

In all ages, hypocrites called priests have put crowns upon the heads of thieves called kings.

Robert C. Ingersoll,
 US lawyer and agnostic, 1884

We are Christians by forcible conversion.

Kaiser Wilhelm,
 claiming that war, despite its lack of apparent Christianity, was good for a nation, 1908

The church should no longer be satisfied to represent only the Conservative Party at prayer.

Maud Royden,
 English social worker and preacher, 1917

I believe in Divine Providence. If I did not I would go crazy.

Woodrow Wilson,
 US president, 1919

My prime motive in going to the White House is to bring America back to God.

Warren G. Harding;
 his conspicuous corruption belied this remark to the Bishop of Cincinnati, 1920

Christ was the greatest early fighter in the battle against the world enemy — the Jews. The work that Christ started but did not finish, I, Adolf Hitler, will conclude.

Adolf Hitler,
 1926

If God were to come to me and say 'Ramsay, would you rather be a country gentleman than a prime minister?', I should reply, 'Please God, a country gentleman.'

Ramsay MacDonald,
 British prime minister, 1930

The Pope! How many divisions has he?

Joseph Stalin,
 rejecting a suggestion from Laval, the French prime minister, that he should mollify Russian Catholics, 1935

Bolshevism is Christianity's illegitimate son.

Adolf Hitler

Praise the Lord and pass the ammunition.

Howell M. Forgy,
 navy chaplain at Pearl Harbour, to men handling ammunition, 1941

The assertion that this universal force can trouble itself about the destiny of each individual being, every smallest earthly bacillus, can be influenced by so-called prayers or other surprising things, depends on a requisite dose of naïvete or else upon shameless professional self-interest.

Martin Bormann,
 Nazi leader, on God

There are no atheists in the foxholes.

Father William T. Cummings,
 in a sermon, 1942

In some sort of crude sense which no vulgarity, no humour, no overstatement can quite extinguish, the physicists have known sin, and this is a knowledge they cannot lose.

Robert J. Oppenheimer,
 head of the Manhattan Project which developed the A-Bomb, in a lecture, 1947

Your cravings as a human animal do not become a prayer just because it is God whom you ask to attend to them.

Dag Hammarskjöld,
 United Nations Secretary-General

Afrikaner history reveals a firm resolve and purpose which makes one feel that Afrikanerdom is not the work of men but the creation of God. . . . Throughout our history, God's plan for our people is clear — we have a divine right to be Afrikaners. No worldly power can destroy our nationhood because God created our people.

D.F. Malan,
   South African premier, 1949

An atheist is a man who watches a Notre Dame — Southern Methodist Union game and doesn't care who wins.

Dwight D. Eisenhower

Mass movements can rise and spread without a belief in God, but never without a belief in a devil.

Eric Hoffer,
   US philosopher: _The True Believer,_ 1951

There is no social evil, no form of injustice, whether of the feudal or capitalist order, which has not been sanctified in some way or another by religious sentiment and thereby rendered more impervious to change.

Reinhold Niebuhr,
   US theologian: _Christian Realism and Political Problems,_ 1953

The communist loves nothing better than to be arrested. But he is not like the martyr for the faith. Saint Joan of Arc did not like being tied to a stake. A communist does.

Bishop Fulton Sheen,
   US clergyman, 1955

The supreme reality of our time is our indivisibility as children of God and the common vulnerability of this planet.

John F. Kennedy,
   US president, 1963

The struggle today is between godless people and the people of God and if you want to put it in its basic form, it is between slavery and freedom. I claim we cannot live with these two philosophies in the world forever.

Senator Barry Goldwater,
   1964

We firmly believe that all will be well with our country and our people because God rules.

Dr Hendrik F. Verwoerd,
   South African prime minister, 1958

Christians, to arms! The enemy is at the gate! Buckle on the armour of the Christian and go forth to battle! With education, evangelism and dedication let us smite the communist foe and if necessary give up our lives in this noble cause! We cry 'We shall not yield!' Lift high the blood-stained banner of the Cross and on to victory! Co-existence is impossible — Communism is total evil! Its methods are evil and its ends are evil. We must hurl this thing back into the pit from whence it came!!

Dr Fred C. Schwarz,
   head of the Christian Anti-Communism Crusade, 1961

Providence will provide for Spain when I go.

Francisco Franco

I have been holding demonstrations for fifteen years, but in a stadium where it was legal. . . . So let me do my work in the stadium, and you do yours in the streets.

Billy Graham,
   US evangelist, to black civil rights leader Martin Luther King

Oh Lord, give us the strength to fight the bastards and the strength to carry on.

US army chaplain
   with the 11th Armoured Cavalry in Vietnam, asked to pray for a big body count

If God, as some now say, is dead, He no doubt died of trying to find an equitable solution to the Arab-Jewish problem.

I.F. Stone,
   US political commentator, 1967

I fear no one but God.

Idi Amin,
   Ugandan president, 1977

GOD ON OUR SIDE

I work only according to God's instruction.

Idi Amin,
    Ugandan president, explaining his many massacres, 1974

God taught us to obey civil law and authority. We must reach compatibility between civil and God's law. If there is disharmony, obey God's law, but accept punishment. Governments have been evolved subsequent to religious construction. Worship first, then civil government, then attempt to make the two compatible.

Jimmy Carter,
    US president, 1976

I have asked You for a moral and spiritual restoration in the land, and give thanks that in Thy sovereignty Thou has permitted Richard M. Nixon to lead us at this momentous hour of our history.

Billy Graham,
    US evangelist, at Nixon's inauguration, 1969

From the time I was six or seven, I have felt that perhaps there is a Supreme Being who is guiding me.

Mohammad Reza Pahlevi,
    former Shah of Iran

First the Communists get the kids hooked on free love and free sex, then they start them on marijuana and then the hard stuff. Before you know it they're on to atheism and socialism and the only way to fight it is with the word of God.

Billy Joe Clegg,
    ex-US Air Force sergeant, fringe candidate for the presidency, 1976

There's no more meaningful feeling in life than the feeling you get making things grow, being in touch with nature like that. It gives you almost a religious *feeling*, you know, seeing that corn come in the Fall. It's just good for a man's soul.

Senator Birch Bayh,
    US presidential candidate, 1976

We should live our lives as though Christ was coming this afternoon.

Jimmy Carter

Am I to be told I cannot promise? That we cannot hope? Life is built on hope. Promises make for hope. Without the promise, there never would be progress. Everything in life is a promise. Marriage is a promise. A child coming into the world is a promise. The Bible itself is a promise. It is filled with promises. That is its message — that life is a promise.

Senator Hubert Humphrey,
1976

I think the establishment of Israel...is a fulfilment of biblical prophecy. I think God wanted the Jews to have somewhere to live.

Jimmy Carter

All Ugandans who believe in God should pray night and day.

Idi Amin,
Ugandan president, 1979

There are eleven things which are impure: urine, excrement, sperm, bones, blood, dogs, pigs, non-Moslem men and women, wine, beer and the sweat of the excrement-eating camel.

Ayatollah Khomeini:
Sayings, 1980

ON AND OFF THE RECORD

No government ought to be without censors, and where the press is free, none ever will.

Thomas Jefferson

There are different ways of assassinating a man — by pistol, sword, poison or moral assassination. They are the same in their results, except that the last is more cruel.

Napoleon Bonaparte

Were it left to me to decide whether we should have a government without newspapers or newspapers without a government, I should not hesitate for a moment to prefer the latter.

Thomas Jefferson,
US statesman, 1787

The press is like the air, a chartered libertine.

William Pitt, Earl Chatham,
British Secretary of State, 1757

A people which is able to say everything becomes able to do anything.

Napoleon Bonaparte:
Maxims, 1804-15

The man who never looked into a newspaper is better informed than he who reads them; in as much as he who knows nothing is nearer to the truth than he whose mind is filled with falsehoods and errors.

Thomas Jefferson,
US president, 1807

For what is history but a kind of Newgate Calendar, a register of the crimes and miseries that man has inflicted on his fellow man? It is a huge libel on human nature.

Washington Irving,
US essayist: *History of New York,* 1809

Our liberty depends on the freedom of the press and that cannot be limited without being lost.

Thomas Jefferson

Four hostile newspapers are more to be feared than a thousand bayonets.

Napoleon Bonaparte

It is no longer an event, it is only an item of news.

Charles Maurice de Talleyrand,
French statesman, on Napoleon's death, 1821

Democracy becomes a government of bullies tempered by editors.

Ralph Waldo Emerson,
US poet and philosopher

The gallery in which the reporters sit has become the Fourth Estate of the realm.

Lord Macaulay,
English historian: *Hallam's Constitutional History,* 1828

Happy are the people whose annals are blank in the history books.

Thomas Carlyle,
Scottish author and historian

What experience and history teaches is this — that people and governments have never learnt anything from history or acted on principles deduced from it.

Georg Friedrich Hegel,
    German philosopher, 1832

Burke said that there were three estates in parliament; but in the reporters' gallery yonder, there sat a Fourth Estate more important far than they all.

Thomas Carlyle,
    Scottish author and historian: *Heroes and Hero-Worship*, 1841

Historical phenomena always happen twice — the first time as tragedy, the second as farce.

Karl Marx

History is nothing but a collection of fables and useless trifles, cluttered up with a mass of unnecessary figures and proper names.

Leo Tolstoy,
    Russian author, 1846

History is the autobiography of a madman.

Alexander Herzen,
    Russian political thinker and writer: *Dr Krupov*

History does nothing. It does not possess immense riches, it does not fight battles. It is men, real, living men who do all this....History is nothing but the activity of men in pursuit of their ends.

Karl Marx:
    ***Critique of Political Economy*, 1859**

I have made arrangements for the correspondents to take the field...and I have suggested to them that they should wear a white uniform to indicate the purity of their character.

General Irvin McDowell,
    Union general in the US Civil War, on the war correspondents, 1861

A newspaper writer is one who has failed in his calling.

Otto von Bismarck,
    German president, 1862

History is the essence of innumerable biographies.

Thomas Carlyle,
    Scottish author and historian: 'Essay on History'

In America the president rules for four years and journalism governs for ever and ever.

Oscar Wilde,
    Irish poet, wit and dramatist

The business of the New York journalist is to destroy the truth, to lie outright, to pervert, to vilify, to fawn at the feet of Mammon, and to sell his race and his country for his daily bread.... We are the tools and the vassals of rich men behind the scenes. We are the jumping jacks, they pull the strings and we dance. Our talents, our possibilities and our lives are all the property of other men. We are intellectual prostitutes.

John Swinton,
    US journalist, 1880

History is past politics and politics present history.

Sir John Seeley,
    English historian, 1895

Please remain. You furnish the pictures and I'll furnish the war.

William Randolph Hearst,
    US press magnate, cable to reporter Frederic Remington who was looking for a purported war in Cuba, 1898

It is better to be making the news than taking it, to be an actor rather than a critic.

Winston Churchill,
    1898

History would be an excellent thing if only it were true.

Leo Tolstoy

Politicians tend to live 'in character', and many a public figure has come to imitate the journalism which describes him.

Walter Lippmann,
    US political commentator: *A Preface to Politics*, 1914

ON AND OFF THE RECORD

History, n. An account, mostly false, of events, mostly unimportant, which are brought about by rulers, mostly knaves, and soldiers, mostly fools.

Ambrose Bierce,
US journalist and author: *The Devil's Dictionary*, 1881-1911

The bourgeoisie is many times stronger than we. To give it the weapon of freedom of the press is to ease the enemy's cause, to help the class enemy. We do not desire to end in suicide, so we will not do this.

V.I. Lenin,
founding *Pravda* (Truth), 1912

History is more or less bunk. It's tradition. We don't want tradition. We want to live in the present and the only history that's worth a tinker's damn is the history we make today.

Henry Ford,
US industrialist, 1916

The first casualty, when war comes, is truth.

Senator Hiram Johnson,
1917

I only read articles attacking me, never those that praise. They are too dangerous.

Georges Clemenceau,
former French prime minister, 1921

History is largely concerned with arranging good entrances for people and later exits, not always so good.

Heywood Broun,
US wit: *Pieces of Hate and Other Enthusiasms*, 1922

Print is the sharpest and the strongest weapon of our party.

Joseph Stalin,
1923

Propaganda, propaganda! All that matters is propaganda!

Adolf Hitler,
1923

History repeats itself. That's one of the things wrong with history.

Clarence Darrow,
US radical lawyer

Where books are burnt, humans will be burnt in the end.

Heinrich Heine,
German philosopher, on seeing a picture of Nazis burning books, 1926

What the proprietorship of these papers is aiming at is power without responsibility — the prerogative of the harlot throughout the ages.

Stanley Baldwin,
British prime minister quoting Rudyard Kipling to condemn Lords Beaverbrook and Rothermere, 1930

Spend less money on foolish propaganda and more money on wise propaganda.

Lord Beaverbrook,
British newspaper magnate: a dictum

Dictators have only become possible through the invention of the microphone.

Sir Thomas Inskip,
British MP, 1936

The propagandist's purpose is to make one set of people forget that certain other sets of people are human.

Aldous Huxley,
English novelist and essayist: *The Olive Tree*, 1937

That propaganda is good which leads to success, and that is bad which fails to achieve the desired result, however intelligent it is. For it is not propaganda's task to be intelligent, its task is to lead to success.

Joseph Goebbels,
Nazi propaganda minister

Repetition is the principal secret of successful propaganda.

Lord Beaverbrook,
British newspaper magnate

All propaganda is lies — even when it is telling the truth.

George Orwell,
    English essayist and critic, in his diary, 1942

Accuracy to a newspaper is what virtue is to a lady, but a newspaper can always print a retraction.

Adlai Stevenson,
    US statesman

One of the greatest of American soldiers, Robert E. Lee, once remarked on the tragic fact that in the war of his day all the best generals were apparently working on newspapers intead of in the army. And that seems to be true in all wars.

Franklin D. Roosevelt

When the political columnists say 'every thinking man', they mean themselves; and when candidates appeal to 'every thinking voter', they mean everybody who is going to vote for them.

Franklin P. Adams,
    US columnist: *Nods and Becks*, 1944

Political or military commentators, like astrologers, can survive almost any mistake, because their more devoted followers do not look to them for an appraisal of the facts, but for the stimulation of nationalistic loyalties.

George Orwell,
    English essayist and critic: 'Notes on Nationalism', 1945

A politician wouldn't dream of being allowed to call a columnist the things a columnist is allowed to call a politician.

Max Lerner,
    US journalist: *Actions and Passions*, 1949

Eisenhower was right for the country for a large number of reasons. Therefore it was *Time*'s duty to explain why the country needed Ike. Any other form of objectivity would have been unfair and uninvolved.

Henry Luce,
    proprietor of *Time* magazine, explaining his unabashed pro-Eisenhower stance, 1952

In our time, political speech and writing are largely the defence of the indefensible.

George Orwell,
    English essayist and critic: 'Politics and the English Language', 1950

An editor is one who separates the wheat from the chaff and prints the chaff.

Adlai Stevenson,
    US statesman

The media, far from being a conspiracy to dull the political sense of the people, could be seen as a conspiracy to disguise the extent of political indifference.

David Riesman,
    US sociologist

Political language. . . is designed to make lies sound truthful and murder respectable, and to give an appearance of solidity to pure wind.

George Orwell,
    English essayist and critic: 'Politics and the English Language', 1950

No TV performance takes such careful preparation as an off-the-cuff talk.

Richard Nixon,
    US vice-president, 1952

I won't sell their cereal for them.

Sam Rayburn,
    Speaker of the House of Representatives, refusing to allow TV cameras covering the debates

I am a protestant, a Republican and a free-enterpriser. Which means I am biased in favour of God, Eisenhower and the stockholders of Time Inc. And if anybody who objects doesn't know this by now, why the hell are they still spending thirty-five cents for the magazine?

Henry Luce,
    proprietor of *Time* magazine

STALIN DEAD OFFICIAL — HOORAY!

Sir Frank Packer,
    Australian newspaper magnate, 1953. He forced his typesetters to run this bill in the Sydney *Daily Telegraph*, announcing Stalin's death

ON AND OFF THE RECORD

If you lose your temper at a newspaper columnist, he'll get rich, or famous, or both.

James C. Hagerty,
    Eisenhower's press secretary, after a row with columnist Art Buchwald

You know very well whether you are on page one or page thirty depends on whether they fear you. It is just as simple as that.

Richard Nixon

Television is democracy at its ugliest.

Paddy Chayevsky,
    TV scriptwriter

Without criticism and intelligent reporting, a government cannot govern.

Walter Lippmann,
    US political commentator

People will say a spot announcement does not give the audience a chance to get to know the candidate. Sometimes that is a good thing for the candidate.

Richard Nixon,
    US vice-president, addressing the Radio and TV Executives Society, 1955

What is history after all? History is the facts which become legends in the end. Legends are lies which become history in the end.

Jean Cocteau,
    French writer, 1957

That men do not learn very much from the lessons of history is the most important of all the lessons that history has to teach.

Aldous Huxley,
    English novelist and essayist: *Collected Essays,* **1959**

Human history, if you read it right, is the record of the attempts to tame Father.

Max Lerner,
    US journalist: *The Unfinished Country,* **1959**

I read the newspaper avidly — it is my one form of continuous fiction.

Aneurin Bevan,
    British Labour politician, 1960

Freedom of the press has passed into history.

Francisco Franco,
    1961

In Cuba, there is only one newspaper. It appears irregularly, from time to time. It is Fidel, when he speaks to the people.

Carlos Franqui,
    Cuban journalist, 1961

As I leave the press, all I can say is this — for sixteen years, ever since the Hiss case, you've had a lot of fun, a lot of fun....You've had an opportunity to attack me...just think about how much you're going to be missing, you won't have Nixon to kick around any more because, gentlemen, this is my last press conference.

Richard Nixon,
    after failing to be elected Governor of California, 1962

We were here before you got here, Ted, and we will be here when you're gone.

James Reston,
    US political commentator, rebuking Kennedy aide Theodore Sorenson for harassing his colleague Tom Wicker, a new member of the White House press corps, 1961

It is the rule, not the exception, that otherwise unemployable public figures inevitably take to writing for publication.

Richard Condon,
    US novelist

Just play the assassination footage over and over again, that's all they want to see.

James T. Aubrey, Jr,
    president of CBS-TV, ordaining the network's coverage of John F. Kennedy's death, 1963

Democracy depends on information circulating freely in society.

Katherine Graham,
    publisher of *The Washington Post* **and** *Newsweek*

There are honest journalists like there are honest politicians — they stay bought.

Bill Moyers,
   Kennedy aide

Any event, once it has occurred, can be made to appear inevitable by a competent historian.

Lee Simonson,
   US historian

This damn thing is going to cost us ten million dollars. Who wants to listen to news? If I had my way we'd have some guy come on at 11 p.m. and say, 'The following six guys made horses' asses of themselves at the Republican Convention,' and he'd give the six names and that would be it.

James T. Aubrey,
   walking out of the Republican Convention,
furious with CBS's saturation coverage of the
event, 1964

The major tasks of the press are to popularize, in a prompt and easy-to-understand manner, with a deep knowledge of the matter under discussion, and using lively, concrete examples; advanced methods of labour, management and administration; to work persistently for their introduction everywhere, and to educate tirelessly in all Soviet people a conscientious, creative attitude to work, a feeling of being master of the country, and a high sense of responsibility to society.

Central Committee of the Communist Party
of the Soviet Union:
   directive to the Soviet press

Halberstam should be barbecued, and I would be glad to supply the fluid and the match.

Madame Nhu,
   a member of Vietnam's ruling Diem family,
after the _New York Times'_ reporter had
commented adversely and regularly on the
family's mismanagement of Vietnam, 1963

The press conference is the politician's way of being informative without actually saying anything.

Emery Kelen

Reporters are puppets. They simply respond to the pull of the most powerful strings.

Lyndon B. Johnson

A free press is not a privilege, but an organic necessity in a great society. . . . A great society is simply a big, complicated urban society.

Walter Lippmann,
   US political commentator, 1965

Television is eerie: all politicians believe their own myths, and television makes those myths even larger. What television sends up these days, it sends up very quickly, but it can bring things down just as quickly.

David Halberstam,
   US journalist

The press are good guys. I have a lot of friends in the press. . . . I like the press guys because basically I'm like them, because of my own inquisitiveness. The press is very helpful with their questions.

Richard Nixon,
   New York lawyer, 1966

In order to avoid the embarrassment of calling a spade and spade, newspapermen have agreed to talk about the credibility gap. This is a polite euphemism for deception.

Walter Lippmann,
   US political commentator, on the Johnson
administration, 1967

Information is the currency of democracy.

Ralph Nader,
   US consumer campaigner

He who attacks the fundamentals of the American system, attacks democracy itself.

William S. Paley,
   chairman of CBS, on broadcasting

What the hell is going on? I thought we were winning the war.

Walter Cronkite,
   US TV news anchorman, off-screen
comment after announcing the Viet Cong's
devastating Tet offensive, 1968

ON AND OFF THE RECORD

Some newspapers are fit only to line the bottom of birdcages.

Spiro T. Agnew,
  US vice-president

It is next to useless to interview a politician. ... To surprise a skilful politician is approximately equal in difficulty to hitting a professional boxer with a bar-room hook.

Norman Mailer,
  US novelist and journalist: *Miami and the Siege of Chicago*, 1968

In dealing with the press, do yourself a favour, stick with one of three responses: (a) I know and I can tell you; (b) I know and I can't tell you; (c) I don't know.

Dan Rather,
  CBS TV reporter, advising politicians

A spirit of national masochism prevails, encouraged by an effete corps of impudent snobs who characterize themselves as intellectuals.

Spiro T. Agnew,
  scourging the media, 1969

I hesitate to get into the gutter with this guy.

Chet Huntley,
  TV news anchorman, responding to Agnew

Nixon depended on television the way a polio victim depends on an iron lung.

Joe McGinnis,
  US journalist: *The Selling of the President*, 1969

I think that probably the attacks on me in the press and in politics have been worse than on any other Prime Minister, even Lloyd George.

Harold Wilson,
  British prime minister, 1969

Politicians and journalists have a peculiar dependence on and contempt for each other.

Alistair Burnet,
  British TV and print journalist, 1971

Without an informed and free press there cannot be an enlightened people.

Justice Stewart,
  US Supreme Court judge, over-ruling the Administration's attempts to suppress publication of the 'Pentagon Papers', the secret government history of The Vietnam War, 1971

The most distressing thing about covering politics is the guy who was absolutely right, whose wisdom was almost breath-taking one election year.... You go back to that same man for wisdom some other year and he'll be dumb as dogshit. That's why it's not a science.

David Broder,
  US political commentator, 1972

One of the lessons of history is that nothing is often a good thing to do and always a clever thing to say.

Will Durant,
  US historian, 1972

They shouldn't try to be objective, they should try to be honest. Their so-called objectivity is just a guise for superficiality.... They never get around to finding out if the guy is telling the truth.... What they pass off for objectivity is just a mindless kind of neutrality.

Brit Hume,
  US investigative journalist, on the political press, 1972

All these reporters care about is 'Who's gonna run, who's gonna win?' And that just isn't enough. The press has a greater responsibility than to do a bunch of handicapping stories.

Brit Hume,
  1972

This is not a warning, but a statement of fact: you have until January to put your houses in order.

J. B. Vorster,
  South African prime minister, to the assembled editors of the nation's press, September 1973

They're like slugs on a snail farm.

Hunter S. Thompson,
   US gonzo journalist, on the White House press corps, 1972

You delude yourself into thinking, 'Well, if I get on the bad side of these guys, then I'm not going to get all that good stuff.' But pretty soon the realization hits that there *isn't* any good stuff, and there isn't going to be any good stuff. Nobody's getting anything you're not getting, and if they are, it's just more of the same bullshit.

Karl Fleming,
   US journalist, on relations with politicians, 1973

In all my life I have treated the press with marked contempt and remarkable success.

Sir Robert Menzies,
   Australian prime minister, talking to Richard Nixon

No one would ever forget Robert Menzies. I learned a lot from him.

Richard Nixon

Political reporters, they're like sports writers. The job's a lot the same. It's fun to do. And the quality isn't very high. Anyone can be a political writer or a sports writer.

Dick Stout,
   US journalist, 1973

We're like the guys who sweep up behind circus elephants. That's all we have dropped on us.

Adam Clymer,
   White House press corps, 1974

No one likes being covered, and covered constantly; none of us likes our face in the mirror, unless we own the mirror.

David Halberstam,
   US journalist, 1974

God help us, you're a rotten bunch!

Senator Barry Goldwater,
   to US journalists after their attacks on Richard Nixon, 1974

If I were basically a liberal by the standards of the press, if I had bugged out on Vietnam, which was what they wanted, Watergate would have been a blip.

Richard Nixon,
   US president, 1974

It is expecting too much for any politician to be sincerely interested in the free flow of information.

Graham Perkin,
   editor of the Melbourne *Age*, 1974

Presidents do not have press problems, they have constituency problems. When they get in trouble with the press it is a symptom of something else — that they are getting into trouble with their constituents. Newsmen live within our society and they react like other Americans do — the things that bother a press about a president will ultimately bother the country.

George Reedy,
   former press secretary to Lyndon B. Johnson, 1974

Those who control a great deal are obsessed by the few things they do not control, particularly if these things, like television reporters, bear constant reminder that you do not control all that you think you do.

David Halberstam,
   US journalist, 1974

Half the reporters in town are looking on you as a Pulitzer Prize waiting to be won.

Senator Lawton Chiles,
   on the upsurge of investigative journalism in Washington in the aftermath of Watergate

Memories don't last as long as you people in the media think.

Harold Wilson,
   British prime minister, 1975

Would a Catholic talk to the devil? That's what the CIA thinks of talking to the press.

Jim Keehner,
   CIA psychologist, 1976

If I rescued a child from drowning, the press would no doubt headline the story 'Benn Grabs Child'.

**Anthony Wedgwood Benn,
British politician, 1975**

If I go on TV and look grim, they say the situation must be even worse; if I smile at all, it's complacency.

**Harold Wilson,
1975**

The interview is an intimate conversation between journalist and politician wherein the journalist seeks to take advantage of the garrulity of the politician, and the politician of the credulity of the journalist.

Emery Kelen

If you look back on politicians who've been popular with the press . . . they've always been the most superficial, the most manipulative, and the most tactical — as opposed to strategic — of politicians.

Sir James Goldsmith,
English businessman and publisher, 1977

The only way a reporter should look at a politician is down.

Frank Kent,
US journalist, 1977

I hate to look another human being in the eye and say 'no comment'.

Andrew Young;
such candour eventually lost him his job as US Ambassador to the United Nations

Information is an equalizer, it breaks down the hierarchy. A lot of institutions are living in a world that is rapidly passing them by.

Jerry Brown,
governor of California, 1978

The perception of power *is* power.

David Garth,
US specialist in political ad campaigns, 1978

Thirty seconds on the evening news is worth a front page headline in every newspaper in the world.

Edward Guthman,
quoted by Paul Dickson: *The Official Rules*, 1978

Back in the fifties I watched the McCarthy hearings on TV. And they really upset me. I kept seeing the good guys get their asses handed to them. They always seemed to be outmanned and outfought. And ya know who finally saved them? It wasn't the goddam establishment. Oh no. It was a guy named Joe Welch and two NBC cameramen who took a tight shot of that bastard's face every time he twitched or scowled.

David Garth,
specialist in political ad campaigns, 1978

Radio and television are allowed if they are used for the broadcasting of news or sermons, for the spreading of good educational material, for publicizing the products and curiosities of the planet; but they must prohibit singing, music, anti-Islamic laws, the lauding of tyrants, mendacious words and broadcasts which spread doubt and undermine virtue.

Ayatollah Khomeini,
religious dictator of Iran: *Sayings*, 1980

Private Eye made me more money than Marmite.

Sir James Goldsmith,
English businessman and publisher, whose Cavenham Foods own the breakfast spread, on his lawsuit against the British satirical fortnightly, 1980

I don't know how good she is for the country, but she's good for me.

Wally Fawkes,
cartoonist 'Trog' of the *Daily Mail*, on Margaret Thatcher, 1980

Three things are specifically excluded from our television: political propaganda against the socialist system, sadism and pornography.

Richard Nagy,
director-general of Hungarian TV, 1978

FRAUDS AT THE POLLS

Persistence in one opinion has never been considered a merit in political leaders.

Cicero:
    Ad Familiares, first century BC

A cock has great influence on his own dunghill.

Pubilius Syrus,
    Roman dramatist and mime: *Moral Sayings*, first century BC

It is easier to appear worthy of a position one does not hold than of the office which one fills.

Duc de la Rochefoucauld:
    Maxims, 1665

If you would be powerful, pretend to be powerful.

Horne Tooke,
    English radical

All political parties die at last of swallowing their own lies.

John Arbuthnot,
    Scottish writer, 1712

The English people fancy they are free; it is only during the election of members of parliament that they are so. As soon as these are elected the people are slaves, they are nothing. In the brief moments of their liberty the abuse made of it fully deserves that it should be lost.

Jean-Jacques Rousseau,
    French philosopher

Give me a grain of truth...and I will mix it up with such a mass of falsehood, so that no chemist shall ever be able to separate them.

John Wilkes,
    British radical politician

To succeed in chaining the multitude, you must seem to wear the same fetters.

Voltaire,
    French author and humanitarian: *Philosophical Dictionary*, 1764

The people never give up their liberties but under some delusion.

Edmund Burke,
    British statesman, 1784

Put a rogue in the limelight and he will act like an honest man.

Napoleon Bonaparte:
    Maxims, 1804-15

The object of oratory alone is not the truth, but persuasion.

Lord Macaulay,
    English historian

In argument truth always prevails finally, in politics falsehood always.

Walter Savage Landor,
    English poet, 1829

In politics as on the sickbed, people toss from side to side, thinking they will be more comfortable.

Johann Wolfgang von Goethe,
   German poet

Fellow citizens, I presume you all know who I am. I am humble Abraham Lincoln. My politics are short and sweet like the old woman's dance. If elected I shall be thankful, if not it will be all the same.

Abraham Lincoln,
   in his first campaign speech, 1832

The conduct and opinions of public men at different periods of their careers must not be curiously contrasted in a free society.

Benjamin Disraeli,
   British politician, 1834

The submission of the individual to society — to the people — is the continuation of human sacrifice...the crucifixion of the innocent for the guilty.... The individual, who is the true, real monad of society, has always been sacrificed to some general concept, some collective noun, some banner or other. What the purpose...of the sacrifice was..., was never so much as asked.

Alexander Herzen,
   Russian political thinker and writer: *From the Other Shore,* **1847-50**

'Vote early and vote often' — the advice openly displayed on the election banners in some of our northern cities.

W.P. Miles,
   US editor, 1858

Something unpleasant is coming when men are anxious to tell the truth.

Benjamin Disraeli

You can always get the truth from an American statesman after he has turned seventy or given up all hope of the presidency.

Wendell Phillips,
   US abolitionist, 1860

The greatest superstition now entertained by public men is that hypocrisy is the royal road to success.

Robert G. Ingersoll,
   US lawyer, 1886

I needed the good will of the legislature of four states. I formed the legislative bodies with my own money — I found it cheaper that way.

Jay Gould,
   US railroad millionaire

Half a truth is better than no politics

G.K. Chesterton,
   English critic, novelist and poet: *All Things Considered,* **1908**

A man who raises new issues has always been distasteful to politicians. He musses up what has been so tidily arranged.

Walter Lippmann,
   US political commentator: *A Preface to Politics,* **1914**

The War Office kept three sets of figures: one to mislead the public, one to mislead the Cabinet and one to mislead themselves.

H.H. Asquith,
   on First World War casualty lists

It is unfortunate, considering that enthusiasm moves the world, that so few enthusiasts can be trusted to speak the truth.

Arthur Balfour,
   British politician, 1918

Democracy's ceremonial, its feast, its great function is the election.

H.G. Wells

Universal suffrage almost inevitably leads to government by mass bribery, an auction of the worldly goods of the unrepresented minority.

William R. Inge,
   Dean of St Paul's

FRAUDS AT THE POLLS

General elections in future will tend to become wage auctions.

Sir Henry Fairfax-Lucy,
    British politician, 1919

The convention will be deadlocked and after the other candidates have gone their limit, some twelve or fifteen men, worn out and bleary-eyed for lack of sleep, will sit down about two o'clock in the morning around a table in a smoke-filled room in some hotel and decide the nomination. When that time comes, Harding will be selected.

Harry M. Daugherty,
    US politician, coining a phrase, 1920

It is easy to settle the world upon a soap box.

David Lloyd George

The nauseous sham good fellowship our democratic public men get up for shop use.

George Bernard Shaw:
    Back to Methuselah, 1921

The gift of rhetoric has been responsible for more bloodshed on this earth than all the guns and explosives that were invented.

Stanley Baldwin,
    British prime minister, 1924

I am a candidate for county judge. The first reason I want to be elected judge is to fill the vacancy created by electing S.F. Bowman in 1921. The second reason is to relieve Mr Bowman of the great burden placed on him by the sheriff laying down on his job, thereby causing Mr Bowman to try to fill two official positions. The third reason I want to be a judge is because the county needs a judge. The fourth reason is I want the salary. Yours for a square deal for the great common people....

Lee Ward,
    his election hand-out to Rockcastle
County, Kentucky, 1925

Safety First. Stanley Baldwin. The Man You Can Trust.

Conservative Party slogan,
    General Election, 1929

The fact that an opinion has been widely held is no evidence whatever that it is not utterly absurd. Indeed, in view of the silliness of the majority of mankind, a widespread belief is more likely to be foolish than sensible.

Bertrand Russell: Marriage and Morals, 1929

If you don't say anything, you won't be called upon to repeat it.

Calvin Coolidge

Any party which takes credit for the rain must not be surprised if its opponents blame it for the drought.

Dwight D. Morrow,
    US diplomat and finance expert, 1930

There's just one rule for politicians all over the world. — Don't say in power what you say in opposition. If you do you will only have to carry out what the other fellows have found impossible.

John Galsworthy,
    English novelist: Maids In Waiting, 1931

I hope you have read the election programme of the Labour Party. It is the most fantastic and improbable programme ever put before the electors.... This is not Socialism. It is Bolshevism run mad.

Philip Snowden,
    British statesman, in an election
broadcast, 1931

It is amazing how wise statesmen can be when it is ten years too late.

David Lloyd George,
    Liberal elder statesman, 1932

The politicians and financiers seem to me to be the plumbers of the modern world — always going back to the country for something they haven't got and pretending that it is only the absence of that particular implement which prevents them from doing their job.

A.P. Herbert,
    English humorist, 1932

BOOK OF POLITICAL QUOTES

Even though counting heads is not an ideal way to govern, at least it is better than breaking them.

**Judge Learned Hand,
    US jurist, 1932**

What matters is not so much what we believe, only that we believe.

**Joseph Goebbels,
    Nazi minister of propaganda, 1933**

It would be desirable if every government, when it comes into power, should have its old speeches burned.

**Philip Snowden,
    British statesman**

What is truth? We must adopt a pragmatic definition: it is what is believed to be the truth. A lie that is put across therefore becomes the truth and may, therefore, be justified. The difficulty is to keep up lying.... It is simpler to tell the truth and if a sufficient emergency arises, to tell one big, thumping lie that will then be believed.

**British Ministry of Information memo
    on the wartime maintenance of civilian morale, 1939**

Eating words has never given me indigestion.

Winston Churchill

Prosperity is necessarily the first theme of a political campaign.

Woodrow Wilson

Our major obligation is not to mistake slogans for solutions.

**Edward R. Murrow,
    US radio journalist**

At the bottom of all the tributes paid to democracy is the little man, walking into the little booth, with the little pencil, making the little cross on the little bit of paper — no amount of rhetoric or voluminous discussion can possibly diminish the overwhelming importance of the point.

**Winston Churchill,
    British prime minister, 1944**

The trouble with this country is that there are too many politicians who believe, with a conviction based on experience, that you can fool all of the people all of the time.

**Franklin P. Adams,
    US columnist: *Nods and Becks*, 1944**

If you can't convince them confuse them.

Harry S. Truman

The Republicans stroke platitudes until they purr like epigrams.

Adlai Stevenson

Man is a credulous animal and must believe *something.* In the absence of good grounds for belief, he will be satisfied with bad ones.

Bertrand Russell: *Unpopular Essays,* 1950

A wise politician will never grudge a genuflexion or a rapture if it is expected of him by the prevalent opinion.

**F.S. Oliver,
    British historian**

Anyone who says he isn't going to resign, four times, definitely will.

**John Kenneth Galbraith,
    Canadian-born US economist**

I am persuaded that there is absolutely no limit to the absurdities that can, by government action, come to be generally believed.

**Bertrand Russell:
    Unpopular Essays, 1950**

A lie is an abomination unto the Lord and a very present help in time of trouble.

**Adlai Stevenson,
    governor of Illinois, 1951**

The professional politician woos the fickle public more as a man engaged than married, for his is a contract that must be renewed every few years and the memory of the public is short.

J.T. Salter

Our great democracies still tend to think that a stupid man is more likely to be honest than a clever man and our politicians take advantage of this by pretending to be even more stupid than nature made them.

Bertrand Russell:
New Hopes for a Changing World, **1951**

When Republican speech-makers think they are thinking, they are only rearranging their prejudices.

Adlai Stevenson

There are no political panaceas — except in the imagination of political quacks.

Francis Parkman,
US historian

The voting machines won't hold me up. If I have the right commissioners, I can make those machines play Home Sweet Home.

Earl Long,
Governor of Louisiana

Successful democratic politicians are insecure and intimidated men. They advance politically only as they placate, appease, bribe, seduce, bamboozle or otherwise manage to manipulate the demanding and threatening elements in their constituencies.

Walter Lippmann,
US political commentator: *The Public Philosophy,* **1955**

Politicians speak for their parties and parties never are, never have been, and never will be wrong.

Walter Dwight

Voting is simply a way of determining which side is the stronger without putting it to the test of fighting.

H.L. Mencken,
US philologist, editor and satirist: *Minority Report,* **1956**

Politicians are the same all over. They promise to build a bridge even where there is no river.

Nikita Khruschev,
1960

You will find that the truth is often unpopular and the contest between agreeable fancy and disagreeable fact is unequal. For, in the vernacular, we Americans are suckers for good news.

Adlai Stevenson,
US statesman addressing a Harvard graduating class, 1958

You believe politicians, what they say. It's a device to get elected. If you were to follow Adlai Stevenson from New York to Alabama you would shit from the changes.

Lenny Bruce,
US satirist

Never tell them what you wouldn't do.

Adam Clayton Powell,
US politician

Since a politician never believes what he says, he is surprised when others believe him.

Charles de Gaulle,
1962

IN YOUR HEART YOU KNOW HE'S RIGHT

Barry Goldwater,
his presidential campaign slogan, 1964

If the British public falls for this, I say it will be stark, staring bonkers.

Quintin Hogg,
British jurist and politician, on the Labour Party manifesto, 1964

If you feed the people just with revolutionary slogans they will listen today, they will listen tomorrow, they will listen the day after tomorrow, but on the fourth day they will say 'To hell with you!'

Nikita Khruschev,
1964

The ability to foretell what is going to happen tomorrow, next week, next month and next year. And to have the ability afterwards to explain why it didn't happen.

Winston Churchill
on political skill

Richarc Nixon in 1950/Popperfoto

I should say this: Pat doesn't have a mink coat, but she does have a respectable Republican cloth coat....One other thing I should probably tell you, because if I don't they'll be saying this about me too. We did get something, a gift, after the election...a little cocker spaniel in a crate, all the way from Texas....And our little girl, Trisha, the six-year-old, named it Checkers. And you know, the kids love that dog, and I just want to say this right now, that regardless of what they say about it, we're gonna keep it!

Richard Nixon,
US vice-president, in the 'Checkers Speech', after he had been accused of using campaign funds for his personal gain, 1952

A little nonsense now and then is not a bad thing. Where would we politicians be if we were not allowed to talk it sometimes?

Enoch Powell,
British politician, 1965

The right to lie.

Arthur Sylvester,
press secretary to Robert MacNamara, US Secretary of Defense, defining the basis of his role as a news filter

Look, if you think any American official is going to tell you the truth, then you're stupid.

Arthur Sylvester,
briefing reporters in Saigon, 1965

FRAUDS AT THE POLLS

People rather like all the talk of cliff-hanging. It makes politics more interesting.

Harold Wilson,
British prime minister, 1965

For every credibility gap there is a gullibility fill.

Richard Clopton,
quoted by Dr Lawrence Peter: *Peter's Quotations*

Every government is run by liars and nothing they say should be believed.

I. F. Stone,
US political commentator

The professional politician can sympathise with the professional advertiser. Both must resign themselves to a low public estimation of their veracity and sincerity.

Enoch Powell,
British politician, 1965

You cannot quantify an élan.

Harold Wilson,
parrying demands for a statement of English economic development under his government

The political lie has become a way of bureaucratic life. It has been called by the more genteel name of 'news management'. I say here and now, let's call it what it is: lying.

Walter Cronkite,
US TV anchorman, 1966

It does not mean, of course, that the pound here in Britain in your pocket or purse or in your bank has been devalued.

Harold Wilson,
British prime minister, announcing the devaluation of the pound, 1967

I am a firm believer in the idea that to acknowledge my mistakes of yesterday is but another way of saying that I am a wiser man today.

Senator William Fulbright,
1968

Propaganda is the art of persuading others of what one does not believe oneself.

Abba Eban,
Israeli politician

Experience suggests that the first rule of politics is never to say never. The ingenious human capacity for manoeuvre and compromise may make acceptable tomorrow what seems outrageous or impossible today.

William V. Shannon,
US journalist, 1968

You don't win campaigns with a diet of dishwater and milk toast

Richard Nixon

I am afraid that a lot of the things that many of us have said in the past three years are going to have to be unsaid.

Denis Healey,
British politician, 1968

It is dangerous for a national candidate to say things that people might remember.

Senator Eugeno McCarthy

In order to become the master, the politician poses as the servant.

Charles de Gaulle,
1969

Nothing is so admirable in politics as a short memory.

John Kenneth Galbraith,
Canadian-born US economist

You can say that this Administration will have the first complete, far-reaching attack on the problem of hunger in history. Use all the rhetoric, as long as it doesn't cost money.

Richard Nixon,
speaking on the record to the President's Urban Affairs Council, 1969

I'm sure that if we could get a more euphemistic name for the Labour Party we would get thousands of votes.

S. Rubensohn,
Australian advertising executive, 1969

YESTERDAY'S MEN

**Labour Party slogan,
beneath a picture of caricatured
Conservative leaders, 1970**

The President is aware of what is going on.
That is not to say that something is going
on.

**Ron Ziegler,
White House press secretary, 1971**

Every aspect of the war is layered over by
mistruth, misinformation, mis-statement and
silence. None of this lying and hiding has a
jot to do with military security.....It's done
to conceal graft, stupidity, bad judgement
from our own people. It's done in the hopes
that you can execute policies in secret that
you wouldn't dare attempt if they were
known.

**Nicholas von Hoffman,
US columnist, 1971**

If the people of a democracy are allowed to
do so, they will vote away the freedoms
which are essential to that democracy.

**Snell Putney,
US author: *The Conquest of Society*, 1972**

For the first time in many years, the
government will approach this election quite
frankly not knowing what the result will be.

**Robert Southey,
Australian Liberal Party federal president,
1972**

The gut question for the Committee and
country alike is and was: how much truth
do we want? A few men gambled that
Americans wanted the quiet of efficiency
rather than the turbulence of truth.

**Senator Lowell Weicker,
in his opening speech to the Congressional
Committee on Watergate, 1973**

My non-voters, who are called apathetic,
really just think unacceptable alternatives are
being offered to them. The lesser of two
evils is still evil.

**Sy Leon,
head of the US League of Non-Voters, 1976**

The art of being a political winner is the art
of being there at the right time.

**Tom Burns,
Australian politician, 1974**

Going round the country stirring up
complacency.

**William Whitelaw,
British Conservative MP, on the Labour
Party electioneering, 1974**

Politicians cannot be compelled to be honest.

**D.J. Killen,
Australian politician, 1975**

Sometimes you can have competing election
promises.

**Malcolm Fraser,
Australian parliamentary candidate, 1976**

I'm not from Washington and I'm not a
lawyer.

**Jimmy Carter,
US presidential candidate, endearing
himself to post-Watergate America, 1976**

I wish I had some of that talent.

**Gerald Ford,
US presidential candidate, looking at a
hand-crocheted American flag during his
campaign, 1976**

I feel a special kinship with you, because
potatoes and peanuts are the only major
crops that grow underground.

**Jimmy Carter,
campaigning in potato growing Idaho, 1976**

I'm not going to re-arrange the furniture on
the deck of the Titanic.

**Rogers Morton,
Ford aide, refusing any last-ditch attempts
to salvage his campaign, 1976**

Social workers are my favourite kind of
people.....To see the pride that exists now
in those women who are doing something
useful in God's sight will bring tears to the
eye.

**Jimmy Carter,
addressing social workers, 1976**

FRAUDS AT THE POLLS

Trust is not having to guess what a candidate means.

Gerald Ford,
  1976

I regret that some people in this country have disparaged and demeaned the role of the homemaker. I say — and I say it with emphasis and conviction — that homemaking is good for America.... You should never be embarrassed to say anywhere on the face of this earth: 'I am an American homemaker and I'm proud of it.'

Gerald Ford,
  campaigning among North Carolina's Future Homemakers of America, 1976

I really could not think of a good reason not to. A little vagueness goes a long way in this business.

Jerry Brown,
  governor of California, on his reasons for joining the presidential race, 1976

There is no connection between voting and what comes out at the bottom of the machine. Nixon pledges law and order and receives votes on that issue, and you get crime and corruption. Why vote? Rather than controlling the levers of power, the president seems to be playing a slot machine and you don't know when it's going to come up lemons.

Samuel Popkin,
  US psephologist, 1976

I hope you'll look not at who is most handsome, or who has the best rhetoric, the rhetoric that stirs your soul. It does no good to find someone who turns you on if they aren't electable.

Morris Udall,
  US presidential candidate, 1976

Amend my statements last night and insert the word 'lose' where I had the word 'win'.

Morris Udall,
  referring to a premature victory speech at the Wisconsin primary when, despite media predictions, he did not win, 1976

It doesn't matter what I say as long as I sound different from other politicians.

Jerry Brown,
  US presidential candidate, 1976

You don't tell deliberate lies, but sometimes you have to be evasive.

Margaret Thatcher,
  British Conservative Party leader, 1976

Vote Cederberg — he spends your money like it was his own!

Al Cederberg,
  veteran Republican congressman, seeking re-election in Michigan, 1976

Anyone who says he likes it is sick.

Morris Udall,
  US presidential candidate, on campaigning, 1976

Do you know why I have credibility? Because I don't exude morality.

Bob Hawke,
  Australian trade union leader, 1977

The candidate who is expected to do well because of experience and reputation (Douglas, Nixon) must do *better* than well, while the candidate who is expected to fare poorly (Lincoln, Kennedy) can put points on the media board simply by surviving.

Vic Gold,
  US author: *PR as in President,* 1977

Some statements you make in public...are reported as 'an unnamed source'...Nobody believes the official spokesman, but everyone trusts an unidentified source.

Ron Nessen,
  Gerald Ford's press secretary, 1977

If voting changed anything, they'd make it illegal.

Graffito
  on a London wall, 1979

Advertising men and politicians are dangerous if they are separated. Together they are diabolical.

Phillip Adams,
    Australian advertising executive, 1977

It's very close. They're not going to be able to tell who's the winner until the votes are counted.

Anonymous aide,
    to aspirant Democratic congressman Joseph Vigorito, 1978

Last guys don't finish nice.

Professor Stanley Kelley,
    US academic, on the increasing bitterness of US elections, quoted by Paul Dickson: *The Official Rules*, 1978

They're just words.

Jerry Brown
    on his various official and public statements

The American people aren't interested in details.

Lyn Nofziger,
    member of Ronald Reagan's campaign staff, on the candidate's threadbare speechifying

Campaigns are like childbirth. Before you remember how awful it is, you're back in there having another one.

Margaret Whitlam,
    wife of Australian Labour leader Gough Whitlam, 1977

Margaret Whitlam with her two children/Publisher's files

VOX POPULI

Let the people think they govern and they will be governed.

William Penn,
   founder of Pennsylvania, 1693

A mob has many heads, but no brains.

Thomas Fuller,
   British doctor and writer: *Gnomologia*, 1732

The tyranny of a prince in an oligarchy is not so dangerous to the public welfare as the apathy of a citizen in a democracy.

Charles Baron de Montesquieu,
   French philosopher

The public seldom forgive twice.

Johan Kaspar Lavater,
   Swiss divine and poet, 1788

The tyranny of the multitude is multiplied tyranny.

Edmund Burke,
   British statesman, 1790

The mass of the people have nothing to do with the laws but to obey them.

Samuel Horsley,
   Bishop of Rochester, 1795

When people cease to complain, they cease to think.

Napoleon Bonaparte

If obedience is the result of the instinct of the masses, revolt is the result of their thought.

Napoleon Bonaparte

The mobs of great cities add just so much to the support of pure government as sores do to the strength of the human body.

Thomas Jefferson

I am ashamed to think how easily we capitulate to badges and names, to large societies and dead institutions. We ought to go upright and vital and speak rude truth in all ways.

Ralph Waldo Emerson,
   US poet and philosopher

Enlighten the people generally and oppression of body and mind will vanish like spirits in the dawn of day.

Thomas Jefferson

If any ask me what a free government is, I answer, that for any practical purpose, it is what the people think so.

Edmund Burke,
   British statesman: 'Letter to the Sheriffs of Bristol', 1777

The people feel the need of potatoes, but none whatsoever of a constitution. That is desired only by educated townspeople who are quite powerless.

Vissarion G. Belinsky,
   Russian critic, 1846

The people are capable of good judgement when they do not listen to demagogues.

Napoleon Bonaparte

Public opinion is a weak tyrant, compared with our own private opinion. What a man thinks of himself, that is which determines, or rather indicates his fate.

Henry David Thoreau,
US philosopher

A mob is a society of bodies voluntarily bereaving themselves of reason.... A mob is man voluntarily descending to the nature of the beast.

Ralph Waldo Emerson,
US poet and philosopher

The great unwashed.

Lord Brougham of Vaux,
Scottish law reformer, on the masses. Also attributed to Edmund Burke, Thomas Carlyle and Sir Walter Scott

The public is an old woman. Let her maunder and mumble.

Thomas Carlyle,
Scottish author and historian: *Journal,*
1835

To sin by silence when they should protest makes cowards of men.

Abraham Lincoln

The masses want to stay the hand which impudently snatches from them the bread which they have earned.... They are indifferent to individual freedom, liberty of speech — the masses love authority. They are blinded by the arrogant glitter of power, they are offended by those that stand alone. By equality, they understand equality of oppression.... They want a social government to rule for their benefit.... But to govern themselves doesn't enter their heads.

Alexander Herzen,
Russian political thinker and writer: *From the Other Shore,* **1847-50**

What men call social virtues, good fellowship, is commonly but the virtue of pigs in a litter, which lie close together to keep each other warm.

Henry David Thoreau,
US philosopher: *Journal,* **1851**

No man is good enough to govern another without the other's consent.

Abraham Lincoln

A universal feeling, whether ill or well formed, cannot be safely disregarded.

Abraham Lincoln

The worth of a state, in the long run, is the worth of the individuals composing it.

John Stuart Mill,
English philosopher, 'On Liberty', 1859

Away with this hurrah of masses, and let us have the considerate vote of single men.

Ralph Waldo Emerson,
US poet and philosopher: *The Conduct of Life,* **1860**

Universal suffrage is the government of a house by its nursery.

Otto von Bismarck

Public opinion is stronger than the legislature and nearly as strong as the Ten Commandments.

Charles Dudley Warner,
US essayist: *My Summer,* **1870**

That mysterious independent variable of political calculation — Public Opinion.

T.H. Huxley,
English biologist, 1874

What we call public opinion is generally public sentiment.

Benjamin Disraeli,
British prime minister, 1880

Whenever the cause of the people is entrusted to professors, it is lost.

V.I. Lenin

The one pervading evil of democracy is the tyranny of the majority, or rather of that party, not always the majority, that succeeds by force or fraud in carrying elections.

Lord Acton,
  English historian

As long as there are no myths accepted by the masses, one may go on talking of revolts indefinitely, without ever provoking any revolutionary movement.

Georges Sorel,
  French syndicalist philosopher: *Reflections On Violence*, 1908

The public is not made up of people who get their names in the papers.

Woodrow Wilson

Once lead this people into a war and they will forget there ever was such a thing as tolerance. To fight, you must be brutal and ruthless and the spirit of ruthless brutality will enter into the very fibre of our national life.

Woodrow Wilson,
  US president, 1917

The legitimate aspirations of the proletarian masses are frittered away by the fantastic political programmes of their leaders, who feed the imagination of simple folk on impossible themes.

Antonio de Salazar,
  Portuguese dictator

History is made in the street. The street is the political characteristic of this age.

Joseph Goebbels,
  Nazi minister of propaganda, 1926

A man may have strong humanitarian and democratic principles, but if he happens to have been brought up as a bath-taking, shirt-changing lover of fresh air, he will have to overcome certain physical repugnancies before he can bring himself to put these principles into practice.

Aldous Huxley,
  English novelist and essayist: *Jesting Pilate*, 1926

The chief business of the nation, as a nation, is the setting up of heroes, mostly bogus.

H.L. Mencken,
  US philologist, editor and satirist: *Prejudices*, third series, 1922

Like a woman...the masses love a dominator rather than a suppliant and feel inwardly more satisfied by a doctrine which tolerates no other beside itself than by the granting of liberal freedom. They have no idea what to do with it as a rule, and tend to feel they have been abandoned.

Adolf Hitler:
  ***Mein Kampf*, 1924**

No secretary of state worthy of his name can permit himself to be influenced in a matter of this kind by public clamour. Mob mercy is as bad as mob execution.

Sir William Joynson-Hicks,
  British Home Secretary, refusing to accept a huge petition against the hanging of a murderer, 1928

One should respect public opinion in so far as is necessary to avoid starvation and keep out of prison, but anything that goes beyond this is voluntary submission to an unnecessary tyranny.

Bertrand Russell:
  ***The Conquest of Happiness*, 1930**

Minorities are indiviuals or groups especially qualified. The masses are the collection of people not specially qualified.

Jose Ortega y Gasset,
  Spanish philosopher, 1930

In most cases, when the lion, weary of obeying its master, has torn and devoured him, its nerves are pacified, and it looks around for another master before whom to grovel.

Paul Valéry,
  French poet: *Reflections on the World Today*, 1931

VOX POPULI

Brutality is respected. The people need wholesome fear. They want to fear something. They want someone to frighten them and make them shudderingly submissive.... Why babble about brutality and get indignant about tortures? The masses want them. They need something that will give them a thrill of horror.

Ernest Röhm,
Nazi leader

A government can be no better than the public opinion that sustains it.

Franklin D. Roosevelt,
US president, 1936

The most popular man under a democracy is not the most democratic man but the most despotic man. The common folk delight in the exactions of such a man. They like him to boss them. Their natural gait is the goosestep.

H.L. Mencken,
US philologist, editor and satirist

The democratic disease which expresses its tyranny of reducing everything to the level of the herd.

Henry Miller,
US author: *The Wisdom of the Heart*, 1941

The public, with its mob yearning to be instructed, edified and pulled by the nose, demands certainties — but there are no certainties.

H.L. Mencken,
US philologist, editor and satirist

Never take notice of anonymous letters, unless you get a few thousand on the same subject.

Sir Robert Menzies,
Australian prime minister

There has never been a war yet which, if the facts had been put calmly before the ordinary folk, could not have been prevented. The common man is the greatest protection against war.

Ernest Bevin,
British Labour politician, 1945

The death of democracy is not as likely to be assassination from ambush. It will be a slow extinction from apathy, indifference and undernourishment.

Robert M. Hutchins,
US editor

Government in the last analysis is organized opinion. Where there is little or no public opinion, there is likely to be bad government, which sooner or later becomes autocratic government.

W.L. Mackenzie King,
Canadian prime minister

There is no tyranny so despotic as that of public opinion among a free people.

Donn Platt

If people have to choose between freedom and sandwiches, they will take sandwiches.

Lord Boyd Orr,
Scottish biologist, 1955

In the crowd, herd or gang, it is the mass mind that operates — that is to say, a mind without subtlety, a mind without compassion, a mind, finally, uncivilized.

Robert Lindner,
US psychoanalyst: 'Must You Conform?',
1956

Men need heroes in order to transcend the limitations and disappointment they experience in their everyday lives...but the *creation* of heroes depends upon the compliance of history, the coming together of special events and situations, with unusual men,...who take hold of these circumstances, force them upon their own actions and personalities, and transform them along the lines of their own dreams.

Tawfiq al-Hakim,
Egyptian author, on President Nasser of
Egypt: *Return of Consciousness*

In the last analysis, all power rests on opinion.

Enoch Powell,
British politician

BOOK OF POLITICAL QUOTES

There are not enough jails, not enough policemen, not enough courts to enforce a law not supported by the people.

**Senator Hubert Humphrey,
1965**

The citizen is influenced by his principles in direct proportion to his distance from the political situation.

**Milton Rakove,
US academic, in *Virginia Quarterly*, 1965**

The government has become attuned to falsehood as a routine way of conducting its affairs. Official lies on matters large and small, official and domestic, are the daily fare of the Washington press corps.

**William McGuffin and Erwin Knoll,
US authors: *Anything But the Truth*, 1968**

In public life we have seen reputations destroyed by smear...., we have heard the sly voices of malice twisting the facts.

**Richard Nixon,
US president, 1969**

A merely random collection of people becomes an operative crowd when each of its members begins to feel a strong sense of equality with all the others. Whatever the crowd's larger social purposes, its first purpose is to exist as a crowd.

**Arthur Miller,
US playwright, watching the Democratic National Convention, 1972**

It would be shameful if you let politicians travel the safe middle ground to victory. For if they are to govern well, they need to be forced out of their safe harbours and into the storms that challenge the ship of state.

**Edward Kennedy,
1972**

People will feel differently when it works out....An efficient organization silences all opposition by declaring high quarterly returns.

**Ron Ziegler,
Richard Nixon's press secretary,
countering attacks on the US involvement in Vietnam**

Bad news does not improve with age.

**Jody Powell,
Jimmy Carter's press secretary**

The American people won't buy political double-talk for ever.

Gerald Ford

Everyone is so anaesthetized by scandal that if it turned out that Richard Nixon was the illegitimate son of Golda Meir, it wouldn't make the front pages.

**Gore Vidal,
US author, 1976**

You know, they tell me at a lot of élitist cocktail parties, 'Fred, we love what you say, but will *they* get it?' Meaning, of course, the great unwashed. Well, I'm a member of the great unwashed and let me tell you something — they get it quickest!

**Fred Harris,
US presidential candidate, 1976**

Indifference is the only sure defence.

**Jody Powell,
Jimmy Carter's press secretary**

Freedom of thought, freedom of thought! Democracy, democracy! With five-year-old children going on strike and parading through the streets. That's democracy? That's freedom of thought?

**Mohammad Reza Pahlevi,
Shah of Iran, 1979**

FAMOUS LAST WORDS

There is every reason to believe that our system will soon attain the highest degree of perfection of which human institutions are capable.

James Monroe,
  US president, 1820

I am besieged by a thousand or more of the Mexicans under Santa Anna. I have sustained a continuous bombardment for twenty-four hours and have not lost a man. The enemy have demanded a surrender....I have answered the summons with a cannon shot and our flag still waves proudly from the walls.

W. Barret Travis,
  US commander at the Alamo, sending off a last message shortly before the wholesale slaughter of the 182 American defenders, 1836

How miserable is a society which knows no better method of defence than the executioner.

Karl Marx

But are they allowed to do that?

Emperor Ferdinand of Austria,
  to an adviser as he watched Viennese workers and students erecting barricades, 1848

All we ask is to be left alone.

Jefferson Davis,
  president of the Confederate States, 1861

Kapital will not pay for the cigars I smoked writing it.

Karl Marx,
  1867

There is no doubt that Jefferson Davis and the other leaders of the South have made an army. They are making, it seems, a navy. And they have made, what is more than either: they have made a nation.

William Gladstone,
  leader of the British House of Commons, 1865

Assassination can be no more guarded against than death by lightning and it is best not to worry about either.

James A. Garfield,
  US president, assassinated after four months in office, 1881

In a higher plane of communist society, after the enslaving subordination of the individual to the division of labour, and therewith also the antithesis between mental and physical labour has vanished; after labour has become not only a means of life but life's prime want; after the productive forces have also increased with the all-round development of the individual, and all the springs of co-operative wealth flow more abundantly — only then can the narrow horizon of bourgeois right be crossed in its entirety and society inscribe on its banners 'From each according to his ability, to each according to his need'!

Karl Marx:
  his ultimate vision

We are not interested in the possibilities of defeat. They do not exist.

Queen Victoria,
  on the Boer War — which England lost — 1900

225

BOOK OF POLITICAL QUOTES

Sensible and responsible women do not want to vote. The relative positions to be assumed by men and women in the working out of our civilization were assigned long ago by a higher intelligence than ours.

Grover Cleveland,
  former US president, 1905

Bullets have little stopping power against the horse.

Sir Douglas Haig,
  British general in the First World War, 1914

In my opinion the attempt to build up a Communist republic on the lines of a strongly centralized State Communism under the iron rule of the dictatorship of a party is ending in failure.

Prince Kropotkin,
  Russian revolutionary, on the Russian Revolution, 1920

I have often said to myself that the history of South Africa is the one true and great romance of modern history.

General Jan Smuts,
  South African leader, 1917

What is our task? To make Britain a fit country for heroes to live in.

David Lloyd George,
  British prime minister, planning the post-war revival, 1918

I have been over into the future and it works.

Lincoln Steffens,
  US journalist, on returning from Soviet Russia, 1919

The government will go on with patience and courage until the last revolver is picked out of the hands of the last assassin in Ireland.

Sir Hamar Greenwood,
  Secretary of State for Ireland, 1921

Mother, I want to be an old-fashioned lawyer, a honest lawyer who can't be bought by crooks.

Richard Nixon,
  aged twelve, 1925

The bonds, social, economic, commercial and industrial, which are always drawing North and South Ireland together, will prove too powerful for the bigots and revolutionaries.

J.R. Devlin,
  Irish journalist and nationalist, 1924

England is at last ripe for revolution.

Leon Trotsky,
  1925

I do not think we shall hear much more of the General Strike in our life.

Ramsay MacDonald,
  British prime minister, 28th May 1926

Not a penny off the pay, not a second on the day.

A.J. Cook,
  secretary of the National Union of Miners, coining an over-optimistic slogan for the General Strike, 1926

WE CAN CONQUER UNEMPLOYMENT

Liberal Party Pamphlet,
  1929

It would be a mistake to think that everything is quite all right in our country.

Joseph Stalin,
  1933

We shall win, or we shall return upon our shields.

Sir Oswald Mosley,
  British Fascist leader

Herr Hitler has one of the endearing characteristics of Ferdinand the Bull. Just when the crowds expect him to be most violent he stops and smells the flowers. I have a feeling, and I hope I am right, that for the next month or so Herr Hitler is going to take things a little easier and smell the flowers and listen to the nightingales.

Beverley Nichols,
  English journalist, in the _Sunday Graphic_

FAMOUS LAST WORDS

The idea of National Socialism is an accomplishment of the human soul that ranks with the Parthenon, the Sistine Madonna and the Ninth Symphony of Beethoven.

Alfred Rosenberg,
 Nazi theorist, 1935

Something ought to be done to find these people employment...something will be done.

Edward VIII,
 visiting the impoverished South Wales coalfields, 1936

I do not believe in the probability of anything much worse than mustard gas being produced.

Professor J.B.S. Haldane,
 British scientist, 1937

We shall reach the helm in five years.

Sir Oswald Mosley,
 British Fascist leader, 1938

I am a Comintern agent.

Guy Burgess,
 British diplomat, making a factual statement that was ignored for the next thirteen years, 1938

This is the second time in history that there has come back from Germany to Downing Street peace with honour. I believe it is peace for our time.

Neville Chamberlain,
 British prime minister, returning from appeasing Hitler and referring to Disraeli's 1878 visit to the Congress of Berlin, 1938

No enemy bomber can reach the Ruhr. If one reaches the Ruhr my name is not Goering. You can call me Meier.

Hermann Goering,
 Nazi leader, 1939

C'est une drôle de guerre. [It's a phoney war.]

Edouard Daladier,
 French prime minister, 1939

Whatever may be the reason, whether it was that Hitler thought he might get away with what he had without fighting for it, or whether it was that, after all, the preparations are not sufficiently complete, one thing is certain — he has missed the bus.

Neville Chamberlain,
 British prime minister, 1940

Are you aware it is private property? Why, you will be asking me to bomb Essen next!

Sir Kingsley Wood,
 Chamberlain's Air Minister, refusing to consider sending bombers to destroy Germany's valuable forests

I assure you, we are all appalled by these persecutions and atrocities. It is simply not typically German. Can you imagine that I could kill anyone? Tell me honestly, do any of us look like murders?

Joachim von Ribbentrop,
 former Ambassador to England, duly hanged for war crimes, to the Nuremburg Tribunal, 1945

When you see something that is technically sweet, you go ahead and do it.

Robert Oppenheimer,
 head of the Manhattan Project, on the development of the atomic bomb, 1945

In the course of thirty years the human race will have been biologically restored. It will come into the world without any trace of fascist distortion.

Wilhelm Reich,
 Austrian-born US psychiatrist, 1946

Wanted: Congressman candidate with no previous political experience to defeat a man who has represented the district in the House for ten years. Any young man, resident of the district, preferably a veteran, fair education, may apply for the job.

Advertisement
 in the Whittier, California Press, 1946. Richard Nixon won the job, promptly branded his rival, Jerry Voorhis, a Communist and launched his political career

We conclude that in the field of public education the doctrine of 'separate but equal' has no place. Separate educational facilities are inherently unequal.

Earl Warren,
US Supreme Court Chief Justice, ruling on the legal integration of US schools, 1954

Well, that's good. That takes care of the problem.

Henry Luce,
US publisher, on hearing of the above decision, 1954

You've never had it so good.

Harold Macmillan,
British prime minister, 1957

The employers will love this generation. They aren't going to press many grievances. They are going to be easy to handle. There aren't going to be any riots.

Clark Kerr,
University of California chancellor, forecasting the 1960s, 1959

The class war is obsolete.

Harold Macmillan,
British prime minister, 1959

The Cuban movement is not a communist movement. Its members are Roman Catholics, mostly.

Fidel Castro,
Cuban prime minister, 1959

We have developed an affluent, open and democratic society in which the class escalators are continually moving and in which people are divided not so much between the 'haves' and 'have-nots', but between the 'haves' and the 'have-mores'.

R.A. Butler,
British Conservative politician, 1960

I myself have always deprecated, perhaps rightly, perhaps wrongly, in crisis after crisis, appeals to the Dunkirk spirit as an answer to our problems.

Harold Wilson,
British opposition leader, 1961

I believe that the spirit of Dunkirk will once again carry us through to success.

Harold Wilson,
British prime minister, 1964

Whenever any mother or father talks to their child, I hope he can look at the man in the White House and, whatever he may think of his politics, he will say, 'Well, there's a man who maintains the kind of standards personally that I would want my child to follow.'

Richard Nixon,
US presidential candidate, debating John F. Kennedy, 1960

I was an expert on migration problems.

Adolf Eichmann,
Nazi war criminal, on trial, 1961

I found nothing but progress and hope for the future.

Robert MacNamara,
US Secretary of Defense, after visiting Vietnam, 1962

What is mobility? Mobility means vehicles and aircraft. You have seen the way our Vietnamese units are armed: fifty radios, thirty or forty vehicles, rockets, mortars and airplanes. The Viet Cong have no vehicles and no airplanes. How can they be mobile?

Aide to General Paul Harkins,
US commander in Vietnam, 1963

A great party is not to be brought down because of a squalid affair between a woman of easy virtue and a proven liar.

Lord Hailsham,
British jurist on the Profumo Affair, 1963

You can't say the people of Dallas haven't given you a nice welcome.

Mrs John Connally,
wife of the Governor of Texas, to John F. Kennedy before they drove through Dallas on 22nd November 1963

I can safely say the end of the war is in sight.

General Paul Harkins,
on Vietnam, 1963

It was incomprehensible. Americans don't get assassinated. Europeans do. That's how they solved problems.

Benjamin Bradlee,
    US editor, on John Kennedy's death, 1963

I'm not going to lose Vietnam. I am not going to be the president who saw South East Asia go the same way China went.

Lyndon B. Johnson,
    US president, 1963

I wanted to show them a Jew has guts.

Jack Ruby,
    assassin of the alleged Kennedy killer, Lee Harvey Oswald. Ruby died in his cell, 1963

I draw the line in the dust and toss the gauntlet before the feet of tyranny and I say segregation now, segregation tomorrow and segregation forever!

George Wallace,
    pledging himself at his inauguration as governor of Alabama, 1963

We are re-defining and we are re-stating our socialism in terms of the scientific revolution.... The Britain that is going to be forged in the white heat of this revolution will be no place for restrictive practices or outdated methods on either side of industry.

Harold Wilson,
    British Opposition leader, 1963

Our one desire, our one determination, is that the people of South East Asia be left in peace to work out their own destinies in their own way.

Lyndon B. Johnson,
    US president, 1964

Our constant aim, our steadfast purpose, our undeviating policy is to do all that strengthens the hope of peace.

Lyndon B. Johnson,
    three months prior to increasing the US advisers in Vietnam by thirty per cent, 1964

Peace ought to be possible in South East Asia without any extension of the fighting.

Dean Rusk,
    US Secretary of State, 1964

We are not going to send American boys nine or ten thousand miles away from home to do what Asian boys ought to be doing for themselves.

Lyndon B. Johnson,
    US president, announcing 'Vietnamization', 1964

I am going to build the kind of nation that President Roosevelt hoped for, President Truman worked for and President Kennedy died for.

Lyndon B. Johnson,
    1964

The major part of the US military task in Vietnam can be completed by the end of 1965.

Robert MacNamara,
    US Secretary of Defense, 1965

Victory for the Viet Cong would mean ultimately the destruction of freedom of speech for all men for all time, not only in Asia, but in the United States as well.

Richard Nixon,
    US lawyer, 1965

There is little evidence that the Viet Cong have any significant following in South Vietnam.

Dean Rusk,
    US Secretary of State, 1965

We are making war in Vietnam to show that guerilla warfare does not pay.

General William Westmoreland,
    Commander in Chief US forces in Vietnam, 1966

If we quit Vietnam, tomorrow we'll be fighting in Hawaii and next week we'll have to fight in San Francisco.

Lyndon B. Johnon,
    US president, 1967

John Profumo dances with his wife/Popperfoto

There was no impropriety whatsoever in my acquaintanceship with Miss Keeler.

John Profumo,
    British Minister of Defence, lying in the House of Commons, 1963

If we just keep up the pressure, these little guys will crack.

General Earle Wheeler,
    Joint Chiefs of Staff chairman, on the Viet Cong

FAMOUS LAST WORDS

In about seven or eight years the psychedelic population of the United States will be able to vote anybody into office they want to. Allen Ginsberg? Sure. Imagine what it would be like to have anyone in high office with our understanding of the universe. I mean, let's imagine that Bobby Kennedy had a fully expanded consciousness. Just imagine him, in his position, what he would be able to do.

Dr Richard Alpert
  (Baba Ram Dass), US psychedelic guru, 1967

This is our great adventure, and a wonderful one it is.

Hubert Humphrey,
  US vice-president, on Vietnam, 1967

The war is far from being over yet, and the Viet Cong may yet pull off a few spectacular feats, but the war is increasingly taking on the form of a series of mopping-up exercises. These will be a bloody and horrible business, but there is little doubt that it can now be successfully accomplished.

Peter Samuel,
  Australian journalist, 1966

Our country is big enough to support a war in Vietnam and a successful war on poverty at home.

Sargent Shriver,
  director of the Office of Economic Opportunity, 1966

Make no mistake about it, we are going to win.

Lyndon B. Johnson,
  US president, 1968

I promise that truth shall be the policy of the Nixon administration.

Spiro T. Agnew,
  US vice-president, 1968

We thought we could put the economy right in five years — we were wrong. It will probably take ten.

Anthony Wedgwood Benn,
  British politician, 1968

To some extent, if you've seen one city slum, you've seen them all.

Spiro T. Agnew,
  explaining why he visited no black ghettoes on his campaign, 1968

I suppose one day someone might throw something other than rotten eggs at me.

George Wallace,
  Governor of Alabama, prophesying his near-assassination of 1972, 1968

Let us begin by committing ourselves to the truth, to see it like it is and to tell it like it is, to find the truth, to speak the truth and live with the truth. That is what we will do.

Richard Nixon,
  accepting the Republican nomination, 1968

This is not a rout. This is a planned withdrawal.

Andrew Peacock,
  Australian Army Minister, on the Australian disengagement from Vietnam

I have often been accused of putting my foot in my mouth, but I will never put my hand in your pockets.

Spiro T. Agnew,
  US vice-president, subsequently to be fired for economic corruption

Let us be united for peace. Let us be united against defeat. Because, let us understand, North Vietnam cannot defeat or humiliate the United States — only Americans can do that.

Richard Nixon,
  US president, 1969

Truth will become the hallmark of the Nixon Administration....It will eliminate any possibility of a credibility gap.

Herb Klein,
  US Director of Communications, 1969

I would walk over my grandmother if necessary for Richard Nixon.

Charles Colson,
  White House special assistant

We shall not defeat America by organizing a political party. We shall do it by building a new nation, a nation as rugged as the marijuana weed born from the seeds of the Woodstock Festival. The nation will be built on love, but in order to love we must survive, and in order to survive we must fight. The styles of our struggle might look strange, but the spirit is time-honoured. Victory or death!

Abbie Hoffman,
   Yippie! leader, in *Woodstock Nation,* **1969**

After all, what does a politician have but his credibility?

Spiro T. Agnew,
   US vice-president, 1969

This would, at a stroke, reduce the rise in prices, increase productivity and reduce unemployment.

Conservative Party press release,
   on economic plans and generally, but erroneously, attributed to Prime Minister Edward Heath, 1970

Writing about the Nixon Administration is about as exciting as covering the Prudential Life Assurance Company.

Art Buchwald,
   US humorist, 1970

Contrary to reports that you noticed in the last day or so in the papers, this was not a rout, this was an orderly retreat.

Spiro T. Agnew,
   US vice-president, on troop movements in Vietnam, 1971

I want to see peace, prosperity and happiness in my country, and I think we are going about achieving it in the best way.

Joe Cahill,
   leader of the Provisional IRA in Belfast, 1971

We have the happiest Africans in the world.

Ian Smith,
   Rhodesian prime minister, 1971

How much do you think I'll get for my autobiography?

Arthur Bremer,
   after his assassination attempt on George Wallace, 1972

Let him hang there, let him twist slowly, slowly in the wind.

John Ehrlichman,
   Nixon aide, on FBI director, Patrick Gray, who was 'hanging tough' on Watergate, 1972

I am one thousand per cent for Tom Eagleton and I have no intention of dropping him from the ticket.

Senator George McGovern,
   shortly before dropping Eagleton from his presidential ticket, 1972

It won't be a convention, but a coronation.

Frank Mankiewicz,
   McGovern aide, on the nomination that sent McGovern towards the worst-ever defeat in a US presidential election, 1972

The intricate tangle of criminal charges levelled at me...boils down to the accusation that I permitted my fund-raising activities and my contract-dispensing activities to overlap in an unethical and an unlawful manner. Perhaps, judged by the new, post-Watergate morality, I did.

Spiro T. Agnew,
   US vice-president, TV resignation speech, 1973

I was not there to think, I was there to follow orders.

Bernard 'Macho' Barker,
   White House 'plumber', 1973

Until they show me different I've got to stick with the Prez.

Bob Hope,
   US comedian, refusing to abandon Nixon, 1974

Something here is not kosher.

Tony Ulascewicz,
   Watergate bagman, on his money-dispensing activities

FAMOUS LAST WORDS

Our problem at the moment is a problem of success.

Edward Heath,
   British prime minister, four months before an ignominious election defeat, 1973

It will be open house. Caviar, vodka, no problems about visas.

Vladimir Bromislov,
   mayor of Moscow, looking forward to hosting the 1980 Olympics, 1974

The country needs good farmers, good businessmen, good plumbers...

Richard Nixon,
   in his resignation speech, 1974

He no playa da game, he no make-a da rules.

Earl Butz,
   US Secretary of Agriculture, referring to Pope Paul VI's stance against birth control, 1974

Portions of the tapes of these June 23 conversations are at variance with certain of my previous statements....I recognize that this...may further damage my case.

Richard Nixon,
   US president, 1974

The men of violence are not going to bomb their way to the conference table. Nor must they be allowed to bomb Northern Ireland into the abyss.

Harold Wilson,
   British prime minister, 1974

My own view was that the taping of conversations for historical purposes was a bad decision.

Richard Nixon,
   former US president, 1974

Our advice to them is to run away if they can.

Prince Norodom Sihanouk,
   warning the Lon Nol regime as the Khmer Rouge took over Cambodia, 1975

There are going to be no dramatic changes in Rhodesia.

Ian Smith,
   Rhodesian prime minister, 1975

It is very likely that I will never seek public office again.

Spiro Agnew,
   former US vice-president, 1976

I never thought a man like Dr Kissinger would deliver our people to such a disastrous fate.

Nguyen Van Thieu,
    South Vietnamese president, 1975

Coloureds only want three things: first, a tight pussy; second, loose shoes, and third, a warm place to shit.

Earl Butz,
    speaking to John Dean, in his capacity as *Rolling Stone* **reporter. Butz was forced to resign after this, 1976**

I don't have to be president. There are a lot of things I would not do to be president. I will never make a misleading statement. I will never lie to you.

Jimmy Carter,
    electioneering, 1976

The election of Ted Kennedy would mean the end of our society as we have known it. We are convinced that the consequences would be tragic for the United States.

Citizens Against Kennedy,
    in an advertisement attacking the senator, 1976

You and I know that if I had ever been corrupted, I wouldn't still be around.

Richard Daley,
    greatest of the US political bosses, two weeks before his death, 1976

There is no Soviet domination of Eastern Europe, and there never will be under a Ford Administration.

Gerald Ford,
    US president, 1976

It's all right Prez. We've given up a couple of runs, but the ballgame is only in the top of the fourth, we've got a long way to go.

Joe Garagiola,
    former baseball star turned baseball commentator, trying to cheer up Gerald Ford as Carter won the election, 1976

If, after the election, you find a Cy Vance as Secretary of State and a Zbigniew Brzezinski as head of National Security, then I would say we failed. And I'd quit.

Hamilton Jordan,
    Jimmy Carter's aide, during the campaign. He failed to keep this promise, 1976

The majority of black people are grateful for what the government is doing to uplift them.

James Kruger,
    South African police and justice minister, 1976

We have no political prisons. We have political internal exiles.

Auguste Pinochet,
    Chilean dictator, 1976

There has been a serious problem. There's been an accident.

Jimmy Carter,
    on hearing of the breakdown and failure of his disastrous rescue mission in to Iran, fifty-three US hostages from Iran, 1980

I think most people who have studied the situation, who have looked at the map, who have seen where the embassy is located in Teheran, can see that a strike force or a military action would almost certainly end in failure and almost certainly in the death of the hostages.

Jimmy Carter,
    US president, four months before sending his disastrous rescue mission in to Iran, 1980

We wish to avoid at all costs the recurrent experience in some democratic countries where the people give the governments the opposition they deserve.

Mohammad Reza Pahlevi,
    Shah of Iran, 1978

Crisis? What Crisis?

The *Sun***,**
    headline quoting Prime Minister James Callaghan who refused to admit to the obvious chaos in England after his return from a Commonwealth Conference, 1979

FAMOUS LAST WORDS

I should very much like to take a vacation.

Mohammad Reza Pahlevi,
    former Shah of Iran, shortly before he
began his exile, 1979

I wanted to know how women reacted under various circumstances....It was like cutting through red tape. I was very concerned to see how deep the rejection of blacks by whites would go.

Eldridge Cleaver,
    former Black Panther leader, currently a
Born Again Christian, on his raping several
white women for which he was jailed, 1980

I don't want to be prime minister again, it's pretty tough going.

Indira Gandhi,
    former Indian prime minister, temporarily
out of power, 1978

The last thing I wanted was to create a national scandal.

Norman Scott,
    star of the Jeremy Thorpe murder trial,
1979

There are no prisons in Uganda.

Idi Amin,
    Ugandan president, 1977

Idi Amin at the time he was chairman of the Organisation of African Unity/Publisher's files

INDEX

INDEX

INDEX

INDEX

INDEX

INDEX

INDEX

INDEX

ACKNOWLEDGEMENTS

The author and the publishers would like to thank the following people for giving permission to include in this anthology material which is in their copyright. The publishers have made every effort to trace copyright holders. If we have inadvertently omitted to acknowledge anyone, we would be most grateful if this could be brought to our attention for correction at the first opportunity.

George Allen & Unwin Ltd for 'The Grammar of Politics' by Harold Laski, 'The Revolt of the Masses' by J. Ortega y Gasset, 'Doctrine and Ethics' by H. M. Drucker, 'Reflections on Violence' by Georges Sorel, 'Unpopular Essays', 'The Conquest of Happiness', 'Marriage and Morals', 'New Hopes for a Changing World' and 'Philosophy and Politics' by Bertrand Russell; **Allison & Busby Ltd** for 'Look Out Whitey. . .' by Julius Lester; **Edward Arnold Ltd** for 'Two Cheers for Democracy' by E. M. Forster; **Bantam Books, Inc.** for 'Sayings of the Ayatollah Khomeini: Political, Philosophical, Social and Religious' translated by Harold J. Salemson and specially edited by Tony Hendra with an introduction by Clive Irving (English translation copyright © 1980 by Bantam Books, Inc.; all rights reserved); **Jonathan Cape Ltd** for 'Breakfast of Champions' by Kurt Vonnegut, 'Fighter' by Len Deighton; **Cassell Ltd** for 'The New Face of War' by Malcolm Browne; **Chatto and Windus Ltd** and Mrs. Laura Huxley for 'Jesting Pilate', 'The Olive Tree', 'Collected Essays' and 'Ends and Means' by Aldous Huxley; **J. M. Dent & Sons Ltd** for 'The Selected Writings of George Santayana'; **Doubleday & Co. Inc.** for 'The Opium of the Intellectuals' (translated by Terence Kilmartin) by Raymond Aron (copyright 1957 by Raymond Aron), 'PR as in President' by Vic Gold, 'The Outline of History' by H. G. Wells; **Faber and Faber Ltd** for 'Management and the Unions' by Allan Flanders, 'The Socialist Case' by Douglas Jay; **Victor Gollancz Ltd** for 'Harold Laski' by Kingsley Martin; **Granada Publishing Ltd** for 'The Slow Burning Fuse' by John Quail, 'Black Skin, White Masks' and 'The Wretched of the Earth' by Frantz Fanon; **Hamish Hamilton Ltd** for 'The Rebel' (translated by Anthony Bower) and 'Carnets 1942–1951' (translated by Philip Thody) by Albert Camus; **A. M. Heath & Co. Ltd** for all works by George Orwell; **William Heinemann Ltd** for 'Reminiscences' by Gen. Douglas MacArthur; **Heinemann Educational Books** for 'Death in Beirut' by Tawfiq Yusuf Awwad; **David Higham Associates Ltd** for 'Boring for England' and 'Chronicles of Wasted Time' (vol. I) by Malcolm Muggeridge, 'Points of Departure' by James Cameron; **Hodder & Stoughton Ltd** for 'Soul on Ice' by Eldridge Cleaver; **Houghton Mifflin Company** for 'The Autobiography of Will Rogers' (copyright 1949 by The Rogers Company; copyright © renewed 1977 by Donald Day and Beth Day); **Housmans Bookshop Ltd** for 'Non-Violence in Peace and War' by M. K. Gandhi; **Hutchinson Publishing Group Ltd** for 'Mein Kampf' by Adolf Hitler; **Michael Joseph Ltd** for 'Nobody Knows My Name' by James Baldwin; **Little, Brown and Co.** for 'America Comes of Middle Age' by Murray Kempton, 'The Public Philosophy' by Walter Lippmann; **Longman Group Ltd** for 'Outspoken Essays' by Dean Inge; **Gerard McCauley Agency, Inc.** for 'PR as in President' by Vic Gold; **McGraw-Hill Book Co. (UK) Ltd** for 'Understanding Media' by Marshall McLuhan, 'The Twilight of the American Mind' by W. B. Pitkin; **Macmillan Publishers Ltd** for 'The Wordly Philosophers' by J. M. Keynes; **Macmillan Publishing Co., Inc.** for 'A Sign for Cain' by Frederic Wertham M.D. (copyright © 1966 by Fredric Wertham), 'The Secular City' by Harvey Cox (copyright © Harvey Cox 1965, 1966); **Methuen Children's Books Ltd** for 'Situations' by Jean-Paul Sartre, 'The Enchanted' by Jean Giraudoux, 'Mother Courage', 'Collected Poems', 'The Threepenny Opera' and 'Roundheads and Pealtheads' by Bertolt Brecht; **John Murray Ltd** for 'Parkinson's Law' by C. N. Parkinson; **Harold Ober Associates Inc.** for 'Out of the Red' by Caskie Stinnett; **Oxford University Press** for 'Two Concepts of Liberty' by Isaiah Berlin; **A. D. Peters & Co. Ltd** for 'Janus' by Arthur Koestler; **Philosophical Library, Inc.** for 'The World As I See It' by Albert Einstein; **Pluto Press Ltd** for 'Rights at Work' by Jeremy McMullan; **Random House, Inc.** and **Alfred A. Knopf, Inc.** for 'Out of the Red' by Caskie Stinnett, 'Sketches in the Sand' by James Reston, 'Woodstock Nation' by Abbie Hoffman, 'The I.F. Stone's Weekly Reader' (edited by Neil Middleton) by I. F. Stone, 'Minority Report', 'Prejudices: Third Series' and 'Prejudices: Fourth Series' by H. L. Mencken; **Routledge & Kegan Paul Ltd** for 'The Fear of Freedom' by Erich Fromm, 'Reflections on the World Today' by Paul Valery; **SCM Press Ltd** for 'The Secular City' by Harvey Cox; **Scott Meredith Literary Agency, Inc.** for 'St George and the Godfather' by Norman Mailer (reprinted by permission of the author and the author's agents, Scott

Meredith Literary Agency, Inc., 845 Third Avenue, New York, New York 10022); **Martin Secker & Warburg Ltd** for 'The Opium of the Intellectuals' by Raymond Aron; **Simon & Schuster** for 'Actions and Passions' by Max Lerner (copyright © 1949, 1976 by Max Lerner); **The Society of Authors** for 'Maids in Waiting' by John Galsworthy, 'Back to Methuselah', Man and Superman', 'John Bull's Other Island' and 'Fabian Essays' by George Bernard Shaw; **Souvenir Press Ltd** for 'Quotations for Our Time' by L. J. Peter; **Wadsworth Publishing Co.** for 'The Conquest of Society' by Snell Putney; **A. P. Watt Ltd** and Professor G. P. Wells for 'The Outline of History' by H. G. Wells, and the estate of the late P. G. Wodehouse for 'Carry on Jeeves'; **Weidenfeld Ltd** for 'On the Contrary' by Mary McCarthy, 'Miami and the Siege of Chicago' by Norman Mailer, 'The Diaries of Sir Henry "Chips" Channon'.

Additional Acknowledgments

Delacorte Press/Seymour Lawrence for 'Breakfast of Champions' by Kurt Vonnegut Jr.; **Harcourt Brace Jovanovich, Inc.** for 'Nineteen Eighty-Four', 'Animal Farm', 'Politics and the English Language' from 'Shooting an Elephant and Other Essays', and 'Looking Back on the Spanish War' and 'Notes on Nationalism' both from 'Such, Such Were the Joys' by George Orwell, 'Two Cheers for Democracy' by E. M. Forster; **Harper & Row, Publishers, Inc.** for 'One Man's Meat' by E. B. White, 'The Pursuit of Justice' by Robert F. Kennedy, 'America Is in Danger' by General Curtis E. LeMay, and 'Lyndon Johnson and the American Dream' by Doris Kearns; **International Creative Management, Inc.** for 'The Great Shark Hunt' by Hunter S. Thompson; **Alfred A. Knopf, Inc.** for 'Fighter: the True Story of the Battle of Britain' by Len Deighton; **Liveright Publishing Corporation** for 'The Conquest of Happiness' by Bertrand Russell; **François Maspero Editeur** for 'The Wretched of the Earth' (Les Damnés de la Terre) by Frantz Fanon; **W. W. Norton, Inc.** for 'Revolt of the Masses' by J. Ortega y Gasset; **Princeton University Press** for 'The Collected Works in English' by Paul Valery (Bollingen Series Vol. 10: 'History and Politics', trans. Denise Folliot and Jackson Mathews. Copyright © 1962 by Princeton University Press); **Editions du Seuil** for 'Black Skin, White Masks' (Peau Noire, Masques Blancs) by Frantz Fanon; **Simon and Schuster, Inc.** for 'Unpopular Essays' by Bertrand Russell; The Sterling Lord Agency, Inc. for 'The Selling of the President' by Joe McGinniss; **Joan Daves** for 'Strength to Love' by Martin Luther King Jr. (copyright © 1963 by Martin Luther King Jr.); **Houghton Mifflin Company** for 'The Great Crash' by John Kenneth Galbraith (copyright 1954, 1955, 1961 by John Kenneth Galbraith), 'Parkinson's Law' by C. Northcote Parkinson (copyright 1957 by C. Northcote Parkinson); **A. M. Heath & Co. Ltd.** for 'On the Contrary' by Mary McCarthy.